# THE MALVERN FESTIVAL PLAYS

## MCMXXXIII

ARRANGED FOR PRODUCTION
BY

H. K. AYLIFF

*With an Introduction by*

HUGH WALPOLE

*And Preface by*

SIR BARRY JACKSON

HEATH CRANTON LIMITED
6 FLEET LANE, LONDON, E.C.4
1933

*Printed in Great Britain for Heath Cranton Limited by Purnell and Sons, Paulton (Somerset) and London*

# INTRODUCTION

BY

HUGH WALPOLE

I will confess to a feeling of pride when I read the letter asking me to write a short foreword to this volume. I understood that Sir Barry Jackson was already writing a Preface, and that all that I was asked to do was to express in a general manner what one enthusiast feels about the Festival and the effect of the Plays because of the Festival.

For I *am* an enthusiast, in this instance, and with reason. (I am sometimes an enthusiast *without* reason, a most delightful thing to be, but exasperating to others!)

As I look at the plays in this volume and know that some time in August I shall once again be able to catch that certainty of the continuity and immortality of Art—so that the history or fate of the individual artist matters nothing but that the chain should be unbroken matters everything—I quite frankly lick my lips.

Last summer I had for various reasons what was very nearly the happiest week of my life. The Festival has resemblances to Ben Jonson's Bartholomew Fair. Everyone becomes a little transmuted. I don't know whether the band in the gardens is an especially good one or whether human beings during that one week are more amiable than at any other time in the year—I don't *know* what the reasons for the excitement and expectation are—it *can't* be because Mr. Bernard Shaw is in knickerbockers on the Terrace!—it remains true that this week has magic in it.

I suspect that in reality the reason lies in the plays themselves. *How* they gain by their contiguity the one to another! You would not say that *Oroonoko* was ever a good play, but as you listened to Ralph Richardson's superb declamation with the riot and richness of Ben Jonson's Alchemist still about your ears and the last echo of the bells of "Roister Doister" still ringing down the street, *Oroonoko* takes on a new richness, a fresh importance.

In the same way no one will persuade me that Arthur Jones' *Dancing Girl* is, or ever was, a good play. But it stands nobly for its time. I, who salute you—did I not once see Tree himself coming majestically with a perfect swing of the hip down that grand staircase? And how will *The Dancing Girl* glitter again while the thickly jewelled majesty of "All for Love" is still humming in the eaves of the theatre.

The fact is that this Malvern Festival gives you what you get nowhere else in the world to-day—not in Salzburg, not in Bayreuth, not in Munich—a reassurance about the inevitable vitality of Art. Not Black Deaths, nor Civil Wars, nor Going on the Dole can stay the life, faith and energy of the artist. Up will spring Dr. Bridie with his whale, or Mr. Connelly with his "Green Pastures," or Clemence Dane with her fine tragedy of the Brontës. So Gammer Gurton shakes hands with Noel Coward (a most pleasant meeting) and Dryden nods kindly at the romantic ardour of "Will Shakespeare."

And we, the crowd, at Malvern are also the participants and even for a brief happy moment, the creators.

HUGH WALPOLE.

# PREFACE

## By Sir Barry Jackson

This volume contains the third selection of plays chosen to represent the gradual development of English Drama. With the six here printed, there will have been performed at Malvern eighteen of these historical pieces in the years 1931–33 inclusive.

No language in the world is so rich in dramatic literature as English. Many of its finest treasures, however, are never seen upon the stage to-day; even the texts of some of them lie buried in rare and obscure editions. The Malvern Festival exists to bring these things to life; and that the life thus resurrected is satisfying and abundant, the success of the Festival proves.

There is much in seeing these plays once. But it seems regrettable that, after so brief a re-appearance, they should pass from the ken of theatre-lovers. Accordingly this book has been prepared, giving the acted versions as produced at Malvern, and allowing perpetual renewal of acquaintance with works that hold important place in our dramatic heritage.

"Four hundred Years of English Drama" is no empty phrase. From *The Conversion of St. Paul* to *The Dancing Girl* stretches a period of time covering twelve generations. Each one of the six plays typifies the Drama of its own age—and, therefore, very largely, the age itself. "A compound of poetry and philosophy" was what Macaulay called History, and a series of pictures, drawn in dramatic form by poets and philosophers, should give us a truly historic sense. Whether or not they are poets, good dramatists must evidently be philosophers—and leading examples of the Drama in each century will be found to show, more clearly than anything else, that continuous, unbroken thread which is the chief lesson of History.

# CONTENTS

PAGE

Introduction by Hugh Walpole . . . iii

Preface by Sir Barry Jackson . . . v

The Conversion of Saint Paul . . . 1

Gammer Gurton's Needle . . . . 15

The Fair Maid of the West . . . . 67

All for Love . . . . . . . 129

The Love Chase . . . . . . 211

The Dancing Girl . . . . . . 277

# MALVERN FESTIVAL PROGRAMME

## July 24th to August 12th, 1933

## FOUR HUNDRED YEARS OF ENGLISH DRAMA

*presented*

*Under the direction of* Sir Barry Jackson — *In association with* Roy Limbert

| *Evening* | *Period* | *Play* | *Author* |
|---|---|---|---|
| Monday | 15th Century | The Conversion of St. Paul | Unknown |
| | 1575 .. | Gammer Gurton's Needle | Mr. S., Master of Arts |
| Tuesday | 1630 .. | The Fair Maid of the West | Thomas Heywood |
| Wednes. | 1678 .. | All for Love .. | John Dryden |
| Thursday | 1837 .. | The Love-Chase | Sheridan Knowles |
| Friday | 1891 .. | The Dancing Girl | Henry Arthur Jones |

*The New Play for* 1933, *performed on the Saturday of each week, is not printed in this volume.*

# MONDAY

## THE CONVERSION OF SAINT PAUL

(*Late Fifteenth Century*)

AUTHOR UNKNOWN

## DRAMATIS PERSONÆ

The Poet..........................................................................

Saul..........................................................................

Caiaphas..........................................................................

Annas..........................................................................

1st Knight..........................................................................

2nd Knight..........................................................................

Servant..........................................................................

Groom..........................................................................

God the Father..........................................................................

God the Son..........................................................................

God the Holy Ghost..........................................................................

Ananias..........................................................................

Dancers

# PROLOGUE

*Poet. Rex glorie*, King omnipotent,
Redeemer of the world by the power divine;
And Mary, that pure virgin, queen most excellent,
Which bare that blessed babe Jesu, that for us suffered pain;
Unto whose goodness I do incline,
Beseeching that Lord of his piteous influence,
To preserve and govern this worshipful audience.
Honourable friends, beseeching you of licence,
To proceed our process, we may, under your correction,
Show the conversion of Saint Paul, as the Bible gives experience.
Who lists to read the book *Actum Apostolorum*,
There shall he have the very notition.
But, as we can, we shall us address,
Briefly with your favour, beginning our process.

*A Dance.*

[*Here entereth* SAUL, *richly apparelled as an adventurous Knight.*

*Saul.* Most doughty man I am living upon the ground.
Goodly beseen with many a rich garniment.
My peer alive I trow is not found.
Through the world from the orient to the occident,
My fame is best known under the firmament.
I am most dreaded of people universal;
They dare not displease me most noble.
Saul is my name, I will that ye notify,
Which conspireth the disciples with threat and menace.
Before the princes and priests most noble and high
I bring them to punishment for their trespass.
We will them not suffer to rest in no place,
For they go about to preach and give examples

To destroy our laws, synagogues and temples.
By the god Belial, I shall make progress
Unto the princes, both Caiaphas and Annas,
Where I shall ask of them, in sureness,
To pursue through all Damascus and Libia.
And thus shall we soon after then
Bring them that so do live unto Jerusalem,
Both man and child, as I find them.

[*Here cometh* SAUL *to* CAIAPHAS *and* ANNAS.

Noble prelates and princes of regality,
Desiring and asking of your benign worthiness
Your letters and epistles of most sovereignty
To subdue rebels, that will of frowardness
Against our laws rebel and transgress.

*Caiaphas.* To your desire we give perfect sentence,
According to your petition that ye make postulation;
Because we know your true diligence
To pursue all those that do reprobation
Against our laws by any redarguation.
Wherefore shortly we give in commandment
To put down them that be disobedient.

*Annas.* And by these letters, that be most reverent,
Take them in hand, full agreeing thereto,
Constrain all rebels, by our whole assent.
We give you power so to do.

[*Here* SAUL *receiveth the letters.*

*Saul.* This precept here I take in hand,
To fulfil after your wills both;
Where I shall spare within this land
Neither man nor woman, to this I make an oath,
But to subdue I will not be loth.
Now follow me, knights and servants true,
Unto Damascus as fast as ye can sue.

*1st Knight.* Unto your commandment I do obeisance.

*2nd Knight.* And in me shall be no negligence.
With all my mind, I you insure,
To resist the rebels I will do my cure.

*Saul.* Ever at my need I have found you constant.
But, knights and servants that be so pleasant,
I pray you anon my palfrey ye bring,
To speed my journey without letting.

[*Here* SAUL *goeth aside to make him ready.*

*Servant.* How, Hostler! How! A peck of oats and a pottle of hay!
Come apace, or I will to another inn!
What, Hostler! Why comest thou not thy way?
Hie thee faster, I beshrew thy skin!

*Groom.* I am no hostler, nor no hostler's kin,
But a gentleman's servant, if thou dost know!
Such crabbish words do ask a blow.

*Servant.* I cry you mercy, sir! I wist well somewhat ye were,
Either a gentleman or a knave, methinketh by your philosophy!
If one looked you in the face that never saw you ere,
He'd think you were at the next door by.
In good faith, I thought you had been an hostler, verily.
I saw such another gentleman with you a barrowful bare
Of horse dung, and cow dung, and such other gear.
And how it happened, a marvellous chance! Betide
Your fellow was not sure of foot—and yet he went very wide—
But in a cow-patch both did ye slide;
And, as I ween, your nose therein rode,
Your face was bepainted with cobbler's wax
I saw never such a sight, I make God avow!
You were so begrimed as if you had been a sow.

*Groom.* In faith thou never sawest me 'till this day
I have dwelled with my master this seven year and more.
Full well have I pleased him—he will not say nay.

*Servant.* By my troth, then ye be changed to a new lore!
A servant ye are, and that a good!
There is no better looketh out of a hood.

*Groom.* Forsooth, if a hood I use for to wear
Full well it is lined with silk and camlet.

*Servant.* Yea, it is a double hood and that I'll swear!

[*Here cometh the* 1ST KNIGHT *to the* GROOM.

*1st Knight.* Now stable-groom, shortly bring forth away
The best horse, for our lord will ride.

*Groom.* I am full ready. Here is a palfrey
There can no man a better bestride.

[*Here cometh the* KNIGHT *to* SAUL *with horse.*

*1st Knight.* Behold, Sir Saul, your palfrey is come,
Full goodly beseen, as it is your desire
To take your voyage through every region.
Be not in doubt he will speed your matter.
And we, as your servants, with glad cheer
Shall give attendance. We will not gainsay,
But follow you where ye go by night or day.

*Saul.* Unto Damascus I make my progression,
To pursue all rebels, being froward and obstinate,
Against our laws by any transgression.
With all my diligence myself I will prepare
Concerning my purpose to oppress and separate,
None shall rejoice that doth offend,
But utterly to reprove with mind and intent.

[*Here* SAUL *goeth forth with his* Servants.

*Caiaphas.* Now Saul hath taken his worthy voyage
To pursue all rebels, of what degree they be.
Wherefore I commend his goodly dignity,
That he thus always taketh in hand
By his power to govern all this land.

*Annas.* We honour him as champion in every stand.
There is none such living upon the ground
That may be like him nor be his peer,
By East nor West, far nor near!

*A Dance.*

*Poet.* Finally, of this station thus we make conclusion.
Beseeching this audience to follow and succeed
With all diligence this general procession.
To understand this matter who list, to read
The Holy Bible for the better speed.
There shall he have the perfect intelligence
And thus we command you to Christ's magnificence.

[*Here cometh* SAUL *in with his* Servants.

*Saul.* My purpose to Damascus fully I intend.
To pursue the disciples my life I apply.
For to break down the churches thus I condescend,
None I will suffer that shall edify.
But bound, to Jerusalem, with furious violation,
Before Cæsar, Caiaphas and Annas have presentation.

Thus shall be subdued those wretches of that life;
That none shall enjoy, neither man, child nor wife.

[*Here cometh a flame with a great tempest and* SAUL *falleth down. Then* Godhead *speaketh in Heaven.*

*God.* Saul! Saul! Why does thou me pursue?
It is hard to prick against the spore!
I am thy Saviour that is so true,
Which maketh Heaven and Earth and each creature.
Offend not my goodness! I will thee recure!

*Saul.* Oh Lord, I am afraid! I tremble for fear!
What wouldst I should do, tell me here?

*God.* Arise and go thou with glad cheer
Into the city and I shall succour thee
That no manner of ill shall betide.
And I will there for thee provide
By my great goodness what thou shalt do.
Hie thee as fast as thou mayst go.

*Saul.* Oh merciful God, what aileth me?
I am lame. My legs be taken me from.
My seeing likewise. I may not see.
I cannot tell whither I go.
My men have forsaken me also.
Whither shall I wend, and whither shall I pass?
Lord, I beseech thee, help me of thy grace.

1*st Knight.* Sir, we be here to help thee in thy need.
Withal our affiance we will not cease.

*Saul.* Then to Damascus, I pray you, me lead,
In God's name, according to your promise.

2*nd Knight.* Put forth your hand. We shall you bring
Into the city without tarrying.

[*Here the* KNIGHTS *lead forth* SAUL.

*Poet.* Honourable friends, we beseech you of audience
To hear our intentions and also our process.
Upon our matter, by your favourable licence,
Another part of the story we will address.
Here shall be briefly shown with all our diligence
At this pageant, Saint Paul's Conversion.
Take ye good heed and thereto give attention.

[*Here* CHRIST *appeareth to* ANANIAS

*Christ.* Ananias! Ananias! Where art thou, Ananias?

*Ananias.* Here, Lord; I am here, truly.
*Christ.* Go thy way and make thy course,
As I shall assign thee by mine advice
Into the street *qui dicitus rectus,*
And in a certain house of warrantise,
There shall ye find Saul in humbleness,
As a meek lamb that a wolf before was named.
Do my behest; be nothing ashamed.
He wanteth his sight, by my punishment constrained.
Praying unto me, I assure, thou shalt him find.
With my stroke of pity sore he is pained,
Wanting his sight, for he is truly blind.
*Ananias.* Lord, I am afraid, for always in my mind
I hear so much of his furious cruelty,
That for speaking of thy name to death he will put me.
*Christ.* Nay, Ananias; nay, I assure thee,
He will be glad of thy coming.
*Ananias.* Ah! Lord, but I know of a certainty
That thy saints in Jerusalem to death he doth bring.
*Christ.* Be nothing dread! He is a chosen vessel.
He shall bear my name before the kings and children of Israel;
The true preacher of the high divinity.
A very pinnacle of the faith, I ensure thee.
*Ananias.* Lord, thy commandment I shall fulfil.
Unto Saul I will take my way.
*Christ.* Be nothing in doubt for good nor ill.
Farewell, Ananias! Tell Saul what I do say.
[CHRIST *disappeareth.*
*Ananias.* Blessed Lord, defend me, as thou best may!
Greatly I fear his cruel tyranny
But to do thy precept myself I shall apply.
[*Here* ANANIAS *goeth toward* SAUL.
1*st Knight.* I marvel greatly what it doth mean
To see our master in this hard stound.
The wonder great light that did so shine
Smote him down with its strength to the ground;
And methought I heard a sound
Of one speaking with voice delectable,
Which was to me a wonderful miracle.
But now, sirrah, let us return

Again to Caiaphas and Annas this to tell:
How it befel to us this grievous chance.

[*The two* KNIGHTS *depart.*

*Saul.* Lord, of thy comfort much I desire,
Thou mighty Prince of Israel, King of pity,
Which me hast punished as thy prisoner
That neither ate nor drank these days three.
But, Gracious Lord, for thy visitation I thank thee!
Thy servant shall I be as long as I have breath,
Though I therefore should suffer death.

*Here cometh* ANANIAS *to* SAUL.

*Ananias.* Peace be in this place and goodly mansion!
Who is within? Speak, in Christ's holy name!
*Saul.* I am here, Saul. Come in, on God's benison!
What is your will? Tell, without blame.
*Ananias.* From Almighty God, certainly to thee sent I am;
And Ananias men call me where I dwell.
*Saul.* What would you have, I pray you me tell?
*Ananias.* Give me your hand for your avail:
For as I was commanded by his gracious sentence,
He bade thee be steadfast, for thou shalt be hale.
For this same cause he sent me to thy presence.
Also he bade thee remember his high excellence
By the same token that he did thee meet
Toward the city when he to thee appeared.
There mayest thou know his power celestial
How he disposeth everything as him list.
Nothing may withstand his might essential,
To stand upright or else down to thrust,
This is his power. It may not be missed,
For who that it lacketh wanteth a friend.
This is the message that he doth thee send.
*Saul.* His mercy to me is right welcome!
I am right glad that it is thus.

[*Here the* HOLY SPIRIT *appears above him.*

*Ananias.* Be of good cheer and perfect jubilation
*Descendet super te Spiritus Sanctus,*
Which hath with his grace illumined us.
Put forth thy hand and go with me.
Again to thy sight here I restore thee.

*Saul.* Blessed Lord, thanks to you ever be!
The scales are fallen from my eyes twain!
When I was blind and could not see,
Lord, thou has sent me my sight again.
From sobbing and weeping I cannot refrain,
My pensive heart is full of contrition;
For my offences my body shall have punishment.
Wherefore, Ananias, at the watery stream
Baptise me, heartily I thee pray,
Among your number that I elected and chosen be may.

*Ananias.* Unto this well of much virtue
We will us hie with all our diligence.

*Saul.* Go you before, and after I shall sue
Lauding and praising our Lord's benevolence.
For my great unkindness my heart doth weep.

[*They come to the well.*

*Ananias.* Kneel ye down upon the ground,
Receiving this christening with good intent
Which shall make you whole of your deadly wound.
I christen you with mind full perfect,
Receiving you into our religion,
Ever to be steadfast and never to flinch.
But ever constant without variation.
Now is fulfilled all our observation;
Concluding, thou mayst it ken,
*In nomine Patris et Filii et Spiritus Sancti, Amen!*

*Saul.* I am right glad, as bird on wing,
That I have received this blessed sacrament.

*Ananias.* Come on your way, Saul, for nothing stay.
Take ye some comfort for your body's nourishment.
Ye shall abide with the disciples, verily,
This many days in Damascus city,
Until the time more perfect ye may be.

*Saul.* Go forth your way, I will succeed
Into what place ye will me lead.

[*They go out.*

*Poet.* Thus we commit you all to the Trinity,
Concluding this station as we can or may,
Under the correction of them that lettered be;
How-be-it, unable, as I dare speak or say,
The compiler hereof should be to translate

So holy a story, but with favourable correction
Of my favourable masters of their benign supplexion.

*A Dance.*

The might of the Father's potential deity
Preserve this honourable and worshipful congregation,
That here be present, of high or low degree,
To understand this pageant at this little station,
Which we shall proceed with all our delectation,
If it please you to give audience favourable.
Hark wisely thereto: it is good and profitable.

[*He goeth out.*

[*The two* KNIGHTS *come up to* CAIAPHAS *and* ANNAS.

*1st Knight.* Noble prelates, take heed to our sentence!
A wonderful chance fell and did betide
Unto our master Saul, when he departed hence
A marvellous light from the heavens did glide
Which smote down him to ground before us too.

*2nd Knight.* A sweet dulcet voice spake him unto
And bade him unto Damascus to Ananias go
And there he should receive baptism duly;
And now clean against our laws he is truly.

*Caiaphas.* What! Saul converted from our law!
How say you, Annas, to this matter? This is a marvellous chance!
I cannot believe that this is of assurance!

*Annas.* No, Caiaphas, my mind truly does tell
That he will not turn in no manner wise,
But rather to death put and expel
All miscreants and wretches that do arise
Against our laws, by any enterprise. [*To the* KNIGHTS.
Say the truth without any fraudulence
Or else for your tale ye be like to be shent.

*1st Knight.* All that we declare, I saw it with my eye;
Nothing offending, but truly do justify.

*Caiaphas.* By the Great God, I do marvel greatly!
An this be true that ye do rehearse,
He shall repent his rebellious treachery
That all shall beware of his falseness.
We will not suffer him to prevail doubtless
For many perils that might betide
By his subtle means, on every side.

*Annas.* The law is committed to our adjustment;
Wherefore we will not see it decay,
But rather uphold it, help and augment,
That no reproof to us fall may
Of Caesar the Emperor, by night or day.
We shall to such matters hark and attend,
According to the laws our wits to spend.

[*Here appeareth* SAUL *in a disciple's gown.*

*Saul.* That Lord that is sharper of sight and of sound
And hath wrought with his word all things at his will,
Save this assembly that here sitteth or stands,
For his meek mercy that we do not spill.
Grant me, good Lord, thy pleasure to fulfil,
And send me such speech that I the truth say,
My intentions profitable to move if I may:
Well beloved friends, there be seven mortal sins . . .

*Servant.* What! Is not this Saul that took his voyage
Unto Jerusalem the disciples to oppress?
Bound he would bring them if any did rage
Upon Christ: this was his process,
To the Kings and priests he said, doubtless.

*Saul.* Yes, certainly, Saul is my name.
To hide it from you that were great shame.

*Servant.* To Annas and Caiaphas ye must make your recourse.
Come on your way and make no delation.

*Saul.* I will follow, for better or worse
To the Princes of priests with all delectation.

[*The* SERVANT *leadeth* SAUL *to* CAIAPHAS *and* ANNAS

*Servant.* Holy priests of high potestation,
Here is Saul! Look on him wisely!
He is another man than he was verily.

*Saul.* I am the servant of Jesu Almighty,
Creator and maker of sight and sound
Which is King Omnipotent of heaven's glory,
Chief comfort and solace both to free and bound,
Against whose power nothing may stand.
Emperor he is both of heaven and hell,
Where goodness and grace all things do excell.

[SAUL *withdraws a little.*

*Caiaphas.* Unto my heart this is great admiration,
That Saul is thus marvellously changed
But shortly in this we must have advisement,
For thus against us he may not continue;
Peradventure then of Caesar we may be shent.

*Annas.* Nay, I had liever in fire he were burnt
Than of Caesar we should have displeasure
For such a rebel and subtle false traitor.

*Caiaphas.* We will command the gates to be kept about
And the walls surely on every side
That he may escape nowhere out.
For die he shall, I ensure you indeed.

*Annas.* This traitor rebellious! Evil most be speed
That doth this unhappiness against all!
Now every custadonian keep well his wall!

*Servant.* The gates be shut! he cannot escape.
Every place is kept well and sure,
That in no wise he may, till he be taken,
Get out of the city by any conjecture.
Upon that caitiff and false traitor
Look ye be avenged with death mortal,
And judge him as ye list to what end he shall.

[*An* ANGEL *appears to* SAUL.

*Angel.* Holy Saul, I give you monition,
The princes of the Jews intend certain
To put you to death. But by God's provision
He will ye shall live longer and obtain,
And after thy death thou shalt reign
Above in heaven. With our Lord's grace
Convey yourself quickly into another place.

*Saul.* The Lord's pleasure ever must be done,
Both in Heaven and in hell, as his will is!
In a bearing basket or a sling anon
I shall me convey with help of the disciples,
For every gate is shut and kept with a multitude of men;
But I trust in our Lord that is my succour
To resist their malice and cruel fury.

# EPILOGUE

*Poet.* Thus leave we Saul within the city;
The gates kept by the commandment of Caiaphas and Annas.
But the disciples in the night over the wall truly,
As the Bible sayeth: *dimiserum eum summittentes in sporta.*
And Saul, after that, in Jerusalem, vera,
Joined himself, and there accompanied
With the disciples, where they were unfeigned.
This little pageant thus conclude we
As we can, lacking literary science;
Beseeching you all, of high or low degree,
Our simpleness to hold excused and licensed,
That of rhetoric have not intelligence.
Committing you all to our Lord Jesus,
To whose laud ye sing: *Exultet coelum laudibus!*

# MONDAY

# GAMMER GURTON'S NEEDLE

(1575)

By

"MR. S., MASTER OF ARTS."

(*Identity uncertain.*)

## THE NAMES OF THE SPEAKERS IN THIS COMEDY

DICCON, The Bedlam.

HODGE, Gammer Gurton's Servant.

TIB, Gammer Gurton's Maid.

GAMMER GURTON.

COCK, Gammer Gurton's Boy.

DAME CHAT.

DOCTOR RAT, the Curate.

MASTER BAILEY.

DOLL, Dame Chat's Maid.

SCAPETHRIFT, Master Bailey's Servant.

MUTES

God Save the Queen.

## THE PROLOGUE

As Gammer Gurton, with many a wide stitch
Sat piecing and patching of Hodge her man's breech,
By chance or misfortune, as she her gear tost,
In Hodge leather breeches her needle she lost.
When Diccon the bedlam had heard by report
That good Gammer Gurton was robbed in this sort,
He quietly persuaded with her in that stound
Dame Chat, her dear gossip, this needle had found—
Yet knew she no more of this matter, alas,
Than knoweth Tom our clerk what the Priest saith at mass.
Hereof there ensued so fearful a fray,
Mas' Doctor was sent for these gossips to stay;
Because he was Curate, and esteemed full wise,
Who found that he sought not, by Diccon's device.
When all things were tumbled and clean out of fashion,
Whether it were by fortune, or some other constellation,
Suddenly . . . the needle Hodge found by the pricking
And drew it out of his buttock where he felt it sticking.
Their hearts then at rest with perfect securetie,
With a pot of good ale they struck up their plauditie.

*Enter* DICCON.

*Diccon.* Many a mile have I walked, divers and sundry ways,
And many a good man's house have I been at in my days
Many a gossip's cup in my time have I tasted
And many a broach and spit, have I both turned and basted;
Many a piece of bacon have I had out of their balks,
In running over the country, with long and weary walks;
Yet came my foot never, within those door cheeks,
To seek flesh or fish, garlick, onions, or leeks,
That ever I saw a sort sort in such a plight
As here within this house appeareth to my sight;
There is howling and scowling, all cast in a dump,
With whewling and puling, as though they had lost a trump.
Sighing and sobbing, they weep and they wail
I marvel in my mind, what the devil they ail.
The old Trot sits groaning, with "alas! and alas!"
And Tib wrings her hands, and takes on in worse case.
With poor Cock their boy, they be driven in such fits
I fear me the folks be not well in their wits,
Ask them what they ail, or who brought them in this stay,
They answer not at all, or "alack! and welaway!"
When I saw it booted not, out of doors I hied me—
And caught a slip of bacon, when I saw that none spied me;
Which I intend not far hence, unless my purpose fail,
Shall serve for a shoeing horn to draw on two pots of ale.

*Enter* HODGE.

*Hodge.* See how I am arrayed with dabbling in the dirt!
She that set me to ditching, I would she had the squrt
Was never poor soul that such a life had!
Gog's bones this filthy clay has drest me too bad!
God's soul, see how this stuff tears!
I were better to be a Bear-ward and set to keep Bears!

By the mass, here is a gash! a shameful hole indeed!
If one stitch tear further, a may man thrust in his head.

*Diccon.* By my father's soul, Hodge, if I should now be sworn
I cannot choose but say thy breech is foul betorn.
But the next remedy in such a case and help,
Is to plank on a piece, as broad as thy cap.

*Hodge.* Gog's soul man, 'Tis not yet two days fully ended
Since my dame Gurton, I am sure, these breeches amended.
But I'm made such a drudge, to trudge at every need,
I'd rend it though it were stitched with sturdy pack thread.

*Diccon.* Hodge, let thy breeches go, and speak and tell me soon
What devil aileth Gammer Gurton, and Tib her maid to frown.

*Hodge.* Tush, man, th'art deceived, 'tis their daily look,
They cower so over the coals, their eyes be bleared with smoke.

*Diccon.* Nay, by the mass, I perfectly perceived as I came hither,
That either Tib and her dame hath been by the ears together,
Or else as great a matter, as thou shalt shortly see.

*Hodge.* Now I beseech our Lord, they never better agreed!

*Diccon.* By God's soul there they sit as still as stones in the street,
As though they had been taken with fairies or else with some ill spite.

*Hodge.* Gog's heart, I durst have laid my cap to a crown
I'd learn of some prank as soon as I came to town.

*Diccon.* Why, Hodge, art thou inspired? Or didst thou thereof hear?

*Hodge.* Nay, but I saw such a wonder as I saw not this seven year.
Tom Tankard's cow, by Gog's bones, she set me up her sail
And flinging about his half acre frisking with her tail,
As though there had been on her back a swarm of bees,
If I had not cried "Phroh! woa!" she'd lept out of his lees.

*Diccon.* Why, Hodge, be there knowledge in Tom Tankard's cow's tail?

*Hodge.* Well I've heard some say such tokens do not fail.
But canst you not tell in faith, Diccon, why she frowns
Or whereat?
Hath no man stolen her ducks or hens, or gelded Gib her cat?

*Diccon.* What devil can I tell, man, I could not get one word.
They gave no more heed to my talk than thou wouldst to a lord.

*Hodge.* I can naught do but muse, what marvellous thing it is.
I'll in and know myself what matters are amiss.

*Diccon.* Then farewell, Hodge, a-while, since thou doest inward haste,
For I will into the good wife Chat, to feel how the ale doth taste.

[*Exit.*

*Hodge.* I am aghast, by the mass, I wot not what to do.
I had need bless me well before I go them to.
Perchance some felon sprite may haunt our house indeed,
And then I were but a noddy to venture where I have no need.

*Enter* TIB.

*Tib.* I am worse than mad, by the mass, here at this to stay!
I am chid, I am blamed, and beaten all th' hours of the day.
Lamed and hunger-starved, pricked up all in jaggs;
Having no patch to hide my back, save a few rotten rags.

*Hodge.* I say, Tib, if thou be Tib, as I trow sure thou be,
What devil make ado is this, between our dame and thee?

*Tib.* Gog's bread, Hodge, thou had a good turn thou wast not here this while.
It had been better for some of us to have been hence a mile,
My Gammer is out of course and frantic all at once,
That Cock our boy, and I poor wench, have felt it on our bones.

*Hodge.* What is the matter, say on, Tib, whereat she taketh so on?

*Tib.* She is undone she saith, alas, her joy and life is gone, if she hear not of some comfort, she is she saith, but dead.
Shall never come within her lips, one inch of meat nor bread.

*Hodge.* By'r Lady I am not very glad to see her in this dump.
I hold a noble, her stool hath fallen and she hath broke her rump.

*Tib.* Nay, greater, greater, is her grief, as, Hodge, we shall all feel.

*Hodge.* Gog's wounds, Tib, my Gammer has never lost her needle?

*Tib.* Her needle.

*Hodge.* Her needle?

*Tib.* Her needle by him that made me, it is true, Hodge, I tell thee.

*Hodge.* Gog's sacrament, I would she had lost th' heart out of her belly!
The devil or else his dam, they owe her sure a shame.
How a murrain came this chance, say Tib, unto our dame?

*Tib.* My Gammer sat her down on her stool and bad me reach thy breeches,
And by and by, a vengeance on it, or she had taken two stitches
To clap a clout upon thy seat, by chance aside she peers.
And Gib our cat in the milk pan she spied, over head and ears.
"Ah, there! Out thief," she cried aloud, and swept thy breeches down.
Up went her staff, and Gib leaped out of doors into the town.
And since that time was, never wight could set their eyes upon it.
Gog's malison, have Cock and I bid twenty times light on it.

*Hodge.* And is not then my breeches sewed up? To-morrow them I'd wear.

*Tib.* No, in faith, Hodge, thy breeches lie for all this never the nearer.

*Hodge.* Now a vengeance light on all the lot that better should have kept it.

The cat, the house, and Tib, our maid that better should have swept it!
See where she commeth crawling. Come on in twenty devils way.
Ye have made a fair day's work have you not, pray you say?

*Enter* GAMMER.

*Gammer*. Alas, Hodge! Alas, I may well curse and ban
This day, that ever I saw it! With Gib and the milk-pan!
For these and ill luck together, as knoweth Cock my boy,
Have stuck away my dear needle, and robbed me of my joy:
My fair long straight needle that was mine only treasure.
The first day of my sorrow is, and last end of my pleasure.

*Hodge*. Might ha' kept it when ye had it. But fools will be fools still.
Lose what is fast in your hands! Ye need not but ye will.

*Gammer*. Go hie thee, Tib, and run, thou slut, to th'end here of the town.
Didst carry out dust in thy lap; seek where thou threw it down.
And as thou sawest me raking in the ashes where I mourned,
So see in all the heap of dust, thou leave no straw unturned.

*Tib*. That I will, Gammer, swift and true, and soon be here again.

*Gammer*. Tib, stoop and look; down on the ground to it, and take some pain. [*Exit* TIB.

*Hodge*. Here is a pretty matter! To see this gear how it goes!
By gog's soul I think you would lose your head if it were loose!
Your needle lost! It's a pity you should lack care and endless sorrow!
Gog's death, how shall my breeches be sewed? Must I go thus to-morrow?

*Gammer*. Ah, Hodge, Hodge, if that I could find my needle, by the rood,
I'd sew thy breeches, I promise thee, with full good double thread;
And set a patch on either knee should last these months twain.

Now God and good Saint Sithe I pray to send it home again.

*Hodge.* Whereto served your hands and eyes, not this your needle to keep?
What devil had you else to do? Ye kept, I wot, no sheep,
I'm fain abroad to dig and delve, in water, mire and clay.
Sossing and possing in the dirt, still from day to day
A hundred things that be abroad, I'm set to see them well.
And four of you sit idle at home, and can not keep a needle.

*Gammer.* My needle, alas, I lost it, Hodge, what time I me uphasted
To save the milk set up for thee, which Gib the cat hath wasted.

*Hodge.* The Devil he burst both Gib, and Tib, with all the rest!
I'm alway sure of the worst end, who ever have the best!
Where ha' you been fidging about, since you your needle lost?

*Gammer.* Within the house, and at the door, sitting by this same post,
Where I was looking a long hour, before these folks came here,
But welaway, all was in vain, my needle was never there.

*Hodge.* Set me a candle, let me seek and grope wherever it be.
Gog's heart ye be so foolish, I think, you'll know it not when you see it!

*Gammer.* Come hither, Cock; what Cock I say.

*Cock.* How, Gammer?

*Gammer.* Go hye thee soon, and grope behind the old brass pan,
Which thing when thou hast done,
There shalt thou find an old shoe, wherein if thou look
Thou shalt find lying an inch of a white tallow candle;
Light it, and bring it right away.

*Cock.* That shall be done anon.

*Gammer.* Nay tarry, Hodge, till thou hast light, and then we'll seek each one.

*Hodge.* Come away, ye whoreson boy, are ye asleep? Ye must have a crier.

*Cock.* I cannot get the candle light. There is almost no fire.

*Hodge.* I'll hold thee a penny I'll make ye come if I may catch thine ears!
Art deaf, thou whoreson boy? Cock, I say, why canst not hear?

*Gammer.* Beat him not, Hodge, but help the boy and come up both together.

*Enter* TIB.

*Gammer.* How now, Tib, quick, let's hear what news thou hast brought hither.

*Tib.* I have tost and tumbled yonder heap over and over again,
And winnowed it through my fingers, as I would winnow grain—
Not so much as a hen's leaving but in pieces I tear it;
Or whatsoever clod of clay I found I did not spare it,
Looking within and eke without to find your needle, alas.
But all in vain! And, without help, your needle is where it was.

*Gammer.* Alas, my needle we shall never meet! adieu, adieu for aye!

*Tib.* Not so, Gammer, we might it find if we knew where it lay.

*Enter* COCK.

*Cock.* Gog's cross, Gammer, if ye will laugh, look in but at the door
And see how Hodge lieth tumbling and tossing upon the floor,
Raking there some fire to find among the ashes dead,
Where there is not one spark so big as a pin's head;
At last in a dark corner two sparks he thought he sees
Which were indeed nought else but Gib our cat's two eyes.
"Puff," says Hodge, thinking thereby to have fire without doubt.
With that Gib shuts her two eyes, and so the fire was out!
And by-and-by them opened, even as they were before,
With that the sparks appeared even as they had done of yore:
And even as Hodge blew the fire, as he did think,
Gib, as she felt the blast, straight-way began to wink;

Till Hodge fell a swearing, as came best to his turn,
The fire was sure bewitcht and therefore would not burn.
At last Gib up the stairs, among the old posts and pins,
And Hodge he hied him after till broke were both his shins;
Cursing and swearing oaths that were never of his making,
That Gib would fire the house, if that she were not taken.

*Gammer.* See here is all the thought that the foolish urchin taketh,
And Tib methinks, at his elbow almost as merry maketh.
This is all the wit ye have when others make their moan.
Come down, Hodge, where art thou, and let the cat alone.

*Hodge.* Gog's heart, help and come up! Gib in her tail hath fire,
And is like to burn all if she get a little higher.
Come down, quoth you? nay then you might count me a patch,
The house cometh down on your heads if it catch on the thatch.

*Gammer.* It is the cat's eyes, fool, that shineth in the dark.

*Hodge.* Hath the cat, do you think, in every eye a spark?

*Gammer.* No, but they shine as like fire as ever man see.

*Hodge.* By the mass, an she burns all, you'll bear the blame for me.

*Gammer.* Come down and help to see here our needle that it were found.
Down, Tib, on thy knees, I say; down, Cock, to the ground.
To God I make a vow, and so to good Saint Anne,
A candle shall they have apiece, get it where I can,
If I may my needle find in one place or another.

*Hodge.* Now a vengeance on Gib light, on Gib and his mother,
And all the generation of cats both far and near!
Look on the ground, whoreson. Thinkest thou the needle is here?

*Cock.* By my troth, Gammer, methought your needle here I saw,
But when my fingers toucht it, I felt it was a straw.

*Tib.* See, Hodge, what's this, may it not be within it?

*Hodge.* Break it, fool, with thy hand and see and thou canst find it.

*Tib.* Nay break it you, Hodge, break it for your Tib.

*Hodge*. Gog's sides, fie it stinks; 'twas left there by Gib!
It were well done to make thee eat it by the mass.

*Gammer*. This matter amendeth not! My needle is still where it was.
Our candle is at an end, let us all in quiet
And come another time, when we have more light.

[*They go in.*

### A Song

Back and side go bare, go bare,
Both foot and hand go cold:
But belly, God send thee good ale enough,
Whether it be new or old.

I cannot eat but little meat,
My stomach is not good:
But sure, I think I that can drink
With him that wears a hood.
Though I go bare, take ye no care,
I am nothing acold:
I stuff my skin so full within,
Of jolly good ale and old.
Back and side go bare, go bare,
Both foot and hand go cold:
But belly, God send thee good ale enough
Whether it be new or old.

I love no roast but a nut brown toast
And a crab laid in the fire,
A little bread, shall do me stead
Much bread I not desire:
No frost nor snow, no wind I trow
Can hurt me with its cold
I am so wrapt, and throughly lapt
With jolly good ale and old.
Back and side go bare, go bare,
Both foot and hand go cold:
But belly, God send thee good ale enough,
Whether it be new or old.

And Tib my wife, that as her life
Loveth well good ale to seek,
Full oft drinks she, till ye may see
The tears run down her cheek.
Then doth she trowl, to me the bowl
Even as a malt worm should,
And saith, sweetheart, I took my part
Of this jolly good ale and old.
Back and side go bare, go bare,
Both foot and hand go cold:
But belly, God send thee good ale enough
Whether it be new or old.

Now let them drink till they nod and wink,
Even as good fellows should do;
They shall not miss to have the bliss
Good ale doth bring men to.
And all poor souls that have scoured bowls
Or have them lustily trolled,
God save the lives of them and their wives
Whether they be young or old.
Back and side go bare, go bare,
Both foot and hand go cold:
But belly, God send thee good ale enough
Whether it be new or old.

*Enter* DICCON.

*Diccon*. Well done, by Gog's malt, well sung and well said!
Come on, mother Chat, as thou art true maid;
One fresh pot of ale lets see to make an end;
Against this cold weather, my naked arms to defend.
This gear it warms the soul, now wind blow on the worst,
And let us drink and swill, till that our bellies burst.

*Enter* HODGE.

*Hodge*. I'm goodly rewarded, am I not, do you think?
I've had a goodly dinner for all my sweat and swink!
Neither butter, cheese, milk, onions, flesh nor fish,
Save this poor piece of barley bread. 'Tis a pleasant costly dish!

*Diccon*. Hail, fellow Hodge, and well to fare with thy meat, if you have any!
But by thy words, as I thee smelled, thy dainties be not many!

*Hodge*. Dainties, Diccon! Gods save me, save this piece of dry horsebread,
I've bit no bite this live long day, no crumb come in my head.

*Diccon*. Why, Hodge, was there none at home, thy dinner for to set?

*Hodge*. Gog's bread, Diccon, I came too late; was nothing there to get,
Gib, a foul fiend might on her light, lickt the milk-pan so clean.
See Diccon, 'twas not so well washed this seven year as I ween:
A pestilence light on all ill luck! I'd thought yet for all this
Of a morsel of bacon behind the door at worst I should not miss,
But when I sought a slip to cut, as I was wont to do,
Gog's soul, Diccon, Gib our cat had eat the bacon too.

*Diccon*. Ill luck quotha', marry swear it, Hodge, this day, The truth to tell,
Thou rose not on thy right side, or else blest thee not well!
Thy milk slopt up, thy bacon filched, that was too bad luck, Hodge!

*Hodge*. Nay, nay, there was a fouler fault: my Gammer gave me the dodge.
Seest not how I'm rent and torn, my heels, my knees and my breech?
I'd thought as I sat by the fire, I'd have here and there a stitch:
But there I was fooled indeed.

*Diccon*. How so, Hodge?

*Hodge*. Has she not gone, trowest, thou, and lost her needle?

*Diccon*. Her Eel Hodge, who fished of late? that was a dainty dish.

*Hodge*. Tush tush, her needle, her needle, her needle, man, 'tis neither flesh nor fish.

A little thing with an hole in the end, as bright as any siller.
Small, long, sharp at the point, and straight as any pillar.

*Diccon.* I know not what the devil you meanst, you bringst me more in doubt.

*Hodge.* Knowest not what Tom tailor's man, sits broaching through a clout?
A needle, needle, a needle, my Gammer's needle is gone.

*Diccon.* Her needle, Hodge, now I smell thee. That was a chaunce alone!
By the mass you hadst a shameful loss, if it were but for thy breeches!

*Hodge.* Gog's soul, man, I'd give a crown had it but three stitches.

*Diccon.* How sayest you, Hodge, what should he have, again thy needle got?

*Hodge.* Bym' father's soul, an I had it I'd give him a new groat.

*Diccon.* Canst thou keep counsel in this case?

*Hodge.* Else would my tongue were out.

*Diccon.* Do thou but then by my advice, and I will fetch it without doubt.

*Hodge.* I'll run, I'll ride, I'll dig, I'll delve, I'll toil, I'll trudge, shalt see.
I'll hold, I'll draw, I'll pull, I'll pinch, I'll kneel on my bare knee.
I'll scrape, I'll scratch, I'll sift, I'll seek, I'll bow, I'll bend, I'll sweat,
I'll stoop, I'll stir, I'll cap, I'll kneel, I'll creep on hands and feet.
I'll be thy bondman, Diccon, I swear by sun and moon.
If I cannot somewhat to stop this gap, I'm utterly undone.
[*Pointing behind to his torn breeches.*

*Diccon.* Why, is there any special cause thou takest hereat such sorrow?

*Hodge.* Christian Clack, Tom Simson's maid, by the masse, comes hither to-morrow.
I am not able to say, between us what may hap,
She smiled on me the last Sunday when I put off my cap.

*Diccon.* Well, Hodge, this is a matter of weight, and must be kept close,

It might else turn to both our costs as the world now goes.
Shalt sware to be no blab, Hodge?
*Hodge.* I will, Diccon.
*Diccon.* Then go to,
Lay thine hand here, say after me as thou shalt hear me do.
Hast no book?
*Hodge.* I've no book I.
*Diccon.* Then needs must force us both,
Upon my breech to lay thine hand, and there to take thine oath.
*Hodge.* I, Hodge breechless,
Swear to Diccon, reckless,
By the cross that I shall kiss,
To keep his counsel close
And always me to dispose
To work that his pleasure is.
[*Here he kisseth Diccon's breech.*
*Diccon.* Now, Hodge, see thou take heed
And do as I thee bid.
For so I judge it meet,
This needle again to win
There is no shift therein
But conjure up a spirit.
*Hodge.* What the great Devil, Diccon, I say?
*Diccon.* Yea in good faith, that is the way,
Fetched with some pretty charm.
*Hodge.* Soft, Diccon, be not too hasty yet,
By the mass, for I begin to sweat!
I'm afraid of some harm.
*Diccon.* Come hither then and stir thee not
One inch out of this circle plot,
But stand as I thee teach.
*Hodge.* And shall I be here safe from their claws?
*Diccon.* The master Devil with his long paws
Here to thee cannot reach:
Now will I settle me to this gear.
*Hodge.* I say, Diccon, hear me, hear!
Go softly to this matter.
*Diccon.* What, devil man, art afraid of nought?
*Hodge.* Canst not tarry a little thought?
*Diccon.* Stand still to it, why shouldest thou fear him?

*Hodge.* Gog's sides, Diccon, me think I hear him;
An I tarry I'll mar all.
*Diccon.* The matter is no worse than I told it.
*Hodge.* By the mass, I'm able no longer to hold it.
*Diccon.* Stand to it, Hodge, stir not, you whoreson.
What the devil? Be thy sides a bursting?
Thy self a while but stay,
The devil, I smell him, will be here anon.
*Hodge.* Hold him fast, Diccon. I am gone, I am gone,
I'll not be at that fray. [*Exit.*
*Diccon.* Fie, dirty knave! and out upon thee!
Above all other louts fie on thee!
Is not here a piece of work?
A man I think might make a play,
And need no words but what they say,
Being but half a Clerk.
Soft, let me alone, I will take the charge
This matter further to enlarge
Within a time short,
If ye will mark my toys and note,
I will give ye leave to cut my throat
If I make not good sport.
Dame Chat, I say! where be ye, within?

*Enter* DAME CHAT.

*Chat.* Who have we there maketh such a din?
*Diccon.* Here is a good fellow, maketh no great danger.
*Chat.* What, Diccon! Come near, ye be no stranger.
We be fast set at trump, man, hard by the fire.
Thou shalt set on the king, if thou come a little nigher.
*Diccon.* Nay, nay, there is no tarrying: I must be gone again.
But first for you in counsel I have a word or twain.
*Chat.* Come hither, Doll! Doll! sit down and play this game.
And as thou sawest me do, see thou do even the same
There is five trumps beside the Queen, the hindmost you shalt find her.
Take heed of Sim Glover's wife, she hath an eye behind her.
Now, Diccon, say your will.

*Diccon.* Nay soft a little yet,
I would not tell it my sister, the matter is so great.
There, I will have you swear by our dear Lady of Bullain,
S. Dunstone, and S. Donnyke, with the three Kings of Kullaine,
That ye shall keep it secret.

*Chat.* Gog's bread, that will I do,
As secret as mine own thought, by God and the devil too.

*Diccon.* Here is Gammer Gurton, your neighbour, a sad and heavy wight,
Her goodly fair red cock at home was stole this last night.

*Chat.* Gog's soul, her cock with the yellow legs, that nightly crowed so just?

*Diccon.* That cock is stolen.

*Chat.* What, was he taken out of the hen's roost?

*Diccon.* I cannot tell where the devil he was kept, under key or lock,
But Tib hath tickled in Gammer's ear, that you did steal the cock.

*Chat.* Have I, great whore! By bread and salt——

*Diccon.* What, soft, I say be still!
Say not one word for all this gear.

*Chat.* By the mass that I will.
I will have the young whore by the head, and the old trot by the throat.

*Diccon.* Not one word, dame Chat, I say, not one word for my coat.

*Chat.* Shall such a beggar's brawl as that thinkest you, make me a thief?
The pox light on her whore's sides, a pestilence and a mischief!
Come out, thou hungry needy bitch! O, that my nails be short!

*Diccon.* Gog's bread, woman, hold your peace, this gear will else pass sport.
I would not for an hundred pound, this matter should be known.
That I am author of this tale, or have abroad blown it.
Did ye not swear ye would be ruled, before the tale I told?
I said ye must all secret keep, and ye said, sure ye would.

*Chat*. Would you suffer yourself, Diccon, such a sort, to revile you?
With slanderous words to blot your name, and so to defile you?

*Diccon*. No, goodwife Chat, I would be loth such drabs should blot my name;
But yet ye must so order all, that Diccon bear no blame.

*Chat*. Go to, then, what is your rede? say on your mind, ye shall me rule herein.

*Diccon*. Godamercy to dame Chat. In faith you must the gear begin.
It is twenty pound to a piece of dirt, that my Gammer will not tarry.
But hitherward she comes as fast as her legs can her carry,
To brawl with you about her cock, for well I heard Tib say,
The cock was roasted in your house, to breakfast yesterday.
And when ye had the carcase eaten, the feathers ye out flung,
And Doll your maid the legs she hid a foot deep in the dung.

*Chat*. Oh gracious God, my heart it bursts!

*Diccon*. Well rule yourself a space
And Gammer Gurton, when she cometh anon into this place,
Then to the quean let's see ye tell her your mind and spare not.
[*Aside*] So shall Diccon blameless be, and then go to, I care not.

*Chat*. The whore! Beware her throat! I can abide no longer!
In faith, old witch, it shall be seen which of us two be stronger!
And, Diccon, but at your request, I would not stay one hour.

*Diccon*. Well, keep it in till she be here, and then out let it pour.
In the mean while get you in, and make no words of this.
More of this matter within this hour to hear you shall not miss.
Because I know you are my friend, hide it I could not doubtless.
Ye know your harm, see ye be wise about your own business.
So fare ye well.

*Chat*. Nay, soft Diccon, and drink. What, Doll, I say.
Bring here a cup o' the best ale, let's see. Come quickly away.
[*Exit*.

*Diccon*. Ye see, masters, the one end tapped of this my short device.
Now must we broach t'other too before the smoke arise.

*Enter* HODGE.

*Hodge*. Yea, Gog's soul, art alive yet? What, Diccon, dare I come?
*Diccon*. A man is well paid to trust to thee! I will say nothing but mum.
But an ye come any nearer I pray you see all be sweet.
*Hodge*. Tush, man, is Gammer's needle found? That I'd gladly wot.
*Diccon*. She may thank thee it is not found, for if you had kept thy standing
The devil he would have fetched it out, even, Hodge, at thy commanding.
*Hodge*. Gog's heart, and could he tell nothing where the needle might be found?
*Diccon*. Ye foolish dolt, ye were away. Here we had got our ground,
Therefore his tale so doubtful was, that I could not perceive it.
*Hodge*. Then I see well something was said; I hope one day yet to have it.
But, Diccon, Diccon, did not the devil cry, "Ho, ho, ho?"
*Diccon*. If you hadst tarried where thou stoodst, thou wouldst have said so.
*Hodge*. Durst swear on a book I heard him roar, straight after I was gone.
But tell me, Diccon, what said the knave? let me have it anon.
*Diccon*. The whoreson talked to me. I know not well of what
One while his tongue it ran and paltered of a cat;
Another while he stammered still upon a Rat;

Last of all there was nothing but every word, "Chat" "Chat,"
But this I well percieved before I would him rid,
Between Chat, and the Rat, and the Cat, the needle is hid,
Now whether Gib your cat have eat it in her maw,
Or Doctor Rat our curate have found it in the straw,
Or this Dame Chat your neighbour have stolen it, God he knoweth.
But by to-morrow at this time, we shall learn how the matter goeth.

*Hodge.* Canst not learn to-night, man? Seest not what is here?

[*pointing behind to his torn breeches.*

*Diccon.* 'Tis not possible to make it sooner appear.

*Hodge.* Alas, Diccon, then I have no shift, but lest I tarry too long
Hie me to Sim Glover's shop, there to seek for a thong,
Therewith this breech to 'tatch and tie as I may.

*Diccon.* To-morrow, Hodge, if we chance to meet, shalt see what I will say.
Now this gear must forward go, for here my Gammer commeth,
Be still a while and say nothing, make here a little room.

[*Exit* HODGE.

*Enter* GAMMER GURTON.

*Gammer.* Good Lord, shall never be my luck my needle again to spy?
Alas the while, 'tis past my help, where 'tis still it must lie!

*Diccon.* Now Jesus, Gammer Gurton, what driveth you to this sadness?
I fear me, by my conscience, you will sure fall to madness.

*Gammer.* Who is that? What, Diccon, I am lost man: Fie! fie!

*Diccon.* Marry, fie on them that be worthy! But what should be your trouble?

*Gammer.* Alas! the more I think on it, my sorrow it waxeth double!
My goodly flaunting sewing needle, I have lost I wot not where.

*Diccon.* Your needle! When?

*Gammer.* My needle, alas, I might full ill it spare!
As God himself he knoweth, ne'er one beside I have.

*Diccon.* If this be all, good Gammer, I warrant you all is safe.

*Gammer.* Why, know you any tidings which way my needle is gone!

*Diccon.* Yes that I do doubtless, as ye shall hear anon.
I saw a thing this matter toucheth within these twenty hours,
Even at this gate, before my face, by a neighbour of yours.
She stooped down, and up she took a needle or a pin
I durst be sworn it was even yours, by all my mother's kin.

*Gammer.* It was my needle, Diccon, I wot, for here even at this post
I sat, what time as I started up, and so my needle was lost:
Who was it, dear son? speak I pray thee and quickly tell me that?

*Diccon.* A subtle quean as any in this town, your neighbour here Dame Chat.

*Gammer.* Dame Chat, Diccon? Let me be gone, I'll thither in post haste.

*Diccon.* Take my counsel yet or ye go, for fear ye walk in wast.
It is a murrin crafty drab, and froward to be pleased,
An ye take not the better way, your needle still ye lose it;
For when she took it up, even here before your doors
"What soft, Dame Chat," quoth I, "that same is none of yours."
"Avaunt," quoth she, "Sir knave, what pratest thou of that I find?"
I would you hadst kissed me I wot where—she meant I know behind.
And home she went as brisk as it had been a bodylouse,
And I after as bold as I had been the goodman of the house.

*Gammer.* Gog's bread, and thinks the callet thus to keep my needle me fro?

*Diccon.* Let her alone, and she minds none other but even to dress you so.

*Gammer.* By the mass, I'll rather spend the coat that is on my back.

Thinks the false quean by such a slight, that I'll my needle lack?

*Diccon.* Slip not your gear I counsel you, but of this take good heed.
Let it not be known I told you of it, how well soever ye speed.

*Gammer.* I'll in, Diccon, a clean apron to take, and set before me,
An I may my needle once see, I'll sure remember thee.

[*Exit* GAMMER GURTON.

*Diccon.* Here will the sport begin! if these two once may meet,
Their cheer, durst lay money, will prove scarcely sweet!
Into the town will I, my friends to visit there,
And hither straight again to see the end of this gear.
In the meantime fellows, pipe up your fiddles. I say, take them!
And let your friends hear such mirth as ye can make them.

[*Exit* DICCON.

*Enter* HODGE.

*Hodge.* Sim Glover, to you gramercy, I am meetly well sped now,
Thou art even as good a fellow as ever kissed a cow,
Here is a thong indeed! By the mass, though I speak it,
Tom Tankard's great pie-bald horse, I think could not break it.
And when he spied my need to be so straight and hard
He lent me here this awl, to set the job forward.
As for my Gammer's needle, the fiend fly away w'it.
I'll not now go to the door again with it to meet.
I'd make shift good enough if I'd a candle's end.
The chief hole in my breech, with these two I'll amend.

*Enter* GAMMER GURTON.

*Gammer.* How, Hodge! 'Mayest now be glad! I've news to tell thee:
I know who has my needle, I trust soon shalt it see.

*Hodge.* The devil thou does! Hast heard, Gammer, indeed, or doest but jest?

*Gammer.* 'Tis as true as steel, Hodge.

*Hodge.* Why, knowest thou where didst lose it?

*Gammer*. I know who found it and took it up. Shalt see or it be long.

*Hodge*. God's mother dear! If that be true, farewell both awl and thong!
But who has it, Gammer, say on? I'd fain hear it disclosed.

*Gammer*. That false vixen, that same Dame Chat that counts herself so honest.

*Hodge*. Who told you so?

*Gammer*. That same Diccon the bedlam, which saw it done.

*Hodge*. Diccon? It is a vengeable knave, Gammer. 'Tis a bomndable whoreson.
Can do more things then, else I'm deceived, that be evil:
By the mass, I saw him of late call up a great black devil.
"O," the knave cried, "Ho! ho!" he roared and he thundered
An you'd been there, I'm sure you'd murrainly ha' wondered.

*Gammer*. Was not thou afraid, Hodge, to see him in this place?

*Hodge*. No, an he'd come to me, I'd have laid him on the face, I'd have promised him.

*Gammer*. But, Hodge, had he no horns to push?

*Hodge*. As long as your two arms. Saw ye never Friar Rushe
Painted on a cloth, with a side long cow's tail,
And crooked cloven feet, and many a hooked nail?
For all the world, if I should judge, I'd reckon him his brother.
Look, even what face Friar Rushe had, the devil had such another.

*Gammer*. Now Jesus mercy, Hodge, did Diccon in him bring?

*Hodge*. Nay, Gammer, hear me speak, I'll tell you a greater thing.
The devil, when Diccon had him, I heard him wondrous well,
Said plainly here before us, that Dame Chat had your needle.

*Gammer*. Then let us go, and ask her wherefore she minds to keep it.
Seeing we know so much, 'twere a madness now to slip it.

*Hodge.* Go to her, Gammer, see ye not where she stands in her doors.
Bid her give you the needle, 'tis none of hers but yours.

*Enter* DAME CHAT.

*Gammer.* Dame Chat, I would pray thee fair, let me have what is mine.
I'd not this twenty year take one louse that is thine,
Therefore give me mine own and let me live beside thee.

*Chat.* Why art thou crept from home hither to mine own doors to chide me?
Hence, doting drab, avaunt, or I shall set thee further.
Intends thou and that knave, me in my house to murder?

*Gammer.* Tush! gape not so on me, woman, shalt not yet eat me.
Nor all the friends thou hast in this shall not intreat me.
Mine own goods I will have, and ask thee on belief.
What, woman! poor folks must have right, though the thing you agrieve.

*Chat.* Give thee thy right, and hang thee up, with all thy beggar's brood!
What, wilt thou make me a thief, and say I stole thy goods?

*Gammer.* I'll say nothing, I warrant thee, but that I can prove it well
Thou took my goods even from my door, I am able this to tell.

*Chat.* Did I, old witch, steal ought was thine? how should that thing be known?

*Gammer.* I cannot tell, but up thou tookest it as though it had been thine own.

*Chat.* Marry, fie on thee, thou old gib, with all my very heart!

*Gammer.* Nay, fie on thee, thou ramp, thou rig, with all that take thy part.

*Chat.* A vengeance on those lips that layeth such things to my charge!

*Gammer.* A vengeance on those callats hips, whose conscience is so large!

*Chat.* Come out, Hodge!

*Gammer*, Come out, Hodge, and let me have right!

*Chat.* Thou arrant witch!

*Gammer.* Thou bawdy bitch! I'll make thee curse this night!

*Chat.* A bag and a wallet!

*Gammer.* A cart for a callat!

*Chat.* Why weenest thou thus to prevail?
I hold thee a groat,
I shall patch thy coat!

*Gammer.* Thou slut! Thou cat! Thou rakes! Thou jakes! Will not shame make ye hide thee?

*Chat.* Thou scald! Thou bald! Thou rotten! Thou glutton! I will no longer chide thee,
But I will teach thee to keep home.

*Gammer.* Wilt thou, drunken beast?

*Enter* HODGE.

*Hodge.* Stick to her, Gammer, take her by the head, I'll warrant you this feast!
Smite I say, Gammer!
Bite I say, Gammer!
I trow ye will be keen!
Where be your nails? claw her by the jaws, pull me out both her eyen!
Gog's bones, Gammer, hold up your head!

*Chat.* I trow, drab, I shall dress thee!
Tarry you knave, I hold thee a groat, I shall make these hands bless thee!
Take you this, old whore, for amends, and learn thy tongue well to tame.
And say thou met at this bickering, not thy fellow but thy dame.

*Hodge.* Up, Gammer, and be ye alive, I'll fight now for us both!
Come not near me, thou scald callet, to kill thee I were loth.

*Chat.* Art here again thou hoddy peek! What, Doll, bring me out my spit.

*Hodge.* I'll broach thee with this! By m'father's soul, I'll conjure that foul sprite:
Let door stand, Cock! Why comst indeed? Keep door you whoreson boy!

*Chat.* Stand to it, you dastard, for thine ears, I'll teach thee! A sluttish toy!

*Hodge.* Gog's wounds, whore, I'll make thee avaunt! Take heed,
Cock, pull in the latch!

*Chat.* I faith, sir loose-breech, had ye tarried, ye should have found your match.

*Gammer.* Now ware thy throat, lousel, thou'lt pay for all!

*Hodge.* [*Peeping through door.*] Well said, Gammer, by my soul!
Hoyse her, souse her, bounce her, trounce her, pull out her throat-boule!

*Chat.* Comst behind me, thou withered witch, an I get once on foot,
Thou'lt pay for all, you old tarleather, I'll teach thee what longs to, it!
Take ye this to make up thy mouth, 'till time thou come by more.

[*Exit.*

*Hodge.* Up, Gammer, stand on your feet, where is the old whore?
Faith would I had her by the face! I'd crack her callet crown!

*Gammer.* Ah, Hodge, Hodge, where was thy help when vixen had me down!

*Hodge.* By the mass, Gammer, but for my staff Chat had gone nigh to spill you!
I think the harlot had not cared, if I had not come, to kill you!
But shall we lose our needle thus?

*Gammer.* No, Hodge, I would loth do so.
Thinkest thou I'll take that at her hand? No, Hodge, I tell thee no!

*Hodge.* I would yet this fray were well taken up, and our own needle at home,
'Twill be my chance else some to kill, wherever it be or whom!

*Gammer.* We have a parson, Hodge, thou knowest, a man esteemed wise.
Mast' Doctor Rat, I'll for him send, and let me hear penance straight.

We'll have our needle, else Dame Chat comes ne'er within heaven's gate.

*Hodge*. Yea, marry, Gammer, that I think best. Will you now for him send?
The sooner Doctor Rat be here, the sooner we'll ha' an end.
And hear, Gammer, Diccon's devil, as I remember well,
Of Cat, and Chat, and Doctor Rat, a felonous tale did tell.
I hold you forty pound that is the way your needle to get again.

*Gammer*. I'll ha' him straight, call out the boy, we'll make him take the pain.

*Hodge*. What, Cock, I say! Come out. What, devil, canst not hear?

*Cock*. How now, Hodge? How does Gammer? Is yet the weather clear?
What would you have me to do?

*Gammer*. Come hither, Cock, anon.
Hence away to Doctor Rat, hie thee that thou were gone,
And pray him come and speak with me, I am not well at ease.
Shalt have him at his chamber, or else at mother Bee's.
Else seek him at Hob Filcher's shop, for as I heard it reported,
There is the best ale in all the town, and now is most resorted.

*Cock*. And shall I bring him with me, Gammer?

*Gammer*. Yes, by and by good Cock.

*Cock*. Shalt see that I'll here anon, else let me have one on the dock.

[*Exit*.

*Hodge*. Now, Gammer, shall we go in, and tarry for his coming?
What devil, woman, pluck up your heart, and leave of all this glooming!
Though she were stronger at the first, as I think ye did find her,
Yet there ye dressed the drunken sow, what time ye came behind her.

*Gammer*. Nay, nay, I'm sure I lost not all, for set the end to the beginning

And I doubt not, but she will make small boast of her winning.

*Enter* TIB.

*Tib.* See, Gammer, Gammer, Gib our cat! I'm afraid that she aileth.
She stands me gasping behind the door, as though her wind her faileth.
Now look, I doubt what Gib should mean, that now she doth so dote.

*Hodge.* Hold hither! I hold twenty pound, your needle is in her throat!
Grope her I say! Methinks I feel it! Does not prick your hand?

*Gammer.* I can feel nothing.

*Hodge.* No, I know there's not within this land
A murriener cat than Gib is, betwixt the Thames and Tyne,
She's as much wit in her head almost as I have in mine,

*Tib.* Faith she's eaten something, that will not easily down!
Whether she got it at home, or abroad in the town I cannot tell.

*Gammer.* Alas, I fear it be some crooked pin!
And then farewell Gib, she is undone and lost . . . all save the skin.

*Hodge.* 'Tis your needle, woman, I say! Gog's soul give me a knife,
And I'll have it out of her maw, or else I'll lose my life.

*Gammer.* What, nay, Hodge, fie kill not our cat; 'tis all the cats we have now.

*Hodge.* By the mass, Dame Chat has me so moved, I care not what I kill, my God I vow!

*Enter* COCK.

*Gammer.* Soft, be content, let's hear what news Cock bringeth from Mast' Rat.

*Cock.* Gammer, I have been there as you bad, you wot well about what.
'Twill not be long before he come, I durst swear on a book.
He bids you see ye be at home, and there for him you look.

*Gammer.* Where didst thou find him, boy, was he not where I told thee?

*Cock.* Yes, yes even at Hob Filcher's house, by him that bought and sold me.
A cup of ale had in his hand, and a crab lay in the fire;
I had much ado to go and come, all was so full of mire.
And, Gammer, one thing I can tell, Hob Filcher's awl was lost
And Doctor Rat found it again, hard beside the doorpost.
I hold a penny he can say something your needle again to fet.

*Gammer.* I am glad to hear so much, Cock. Then trust he will not let
To help us herein best he can: therefore till time he come
Let us go in. If there be ought to get thou shalt have some. [*Exeunt.*

*Enter* DOCTOR RAT.

*Dr. Rat.* A man were better twenty times be a bandog and bark,
Than here, among such a sort be parish priest or clerk,
Where he shall never be at rest one breathing while a day!
But he must trudge about the town, this way and that way,
Here to a drab, there to a thief, his shoes to tear and rent;
And that which is worst of all, at every knaves commandment.
I had not sat the space to drink two pots of ale
But Gammer Gurton's sorry boy was straight way at my tail,
For she was sick, and I must come. To do I wot not what.
If once her finger's end but ache, "trudge, call for Doctor Rat!"
And when I come not at their call I only thereby lose.
For I am sure to lack therefore a tithe pig or a goose.
I warrant you, when truth is known and told they have their tale,
The matter where about I come is not worth a halfpenny worth of ale!
Yet must I talk so sage and smooth, as though I were a glosier
Else, or the year come at an end, I shall be sure the loser.

*Enter* GAMMER GURTON.

What work ye, Gammer Gurton? Now, here is your friend, Master Rat.

*Gammer.* Ah, good mast' Doctor, I've troubled, I've troubled you, I wot well that!

*Dr. Rat.* How do ye, woman? Be ye lusty, or be ye not well at ease?

*Gammer.* By Gis, master, I am not sick, but yet I have a disease.
I had a foul turn now of late, I'll tell it you, by Gigs.

*Dr. Rat.* Hath your brown cow cast her calf, or your sandy sow her pigs?

*Gammer.* No, but I had been as good as they had, as this I wot well.

*Dr. Rat.* What is the matter?

*Gammer.* Alas, alas, I've lost my good needle,
My needle I say, and wot ye what? a drab came by and spied it,
And when I asked her for the same, the filth flatly denied it.

*Dr. Rat.* What was she, that?

*Gammer.* A Dame I warrant you! She began to scold and brawl. . . .
Alas! alas! Come hither, Hodge. This wretch can tell you all.

*Enter* HODGE.

*Hodge.* Good morrow, Gaffer Vicar.

*Dr. Rat.* Come on, fellow, let us hear.
Thy dame hath said to me thou knowest of all this gear
Let's see what thou canst say.

*Hodge.* Bym' fay, sir, that ye shall.
What matter so ever here was done, I can tell your ma'ship all.
My Gammer Gurton here, see now,
Sat her down at this door, see now,
And as she began to stir her, see now,
Her needle fell into the floor, see now,
And while her staff she took, see now,
At Gib her cat to fling, see now,

Her needle was lost on the floor, see now,
Is not this a wondrous thing, see now?
Then came the quean Dame Chat, see now,
To ask for her blacke cup, see now,
And even here at this gate, see now,
She took that needle up, see now,
My Gammer then she cried, see now,
Her needle again to bring, see now,
And was caught by the head, see now,
Is not this a wondrous thing, see now!
She tare my Gammer's coat, see now,
And scratched her by the face, see now,
I had thought I had stopt her throat, see now. . . .
Is not this a wondrous case see now,
When I saw this I was wroth, see now
And start between them twain, see now;
Else I durst take a book oath, see now
My Gammer had been slain, see now.

*Gammer.* This is even the whole matter, as Hodge has plainly told.
And I should fain be quiet, for my part, that I should.
But help us, good master, beseech ye that ye do,
Else shall we both be beaten and lose our needle too.

*Dr. Rat.* What would ye have me to do? Tell me, that I be gone;
I will do the best that I can to set you both at one.
But be ye sure Dame Chat hath your needle found?

[DICCON *appears at back.*

*Gammer.* Here comes the man that see her take it up off the ground.
Ask him yourself, Master Rat, if ye believe not me,
And help me to my needle, for God's sake and Saint Charity!

*Dr. Rat.* Come near, Diccon, and let us hear what thou can express.
Wilt thou be sworn thou seest Dame Chat this woman's needle have?

*Diccon.* Nay by St. Benit, will I not, then might ye think I rave.

*Gammer.* Why didst not you tell me so even here? Canst you for shame deny it?

*Diccon.* Aye, marry, Gammer; but I said I would not abide by it.

*Dr. Rat.* Will you say a thing, and not stick to it to try it?

*Diccon.* Stick to it quoth you, Master Rat? Marry, sir, I defy it!
Nay, there is many an honest man, when he such blasts hath blown
In his friends ears, he would be loth the same by him were known.

*Dr. Rat.* Then we be never the nearer, for all that you can tell.

*Diccon.* Yes marry, sir, if ye will do by mine advice and counsel.
If mother Chat see all us here she knoweth how the matter goes
Therefore I rede you three go hence, and within keep close.
And I will into Dame Chat's house, and so the matter use,
That ere you could go twice to church, I warrant you hear news.
She shall look well about her, but I durst lay a pledge
Ye shall of Gammer's needle, have shortly better knowledge.

*Gammer.* Now, gentle Diccon, do so, and, good, sir let us trudge.

*Dr. Rat.* By the mass, I may not tarry so long to be your judge.

*Diccon.* 'Tis but a little while, man. What, take so much pain.
If I hear no news of it I will come sooner again.

*Hodge.* Tarry so much, good master Doctor, of your gentleness.

*Dr. Rat.* Then let us hie us inward, and, Diccon, speed thy business.

[*Exeunt* GAMMER GURTON, DR. RAT, *and* HODGE.

*Diccon.* Now, sirs, do you no more, but keep my counsel just,
And Doctor Rat shall thus catch some good I trust.
But Mother Chat my gossip, talk first withall I must.
For she must be chief captain to lay the Rat in the dust.

*Enter* DAME CHAT.

Good even, Dame Chat, in faith, and well met in this place.
*Chat.* Good even, my friend Diccon. Whither walk ye this pace?
*Diccon.* By my truth even to you, to learn how the world goeth.
Heard ye no more of the other matter, say me now by your troth?
*Chat.* O yes, Diccon, here the old whore, and Hodge that great knave—
But in faith, I would thou hadst seen! O Lord, I drest them brave!
*Diccon.* By the mass, I can thee thank, wench, thou didst so well acquit thee.
*Chat.* And thou'dst seen him, Diccon, it would have made ye split thee
For laughter. The whoreson dolt at last caught up a club,
As though he would have slain the master devil Belsabub.
But I set him soon inward.
*Diccon.* O Lord! there is the thing!
That Hodge is so offended; that makes him start and fling!
*Chat.* Why? Makes the knave any moiling, as ye have seen or heard?
*Diccon.* Even now I saw him last; like a mad man he fared,
And sware by heaven and hell, he would a wreck his sorrow
And leave you never a hen alive by eight of the clock to-morrow.
Therefore mark what I say, and my words see that ye trust—
Your hens be as good as dead if ye leave them on the roost.
*Chat.* The knave dare as well go hang himself as go upon my ground!
*Diccon.* Well, yet take heed I say; I must tell you my tale round.
Have you not about your house, behind your furnace or lead
A hole where a crafty knave may creep in for need?
*Chat.* Yes, by the mass, a hole broke down even within these two days.

*Diccon.* Hodge, he intends this same night to slip in there away.

*Chat.* O Christ, that I were sure of it! In faith he should have his meed.

*Diccon.* Watch well, for the knave will be there as sure as is your creed.
I would spend myself a shilling to have him swinged well.

*Chat.* I am as glad as a woman can be of this thing to hear tell.
By Gog's bones, when he cometh, now that I know the matter,
He shall sure at the first skip to leap in scalding water,
With a worse turn besides. When he will, let him come.

*Diccon.* I tell you as my sister. You know what meaneth "mum".

[*Exit* DAME CHAT.

Now lack I but my Doctor to play his part again.
And lo, where he cometh towards. . . . Peradventure to his pain.

*Enter* DR. RAT.

*Dr. Rat.* What good news, Diccon? Fellow, is mother Chat at home?

*Diccon.* She is, sir, and she is not, but it please her to come
Yet did I take her tardy, as subtle as she was.

*Dr. Rat.* The thing that thou wentest for, hast thou brought it to pass?

*Diccon.* I have done that I have done, be it worse, be it better.
And Dame Chat at her wits end I have almost set her.

*Dr. Rat.* Why, hast thou spied the needle, quickly I pray thee tell?

*Diccon.* I have spied it in faith, sir, I handled myself so well.
And yet the crafty quean had almost taken my trump
But or all came to an end I set her in a dump.

*Dr. Rat.* How, do I pray thee, Diccon?

*Diccon.* In there she sat sewing, a halter or a band,
With no other thing save Gammer's needle in her hand,
Now I, sir, knowing of every door the pin,

Came nicely and said no word till time I was within,
And there I saw the needle, even with these two eyes.
Who ever say the contrary, I will swear he lies.

*Dr. Rat.* O, Diccon, that I was not there then in thy stead!

*Diccon.* Well, if ye will be ordered, and do by my rede,
I will bring you to a place, as the house stands,
Where ye shall take the drab with the needle in her hands.

*Dr. Rat.* For God's sake do so, Diccon, and I will gage my gown
To save thee a full pot of the best ale in the town.

*Diccon.* Follow me but a little, and mark what I will say;
Lay down your gown beside you, go to, come on your way.
See ye not what is here? a hole wherein ye may creep
Into the house, and suddenly unawares among them leap.
There shall ye find the bitch-fox and the needle together.
Do as I bid you, man, come on your ways hither.

*Dr. Rat.* Art thou sure, Diccon, the swill-tub stands not here about?

*Diccon.* I was within myself, man, even now, there is no doubt.
Go softly, make no noise, give me your foot, Sir John.
Here will I wait upon you, 'till you come out anon.

Dr. Rat *climbs through hole in the wall.*

*Dr. Rat.* [*Within*] Help, Diccon! Out alas, I shall be slain among them!

*Diccon.* If they give you not the needle tell them that ye will hang them!
Ware that! hoow, my wenches! have ye caught the fox
That used to make revel among your hens and cocks?
Save his life yet for his order, though he sustain some pain.
Gog's bread, I am afraid, they will beat out his brain!

[*Exit down street.*

*Dr. Rat.* [*Entering*] Woe worth the hour that I came here!
And woe worth him that wrought this gear!
A pack of drabs and queans have me blest!
Was ever creature half so evil drest?
Who ever it wrought, and first did invent it,
He shall I warrant him, ere long repent it!
I will spend all I have, without my skin,

But he shall be brought to the plight I am in.
Master Baily I trow, an he be worth his ears,
Will snaffle these murderers and all that them bears.
I will surely neither bite nor sup
'Till I fetch him hither, this matter to take up. [*Exit.*

*Enter* MASTER BAILEY, DR. RAT *and* SCAPETHRIFT.

*Bailey.* I can perceive none other, I speak it from my heart,
But either ye are in all the fault or else in the greatest part.

*Dr. Rat.* If it be counted his fault besides all his griefs
When a poor man is spoiled and beaten among thieves,
Then I confess my fault herein, at this season.
But I hope you will not judge so much against reason.

*Bailey.* And methinks by your own tale, of all that ye name,
If any played the thief you were the very same.
The women they did nothing, as your words make probation,
But stoutly withstood your forcible invasion.
If that a thief at your window to enter should begin,
Would you hold forth your hand and help to pull him in?
Or you would keep him out? I pray you answer me.

*Dr. Rat.* Marry, keep him out, and a good cause why.
But I am no thief, sir, but an honest learned clerk.

*Bailey.* Yes, but who knoweth that, when he meets you in the dark?
I am sure your learning shines not out at your nose.
Was it any marvel though the poor woman arose
And start up, being afraid of what was in her purse?
Methinks you may be glad that your luck was no worse.

*Dr. Rat.* Is not this evil enough, I pray you as you think?
[*Showing his broken head.*

*Bailey.* Yea, but a man in the dark, if chances do wink,
As soon will smite his father as any other man!
Because for lack of light, discern him not he can.
Might it not have been your luck with a spit to have been slain?

*Dr. Rat.* I think I am a little better! My scalp is cloven to the brain.
If this be all the remedy, I know who bears the knocks.

*Bailey*. By my troth, and well worthy besides to kiss the stocks!
To come in on the back side, when ye might go about!
I know none such, unless they long to have their brains knockt out.

*Dr. Rat*. Well, will you be so good, sir, as talk with Dame Chat
And know what she intended? I ask no more but that.

*Bailey*. Let her be called, fellow, because of Master Doctor.
I warrant in this case she will be her own Proctor,
She will tell her own tale in metre or in prose.
And bid you seek your remedy, and so go wipe your nose.

*Enter* DAME CHAT.

*Bailey*. Dame Chat, master doctor upon you here complained
That you and your maid did him much disorder.
And taketh many an oath that no word be fained,
Laying to your charge, how you thought him to murder.
And on his part again, that same man saith further,
He never offended you in word nor intent.
To hear you answer hereto, we have now for you sent.

*Chat*. That I would have murdered him! Fie on him, wretch!
And evil might he thrive for it, our Lord I beseech!
I will swear on all the books that opens and shuts
He faineth this tale out of his own guts.
For this seven weeks with me I am sure he sat not down.
Nay ye have other minions in the other end of the town,
Where ye were liker to catch a blow
Than anywhere else, as far as I know.

*Bailey*. Belike then, master Doctor, yon stripe here ye got not?

*Dr. Rat*. Think you I am so mad that where I was beat I wot not?
Will ye believe this quean before she hath proved it?
It is not the first deed she hath done and afterward denied it.

*Chat*. What, man, will you say I broke your head?

*Dr. Rat*. How canst thou prove the contrary?

*Chat.* Nay, how provest thou that I did the deed?

*Dr. Rat.* Too plainly, by S. Mary!
This proof I trow may serve, though I no word spoke.
[*Shewing his broken head.*

*Chat.* Because thy head is broken, was it I that it broke?
I saw thee, Rat, I tell thee, not once within this fortnight.

*Dr. Rat.* No, marry, thou sawest me not, for why thou hadst no light.
But I felt thee for all the dark, beshrew thy smooth cheeks!
And thou groped me, this I will declare, any day this six weeks.
[*Shewing his head.*

*Bailey.* Answer me this, Master Rat: when caught you this harm of yours?

*Dr. Rat.* A while ago, sir. God, he knoweth, within less than these two hours.

*Bailey.* Dame Chat, was there none with you, confess i'faith, about that season?
What, woman, let it be what it will, 'tis neither felony nor treason.

*Chat.* Yes, by my faith, master Bailey, there was a knave not far
Who caught one good fillip on the brow with a door-bar.
And well was he worthy, as it seemed to me.
But what is that to this man, since this was not he.

*Bailey.* Who was it then? let's hear.

*Dr. Rat.* Alas, sir, ask you that?
Is it not made plain enough by the own mouth of Dame Chat?
The time agreeth, my head is broken, her tongue cannot lie.
Only upon a bare "nay" she saith it was not I.

*Chat.* No, marry, was it not indeed ye shall hear by this one thing.
This afternoon a friend of mine for good will gave me warning
And bade me well look to my roost and all my Capon pens;
For if I took not better heed, a knave would have my hens.
Then I to save my goods, took so much pains for him to watch,
And, as good fortune served me, it was my chance him for to catch.

What strokes he bare away, or otherwise was his gains
I wot not, but sure I am he had something for his pains.
*Bailey*. Yet tellest thou not who it was.
*Chat*. Who it was? A false thief,
That come like a false fox my pullets to kill and mischief.
*Bailey*. But knowest thou not his name?
*Chat*. I know it. But what then?
It was that crafty scullion Hodge, my Gammer Gurton's man.
*Bailey*. Call me the knave hither, he shall sure kiss the stocks.
I shall teach him a lesson, for filching hens or cocks.
*Dr. Rat*. I marvel, Master Bailey, so bleared be your eyes!
An egg is not so full of meat as she is full of lies!
When she hath played this prank, to excuse all this gear
She layeth the fault on such a one as I know was not there.
*Chat*. Was he not there? Look on his pate, that shall be his witness.
*Dr. Rat*. I would my head were half so whole! I would seek no redress.

*Enter* GAMMER GURTON.

*Bailey*. God bless you, Gammer Gurton!
*Gammer*. God ild you, master mine!
*Bailey*. Thou hast a knave within thy house, Hodge, a servant of thine.
They tell me that busy knave is such a filching one,
That hen, pig, goose or capon, thy neighbour can have none.
*Gammer*. By God, I am much amazed, to hear any such report!
Hodge was not wont I trow, to behave him in that sort.
*Chat*. The thievisher knave is not alive, more filching, nor more false.
Many a truer man than he has hanged up by the halters.
And thou, his dame, of all his theft thou art the sole receiver.
For Hodge to catch and thou to keep, I never knew none better.

*Gammer.* Sir reverence, your masterdom, if you were not adoor,
I should be so bold, for all her brags, to call her arrant whore.
If I knew Hodge so bad as thou, I wish me endless sorrow,
If I should not take the pains to hang him up before to-morrow.

*Chat.* What have I stolen from thee or thine, thou ill-favoured old trot?

*Gammer.* A great deal more, by God's blest, than I ever had by thee got.
That, thou knowest well. I need not say it.

*Bailey.* Stop there I say,
And tell me here, I pray you, this matter by the way.
How chance Hodge is not here? Him would I fain have heard.

*Gammer.* Alas, sir, he'll be here anon, ha' be' handled too bad.

*Chat.* Master Bailey, sir, ye be not such a fool, well I know,
But ye perceive by this lingering there is a toad in the straw.

[*Thinking that* HODGE *his head was broke, and that* GAMMER *would not let him come before them.*

*Gammer.* I'll shew you his face, I warrant thee, lo, now here he is.

*Enter* HODGE.

*Bailey.* Come on, fellow, it is told me thou art a shrew, I'wis.
Why neighbours' hens you takest and playest the two-legged fox?
Their chickens and their capons, too, and now and then their cocks?

*Hodge.* I defy them all that dare to say! I am as true as the best.

*Bailey.* Was't not you taken within this hour, in Dame Chat's hen's-nest?

*Hodge.* Taken there? No, Master, I'd not do it for a house full of gold.

*Chat.* Thou, or the devil in thy coat; swear this I dare be bold.

*Dr. Rat.* Swear me no swearing, quean, the devil he give thee sorrow.
All is not worth a gnat thou canst swear 'till to-morrow!
Where is the harm he hath? Shew it by God's bread.
Ye beat him, with a witness, but the stripes light on my head.

*Hodge.* Beat me? Gog's blessed body, I should first, I trow, have burst thee,
I think if I had my hands loose, harlot, I'd have crushed thee.

*Chat.* Thou dirty knave, I trow, you knowest the full weight of my fist.
I am fouly deceived unless thy head and my door-bar kissed.

*Bailey.* Sir, answer me to this, is thy head whole or broken.

*Chat.* Yea, master Bailey, blest be every good token!

*Hodge.* Is my head whole? I warrant you, 'tis neither scurvy nor scald.
What, you foul beast, does think 'tis either shaven or bald?

*Bailey.* Come nearer here.

*Hodge.* Yes, that I dare.

*Bailey.* By our Lady, here is no harm.
Hodge's head is whole enough, for all Dame Chat's charm.

*Chat.* By Gog's blest, however the thing he cloaks or smoulders,
I know the blows he bare away, either with head or shoulders.
Camest you not, knave, within this hour, creeping into my pens,
And there was caught within my house, groping among my hens?

*Hodge.* A plague both on thy hens and thee! A cart, whore, a cart!
I would I were hanged as high as a tree an I were as false as you art!
Give my Gammer again her whatyoucall, you stole away in thy lap.

*Gammer*. Yea, master Bailey, there is a thing, you know not on, mayhap.
This drab she keeps away my goods, the devil he might her snare!
I pray you that I might have a right action on her.

*Chat*. Have I thy goods, old filth, or any such old sow's?
I am as true, I would thou knew, as skin between thy brows.

*Gammer*. Many a truer hath been hanged though thou escape the danger!

*Chat*. Thou shalt answer, by God's pity, for this thy foul slander!

*Bailey*. Why, what can ye charge her withal? To say so, ye do not well.

*Gammer*. Marry, a vengeance to her heart, that whore has stolen my needle.

*Bailey*. Your talk is such, I can scarce learn who should be most in fault.

*Gammer*. Yet shall ye find no other wight save she, by bread and salt!

*Bailey*. Keep ye content awhile, see that your tongues ye hold.
Methinks you should remember this is no place to scold.
How knowest thou, Gammer Gurton, Dame Chat thy needle had?

*Gammer*. To name, sir, the party, I would not be very glad.

*Bailey*. Yea, but we must needs hear it, and therefore say it boldly.

*Gammer*. Such one as told the tale, full soberly and coldly,
Even he that looked on, will swear on a book,
What time this drunken gossip my fair long needle uptook:
Diccon, Master, the Bedlam, I'm very sure ye know him.

*Bailey*. A false knave, by God's pity, ye were but a fool to trust him!
I durst aventure well the price of my best cap,
That when the end is known, all will turn to a jape,
Told he not you that besides she stole your cock that tide?

*Gammer*. No, master, no indeed, for then he should have lied
My cock is, I thank Christ, safe and well and fine.
*Chat*. Yea, but that ragged colt, that whore, that Tib of thine,
Said plainly thy cock was stolen, and in my house was eaten.
That lying slut is lost that she is not swinged and beaten.
And he that heard it told me, who thou of late didst name,
Diccon, whom all men know; it was the very same.
*Bailey*. This is the case: you lost your needle about the doors;
And she answers again, she has no cock of yours,
Thus in your talk and action, from that you do intend,
She is whole five mile wide, from that she doth defend:
Will you say she hath your cock?
*Gammer*. No, mercy, sir, that I'll not.
*Bailey*. Will you confess her needle?
*Chat*. Will I? No, sir, I will not.
*Bailey*. Then there lieth all the matter.
*Gammer*. Soft, master, by the way,
Ye know she could do little that she could not say nay.
*Bailey*. Yea, but he that made one lie about your cock stealing,
Will not stick to make another what time lies be in dealing.
I ween the end will prove this brawl did first arise
Upon no other ground, but only Diccon's lies.
*Chat*. Though some be lies as you belike have espied them,
Yet other some be true, by proof I have well tried them.
*Bailey*. What other thing beside this, Dame Chat?
*Chat*. Marry, sir, even this,
The tale I told before, the self same tale it was his,
Behaving like a friend, warning against my loss,
Else had my hens been stolen each one, by God's cross.
He told me Hodge would come, and in he came indeed.
But, as the matter chanced, with greater haste than speed.
This truth was said, and true was found, as truly as I report.

*Bailey.* If Doctor Rat be not deceived, it was of another sort.

*Dr. Rat.* By God's mother, thou and he, be a couple of subtle foxes.
Between you and Hodge, I bear away the boxes,
Did not Diccon appoint the place, where you shouldst stand to meet him?

*Chat.* Yes, by the mass, and if he came, bade me not stick to spit him.

*Dr. Rat.* God's sacrament, the villain knave hath drest us round about!
He is the cause of all this brawl, that dirty sinful lout!
When Gammer Gurton here complained and made a rueful moan,
I heard him swear that you had gotten, her needle that was gone.
He further said full certain, if I would follow his rede,
Into your house a privy way he would me guide and lead,
To where ye had it in your hands, sewing about a clout;
And set me in the back hole, thereby to find you out.
And whiles I sought aquietly, creeping upon my knees,
I found the weight of your door-bar for my reward and fees.
Such is the luck that some men get while they begin to meddle,
In setting at one such as be out, minding to make all well.

*Hodge.* Was not I well blest, Gammer, to scape that scour? An I had been there
Then I had been drest belike as ill, by the mass, as Gaffer Vicar.

*Bailey.* Marry, sir, here is a sport alone! I looked for such an end
If Diccon had not played the knave, this had been soon amend.
My Gammer here he made a fool, and drest her as she was.
And goodwife Chat he set to scold, till both parts cried "alas."
And Dr. Rat was not behind, whiles Chat his crown did pare.
I would the knave had been stark blind, if Hodge had not his share.

*Hodge.* I am meetly well sped already amongst, I am dressed like a colt.
An I had not the better wit, I had been made a dolt.

*Bailey.* Sir knave, make haste Diccon were here. Fetch him where ever he be.

*Chat.* Fie on the villain! fie! fie! that makes us thus agree.

*Gammer.* Fie on him, knave, with all my heart. Now fie, and fie again!

*Dr. Rat.* Now, fie on him, may I best say, whom he hath almost slain!

*Bailey.* Lo, where he cometh at hand! Belike he was not far.
Diccon, here be two or three thy company cannot spare.

*Diccon.* God bless you! If you may be blest so many all at once!

*Bailey.* Nay soft, thou mayst not play the knave and have this language too.
If thou thy tongue bridle awhile, the better mayst thou do.
Confess the truth as I shall ask, and cease a while to fable,
And for thy fault I promise thee, thy handling shall be reasonable.
Hast thou not made a lie or two, to set these two by the ears?

*Diccon.* What if I have? five hundred such have I seen within these seven years!
I am sorry for nothing else but that I see not the sport
Which was between them when they met, as they themselves report.

*Bailey.* The greatest thing, Master Rat, ye see how he is drest.

*Diccon.* What devil need he be groping so deep in goodwife Chat's hen's-nest.

*Bailey.* Yea, but it was thy drift to bring him into the briars.

*Diccon.* God's bread, hath not such an old fool wit to save his ears?

*Dr. Rat.* Well, an ye shift no better, ye losel, lying and lazy,
I will go near for this, to make ye leap at a daisy.
In the king's name, Master Bailey, I charge you set him fast.

*Diccon*. What fast at cards, or fast asleep? It is the thing I did last.

*Dr. Rat*. Nay fast in fetters, false varlet, according to thy deeds.

*Bailey*. Master Doctor that is no remedy, I must entreat you needs,
Some other kind of punishment.

*Dr. Rat*. Nay, by all Hallows!
His punishment, if I may judge shall be naught else but the gallows.

*Bailey*. That were too sore. A spiritual man to be so extreme!

*Dr. Rat*. Is he worthy any better, sir? How do ye judge and deem?

*Bailey*. I grant him worthy punishment, but in no wise so great.

*Gammer*. It is a shame I tell you plain, for such false knaves t'entreat.
He has almost undone us, all: that is as true as steel;
And yet for all this great ado I am never the nearer my needle.

*Bailey*. Canst you not say anything to that, Diccon, with least or most?

*Diccon*. Yea, marry sir, thus much I can say well, the needle is lost.

*Bailey*. Nay, canst thou tell which way that needle may be found?

*Diccon*. No by my fay, sir, though I might have an hundred pound.

*Hodge*. Thou liar lickdish, didst not say the needle would be gotten?

*Diccon*. No, Hodge, by the same token, you were that time shaken
For fear of Hobgobling. You wot well what I mean,
As long as it is since, I fear me yet ye be scarce clean.

*Bailey*. Well, Master Rat, you must both learn, and teach us to forgive.
Since Diccon hath confession made, and is so clean shriven,
If ye to me consent to amend this heavy chance,
I will enjoin him here, some open kind of penance.
Of this condition, where ye know my fee is twenty pence

For the bloodshed I am agreed with you here to dispense,
Ye shall go quiet, so that ye grant the matter now to run,
To end with mirth among us all, even as it was begun.

*Chat.* Say yea, Master Vicar, and he shall sure confess to be your debtor,
And all we that be here present, will love you much the better.

*Dr. Rat.* My part is the worst. But since you all hereon agree,
Go even to, Master Bailey, let it be so for me.

*Bailey.* How sayest thou, Diccon? Art content this shall on me depend?

*Diccon.* Go to, Master Bailey, say on your mind, I know ye are my friend.

*Bailey.* Then mark ye well. To recompence this thy former action,
Because thou hast offended all, to make them satisfaction
Before their faces, here kneel down, and as I shall thee teach
So thou shalt take an oath on Hodge's leather breech
First for Master Doctor, upon pain of his curse,
Where he will pay for all, thou never draw thy purse.
And when ye meet at one pot, he shall have the first pull,
And thou shalt never offer him the cup, but it be full.
To goodwife Chat thou shalt be sworn, even on the same wise,
If she refuse thy money once never offer it twice.
Thou shalt be bound by the same here, as thou dost take it
When thou mayst drink of free cost, thou never forsake it.
For Gammer Gurton's sake, again sworn shalt thou be
To help her to her needle again if it do lie in thee,
And likewise be bound, by the virtue of that,
To be of good abearing to Gib, her great cat.
Last of all, for Hodge, the other to scan,
Thou shalt never take him for fine gentleman.

*Hodge.* Come on, fellow Diccon, I'll be even with thee now.

*Bailey.* Thou wilt not stick to do this, Diccon, I trow.

*Diccon.* No, by my father's skin, my hand down I lay it?
Like as I have promised, I will not deny it.
But Hodge take good heed now, thou do not now smite me.

[*And have him a good blow on the buttocks.*

*Hodge.* Gog's heart thou false villain dost thou bite me?

*Bailey.* What, Hodge, doth he hurt thee or ever he begin?

*Hodge.* He thrust me into the buttock with a bodkin or a pin!
I say, Gammer, Gammer!

*Gammer.* How now, Hodge, how now:

*Hodge.* God's malt, Gammer Gurton!

*Gammer.* Thou art mad, I trow.

*Hodge.* Will you see the devil, Gammer.

*Gammer.* The devil son, God bless us.

*Hodge.* I would I were hanged, Gammer!

*Gammer.* Marry, so ye might dress us.

*Hodge.* I have it, by the mass, Gammer.

*Gammer.* What, not my needle, Hodge?

*Hodge.* Your needle, Gammer, your needle!

*Gammer.* No fie! dost but dodge.

*Hodge.* I've found your needle, Gammer, here in my hand be it.

*Gammer.* For all the loves on earth, Hodge, let me see it.

*Hodge.* Soft, Gammer.

*Gammer.* Good Hodge!

*Hodge.* Soft I say, tarry a while.

*Gammer.* Nay, sweet Hodge, say truth, and do not me beguile.

*Hodge.* I am sure on it. I warrant you it goes no more astray.

*Gammer.* Hodge, when I speak so fairly, wilt still say me nay?

*Hodge.* Go near the light, Gammer, this well in faith good luck!
I was almost undone, 'twas so far in my buttock.

*Gammer.* 'Tis mine own dear needle, Hodge, surely I wot.

*Hodge.* Am I not a good son, Gammer, am I not?

*Gammer.* Christ's blessing light on thee, hast made me for ever.

*Hodge.* I knew that I must find it, else I should a had it never.

*Chat.* By my troth, Gossip Gurton, I am even as glad
As though I mine own self as good a turn had!

*Bailey.* And I, by my conscience, to see it so come forth,
Rejoice so much at it as three needles be worth.

*Dr. Rat.* I am no whit sorry to see you so rejoice.
*Diccon.* Nor I much the gladder for all this noise:
Yet say "gramercy, Diccon, for springing of the game."
*Gammer.* Grammercy, Diccon, twenty times. O, how glad I am!
If that you should do so much, your masterdom, to come hither,
Master Rat, goodwife Chat, and Diccon together—
I've but one halfpenny, as far as I know it,
And I'll not rest this night, 'till I bestow it.
If ever ye love me, let us go in and drink.
*Bailey.* I am content, if the rest think as I think.
Master Rat, it shall be best for you if we so do.
Then shall you warm and dress yourself too.
*Diccon.* Soft, sirs, take us with you, the company shall be the more.
As proud comes behind, they say, as any goes before!
But now my good masters since we must be gone
And leave you behind us here all alone:
Since at our last ending thus merry we be,
For Gammer Gurton's needle sake, let us have a plauditie.

# TUESDAY

# THE FAIR MAID OF THE WEST

(1630)

By

THOMAS HEYWOOD

## DRAMATIS PERSONÆ

| | | |
|---|---|---|
| SPENCER, CARROL, FAWCETT, | Gentlemen | ........ |
| CAPTAIN GOODLACK, Spencer's friend | | ........ |
| ROUGHMAN, a swaggering Gentleman | | ........ |
| CLEM, a Vintner's Apprentice | | ........ |
| TWO CAPTAINS | | ........ |
| THE MAYOR OF FOY | | ........ |
| AN ALDERMAN | | ........ |
| MULLISHEG, King of Fez | | ........ |
| BASHAW ALCADE | | ........ |
| BASHAW JOFFER | | ........ |
| A SPANISH CAPTAIN | | ........ |
| AN ENGLISH MERCHANT | | ........ |
| A FRENCH MERCHANT | | ........ |
| AN ITALIAN MERCHANT | | ........ |
| A SURGEON | | ........ |
| A PREACHER | | ........ |
| DRAWERS, SAILORS, SPANIARDS, MOORS | | ........ |
| SERVANTS, CHORUS | | ........ |
| BESS BRIDGES, the Fair Maid of the West | | ........ |
| A KITCHENMAID | | ........ |
| THE EARL OF ESSEX, THE MAYOR OF PLYMOUTH, PETITIONERS | Mutes personated | ........ |

SCENE—England, The Azores, Morocco.

# PROLOGUE

Amongst the Grecians there were annual feasts,
To which none were invited, as chief guests,
Save princes and their wives. Amongst the men,
There was no argument disputed then,
But who best governed; and as't did appear,
He was esteemed sole sovereign for that year.
The Queens and ladies argued at that time
For virtue and for beauty which was prime,
And she had the high honour. Two here be,
For beauty one, the other majesty,
Most worthy (did the custom still persever)
Not for one year, but to be sovereigns ever.

## ACT I

### SCENE I.

SCENE.—*A Street in Plymouth.*

*Enter* CARROL *and two* CAPTAINS.

*1st Captain.* When puts my lord to sea?
*2nd Captain.* When the wind's fair.
*Carrol.* Resolve me, I entreat; can you not guess
The purpose of this voyage?
*1st Captain.* Most men think
The fleet's bound for the Islands.
*Carrol.* Nay, 'tis like.
The great success at Cales, under the conduct
Of such a noble general, hath put heart
Into the English: they are all on fire
To purchase from the Spaniard. If their carracks
Come deeply laden, we shall tug with them
For golden spoil.
*2nd Captain.* Oh, were it come to that!
*1st Captain.* How Plymouth swells with gallants; how the streets
Glister with gold! You cannot meet a man
But tricked in scarf and feather, that it seems
As if the pride of England's gallantry
Were harboured here. It doth appear, methinks,
A very court of soldiers.
*Carrol.* It doth so.
Where shall we dine to-day?
*2nd Captain.* At the next tavern; there's the best wine.
*1st Captain.* And the best wench, Bess Bridges; she's the flower.
*2nd Captain.* A sweet lass,
If I have any judgment.
*1st Captain.* Now, in troth,
I think she's honest.

*Carrol.* Honest, and live there!
What, in a public tavern!
Honest, said you?
*2nd Captain.* I vow she is, for me.
*1st Captain.* For all, I think.
I'm sure she's wondrous modest.
*Carrol.* But withal
Exceeding affable.
*2nd Captain.* An argument
That she's not proud.
*Carrol.* No; were she proud, she'd fall.
*1st Captain.* Well, she's a most attractive adamant:
Her very beauty hath upheld that house,
And gained her master much.
*Carrol.* That adamant
Shall for this time draw me too: we'll dine there.
*2nd Captain.* No better motion. Come to the Castle then.
[*Exeunt.*

*Enter* SPENCER and CAPTAIN GOODLACK.

*Goodlack.* What, to the old house still?
*Spencer.* Canst blame me, captain?
Believe me, I was never surprised till now,
Or catched upon the sudden.
*Goodlack.* Pray resolve me;
Why, being a gentleman of fortunes, means,
And well revenued, will you adventure thus
A doubtful voyage, when only such as I,
Born to no other fortunes than my sword,
Should seek abroad for pillage?
*Spencer.* Pillage, captain!
No, 'tis for honour; and the brave society
Of all these shining gallants, that attend
The great lord-general, drew me hither first,
No hope of gain or spoil.
*Goodlack.* Ay, but what draws you to this house so oft?
*Spencer.* As if thou knew'st it not.
*Goodlack.* What, Bess?
*Spencer.* Even she.
*Goodlack.* Come, I must tell you, you forget yourself,
One of your birth and breeding thus to dote

Upon a tanner's daughter! Why, her father
Sold hides in Somersetshire, and, being trade-fallen,
Sent her to service.

*Spencer.* Prithee speak no more;
Thou tell'st me that which I would fain forget,
Or wish I had not known. If thou wilt humour me,
Tell me she's fair and honest.

*Goodlack.* Yes, and loves you.

*Spencer.* To forget that were to exclude the rest:
All saving that were nothing. Come, let's enter. [*Exeunt.*

## SCENE II.

*A Room in the Castle Tavern.*

*Enter* SPENCER, CAPTAIN GOODLACK, and two DRAWERS.

1*st Drawer.* You are welcome, gentlemen. Show them into the next room there.

2*nd Drawer.* Look out a towel, and some rolls, a salt and trenchers.

*Spencer.* No, sir, we will not dine.

2*nd Drawer.* I am sure ye would, if you had my stomach.
What wine drink ye, sack or claret?

*Spencer.* Where's Bess?

2*nd Drawer.* Marry, above, with three or four gentlemen.

*Spencer.* Go call her.

2*nd Drawer.* I'll draw you a cup of the neatest wine in Plymouth.

*Spencer.* I'll taste none of your drawing. Go call Bess.

2*nd Drawer.* There's nothing in the mouths of these gallants but "Bess, Bess."

*Spencer.* What say y', Sir?

2*nd Drawer.* Nothing, sir, but I'll go and call her presently.

*Spencer.* Tell her who's here.

2*nd Drawer.* The devil rid her out of the house, for me!

*Spencer.* Say y', sir?

2*nd Drawer.* Nothing but anon, anon, sir.

*Enter* BESS BRIDGES.

*Spencer.* See, she's come!

*Bess.* Sweet Master Spencer, y'are a stranger grown.
Where have you been these three days?
*Spencer.* The last night
I sat up late at game. Here, take this bag,
And lay't up till I call for't.
*Bess.* Sir, I shall.
*Spencer.* Bring me some wine.
*Bess.* I know your taste,
And I shall please your palate.
[*Exit.*
*Goodlack.* Troth, 'tis a pretty soul!
*Spencer.* To thee I will unbosom all my thoughts:
Were her low birth but equal with her beauty,
Here would I fix my thoughts.
*Goodlack.* You are not mad, sir?
You say you love her.
*Spencer.* Never question that.
*Goodlack.* Then put her to't; win Opportunity,
She's the best bawd. If, as you say, she loves you,
She can deny you nothing.
*Spencer.* I have proved her
Unto the utmost test; examined her,
Even to a modest force; but all in vain:
She'll laugh, confer, keep company, discourse,
And something more, kiss; but beyond that compass
She no way can be drawn.
*Goodlack.* 'Tis a virtue
But seldom found in taverns.

*Re-enter* BESS, *with wine.*

*Bess.* 'Tis of the best Graves wine, sir.
*Spencer.* Gramercy, girl: come sit.
*Bess.* Pray pardon, sir, I dare not.
*Spencer.* I'll ha' it so.
*Bess.* My fellows love me not, and will complain
Of such a saucy boldness.
*Spencer.* Pox on your fellows!
I'll try whether their pottle-pots or heads
Be harder, if I do but hear them grumble.
Sit: now, Bess, drink to me.
*Bess.* To your good voyage! [*Drinks.*

*Re-enter* 2ND DRAWER.

*2nd Drawer*. Did you call, sir?

*Spencer*. Yes, sir, to have your absence. Captain, this health.

*Goodlack*. Let it come, sir.

*2nd Drawer*. Must you be set, and we wait, with a——!

*Spencer*. What say you, sir?

*2nd Drawer*. Anon, anon: I come there. [*Exits*.

*Spencer*. What will you venture, Bess, to sea with me?

*Bess*. What I love best, my heart: for I could wish
I had been born to equal you in fortune,
Or you so low, to have been ranked with me;
I could have then presumed boldly to say,
I love none but my Spencer.

*Spencer*. Bess, I thank thee.
Keep still that hundred pound 'till my return
From the Islands with my lord: If never, wench,
Take it, it is thine own.

*Bess*. You bind me to you.

*Re-enter* 1ST DRAWER.

*1st Drawer*. Bess, you must fill some wine into the Portcullis;
The gentlemen there will drink none but of your drawing.

*Spencer*. She shall not rise, sir. Go, let your master snick-up.

*1st Drawer*. And that should be cousin-german to the hick-up.

*Re-enter* 2ND DRAWER.

*2nd Drawer*. Bess, you must needs come. The gentlemen fling pots, pottles, drawers, and all downstairs.
The whole house is in an uproar.

*Bess*. Pray, pardon, sir; I needs must be gone.

*2nd Drawer*. The gentlemen swear if she come not up to them, they will come down to her.

*Spencer*. If they come in peace,
Like civil gentlemen, they may be welcome:
If otherwise, let them usurp their pleasures.
We stand prepared for both.

*Enter* CARROL and the two CAPTAINS

*Carrol.* Save you, gallants! We are somewhat bold, to press
Into your company: it may be held scarce manners;
Therefore, 'tis fit that we should crave your pardon.

*Spencer.* Sir, you are welcome; so are your friends.

*1st Captain.* Some wine!

*Bess.* Pray give me leave to fill it.

*Spencer.* You shall not stir. So, please you, we'll join company.
Drawer, more stools.

*Carrol.* I take't that's a she drawer. Are you of the house?

*Bess.* I am, sir.

*Carrol.* In what place?

*Bess.* I draw.

*Carrol.* Beer, do you not? You are some tapstress.

*Spencer.* Sir, the worst character you can bestow
Upon the maid is to draw wine.

*Carrol.* She would draw none to us.
Perhaps she keeps a rundlet for your taste,
Which none but you must pierce.

*2nd Captain.* I pray be civil.

*Spencer.* I know not, gentlemen, what your intents be,
Nor do I fear, or care. This is my room;
And if you bear you, as you seem in show,
Like gentlemen, sit and be sociable.

*Carrol.* We will. [*To* BESS.] Minx, by your leave.
Remove, I say.

*Spencer.* She shall not stir.

*Carrol.* How, sir?

*Spencer.* No, sir. Could you outface the devil,
We do not fear your roaring.

*Carrol.* Though you may be companion with a drudge,
It is not fit she should have place by us.—
About your business, housewife.

*Spencer.* She is worthy.
The place as the best here, and she shall keep't.

*Carrol.* You lie.

[*They draw and justle.* CARROL *is slain.*

*Goodlack.* The gentleman's slain: away!

*Bess.* O, Heaven! what have you done?

*Goodlack.* Undone thyself, and me too. Come away.
*Exit* GOODLACK *and* SPENCER.

*Bess.* Oh, sad misfortune! I shall lose him ever.
What! are you men, or milksops? Stand you still,
Senseless as stones, and see your friend in danger
To expire his last?

*1st Captain.* Tush! all our help's in vain.

*2nd Captain.* This is the fruit of whores;
This mischief came through thee.

*Bess.* It grew first from your incivility.

*1st Captain.* Lend me a hand, to lift his body hence.
It was a fatal business. [*Exit the* CAPTAINS, *bearing the body.*

*Re-enter the two* DRAWERS.

*1st Drawer.* One call my master, another fetch the constable.
Here's a man killed in the room.

*2nd Drawer.* How! a man killed, say'st thou? Is all paid?

*1st Drawer.* How fell they out, canst thou tell?

*2nd Drawer.* Sure, about this bold Bettrice. 'Tis not so much for the death of the man, but how shall we come by our reckoning? [*Exeunt* DRAWERS.

*Bess.* What shall become of me? Of all lost creatures,
The most unfortunate. I by this
Have lost so worthy and approved a friend.
Whom to redeem from exile, I would give
All that's without and in me.

*Enter* FAWCETT.

*Fawcett.* Your name's Bess Bridges?

*Bess.* An unfortunate maid,
Known by that name too well in Plymouth, here.
Your business, sir, with me?

*Fawcett.* Know you this ring?

*Bess.* I do: it is my Spencer's.
I know, withal, you are his trusty friend,
To whom he would commit it. Speak: how fares he?
Is he in freedom, know ye?

*Fawcett.* He's in health
Of body, though in mind somewhat perplexed
For this late mischief happened.

*Bess.* Is he fled,
And freed from danger?
*Fawcett.* Neither. By this token
He lovingly commends him to you, Bess,
And prays you, when 'tis dark, meet him o' th' Hoe,
Near to the new-made fort, where he'll attend you,
Before he flies, to take a kind farewell.
There's only Goodlack in his company:
He entreats you not to fail him.
*Bess.* Tell him from me, I'll come, I'll run, I'll fly,
Stand death before me; were I sure to die.
[*Exeunt.*

## SCENE III.

*The Hoe.*

*Enter* SPENCER *and* CAPTAIN GOODLACK.

*Goodlack.* You are too full of passion.
*Spencer.* Canst thou blame me,
So sweet, so fair, so amorous, and so chaste,
And all these at an instant! Art thou sure
Carrol is dead?
*Goodlack.* I can believe no less.
You hit him in the very speeding place.
*Spencer.* Oh! but the last of these sits near'st my heart.
*Goodlack.* Sir, be advised by me:
Try her, before you trust her.
*Spencer.* Thou counsell'st well.
I'll put her to the test and utmost trial,
Before I trust her further. Here she comes.

*Enter* BESS *with bag and* FAWCETT.

*Fawcett.* I have done my message, sir.
*Bess.* Fear not, sweet Spencer; we are now alone,
And thou art sanctuarèd in these mine arms.
*Goodlack.* While these confer, we'll sentinel their safety.
This place I'll guard.
*Fawcett.* I this.
*Bess.* Are you not hurt,
How is it with you?
*Spencer.* Bess, all my afflictions
Are that I must leave thee: thou know'st, withal,

I am not near my country; and to stay
For new supply from thence might deeply engage me
To desperate hazard.
*Bess.* Is it coin you want?
Here is the hundred pound you gave me of late:
Use that, beside what I have stored and saved,
Which makes it fifty more. Were it ten thousand,
Nay, a whole million, Spencer, all were thine.
*Spencer.* No; what thou hast, keep still; 'tis all thine own.
Here be my keys: my trunks take to thy charge:
Such gold fit for transportage as I have,
I'll bear along: the rest are freely thine.
Money, apparel, and what else thou findest,
Perhaps worth my bequest and thy receiving,
I make thee mistress of.
*Bess.* Before, I doted;
But now you strive to have me ecstasied.
What would you have me do, in which to express
My zeal to you?
*Spencer.* I enjoin thee to keep
Ever my picture, which in my chamber hangs:
For when thou part'st with that, thou losest me.
*Bess.* My soul from my body may be divorced,
But never that from me.
*Spencer.* I have a house in Foy, a tavern called
The windmill; that I freely give thee, too;
And thither, if I live, I'll send to thee.
*Bess.* Is there else
Aught that you will enjoin me?
*Spencer.* Thou art fair:
Join to thy beauty virtue. Many suitors
I know will tempt thee: beauty's a shrewd bait,
But unto that if thou add'st chastity,
Thou shalt o'ercome all scandal. Time calls hence;
We now must part.
*Bess.* Oh, that I had the power to make Time lame,
I could dwell here for ever in thine arms,
And wish it always night.
*Spencer.* We trifle hours. Farewell!
*Bess.* First take this ring:
'Twas the first token of my constant love

That passed betwixt us. When I see this next,
And not my Spencer, I shall think thee dead;
For, 'till death part thy body from my soul,
I know thou wilt not part with it.

*Spencer*. Swear for me, Bess; for thou mayst safely do't.
Once more, farewell: at Foy thou shalt hear from me.
I shall not live to lose thee.

*Fawcett*. Best be gone;
For hark, I hear some tread.

*Spencer*. A thousand farewells are in one contracted.
Captain away! *Exeunt* SPENCER *and* GOODLACK.

*Bess*. Oh! I shall die.

*Fawcett*. What mean you, Bess? Will you betray your friend.
Or call my name in question? Sweet, look up.

*Bess*. Ha, is my Spencer gone?

*Fawcett*. With speed towards Foy,
There to take ship to Fayal.

*Bess*. Let me recollect myself,
And what he left in charge—virtue and chastity;
Next, with all sudden expedition
Prepare for Foy: all these will I conserve,
And keep them strictly, as I would my life.
Plymouth, farewell: in Cornwall I will prove
A second fortune, and for ever mourn,
Until I see my Spencer's safe return. [*Exeunt*.

*Enter the two* DRAWERS.

1*st Drawer*. 'Tis well that we have gotten all the money due to my master. It is the commonest thing that can be, for these captains to score and to score; but when the scores are to be paid, *non est inventus*.

2*nd Drawer*. 'Tis ordinary amongst gallants, nowadays, who had rather swear forty oaths than only this one oath—"God, let me never be trusted!"

1*st Drawer*. But if the captains would follow the noble mind of the general, before night there would not be one score owing in Plymouth.

2*nd Drawer*. Little knows Bess that my master hath got in these desperate debts. But she hath cast up her account, and is going.

*1st Drawer*. Whither, canst thou tell?

*2nd Drawer*. They say, to keep a tavern in Foy, and that Master Spencer hath given her a stock, to set up for herself. Well, howsoever, I am glad, though he killed the man, we have got our money. [*Exeunt.*

## SCENE IV.

*The Windmill Tavern, Foy.*

*Enter* FAWCETT *and* ROUGHMAN.

*Fawcett*. In your time have you seen a sweeter creature?

*Roughman*. Some week, or thereabouts.

*Fawcett*. And in that time she hath almost undone all the other taverns: the gallants make no rendezvous now but at the Windmill.

*Roughman*. Spite of them, I'll have her. It shall cost me the setting on, but I'll have her.

*Fawcett*. Why, do you think she is so easily won?

*Roughman*. Easily or not, I'll bid as fair and far as any man within twenty miles of my head, but I will put her to the squeak.

*Fawcett*. They say there are knights' sons already come as suitors to her.

*Roughman*. 'Tis like enough, some younger brothers, and so I intend to make them.

*Fawcett*. If these doings hold, she will grow rich in short time.

*Roughman*. There shall be doings that shall make this Windmill my grand seat, my mansion, my palace, and my Constantinople.

*Enter* BESS BRIDGES *and* CLEM.

*Fawcett*. Here she comes. Observe how modestly she bears herself.

*Roughman*. I must know of what burden this vessel is. I shall not bear with her till she bear with me; and till then I cannot report her for a woman of good carriage.

[ROUGHMAN *and* FAWCETT *move aside.*

*Clem*. My father was a baker; and, by the report of his neighbours, as honest a man as ever lived by bread.

*Bess*. And where dwelt he?

*Clem.* Below here, in the next crooked street, at the sign of the Leg. He was nothing so tall as I; but a little wee man, and somewhat huck-backed.

*Bess.* I think I have heard of him.

*Clem.* Then I am sure you have heard he was an honest neighbour, and one that never loved to be meal-mouthed.

*Bess.* Well, sirrah, prove an honest servant, and you shall find me your good mistress. What company is in the Mermaid?

*Clem.* There be four sea-captains. I believe they be little better than pirates, they be so flush of their ruddocks.

*Bess.* No matter; they're my good customers,
And still return me profit.

*Clem.* Wot you what, mistress, how the two sailors would have served me, that called for the pound and a half of cheese?

*Bess.* How was it, Clem?

*Clem.* When I brought them a reckoning, they would have had me to have scored it up. They took me for a simple gull, indeed, that would have had me to have taken chalk for cheese.

*Bess.* Well, go wait upon the captains: see them want no wine.

*Clem.* Nor reckoning neither, take my word, mistress.

*Roughman.* She's now at leisure: I'll go to her.—
Lady, what gentlemen are those above? [*Coming forward.*

*Bess.* Sir, they are such as please to be my guests,
And they are kindly welcome.

*Roughman.* Give me their names.

*Bess.* You may go search the church-book where they were christened:
There you perhaps may learn them.

*Roughman.* Minion, how!

*Bess.* Pray, hands off!

*Roughman.* I tell thee, maid, wife, or whate'er thou beest,
No man shall enter here but by my leave.
Come, let's be more familiar.

*Bess.* 'las, good man!

*Roughman.* Why, knowest thou whom thou slightest? I am Roughman,

The only approved gallant of these parts,
A man of whom the roarers stand in awe,
And must not be put off.

*Bess.* I never yet heard a man so praise himself.
But proved in the end a coward.

*Roughman.* Coward, Bess!
You will offend me, raise in me that fury
Your beauty cannot calm. Go to; no more.

*Bess.* Sir, if you thus persist to wrong my house,
Disturb my guests, and nightly domineer,
To put my friends from patience, I'll complain
And right myself before the magistrate.

*Roughman.* Go to, wench:
I wish thee well; think on't, there's good for thee
Stored in my breast; and when I come in place,
I must have no man to offend mine eye:
My love can brook no rivals.

*Bess.* Sir, if you come
Like other free and civil gentlemen,
You're welcome; otherwise my doors are barred you.

*Roughman.* That's my good girl,
I have fortunes laid up for thee: what I have,
Command it as thine own. Go to; be wise.

*Bess.* Well, I shall study for't.

*Roughman.* Consider on't. Farewell.

[*Exit* ROUGHMAN *and* FAWCETT.

*Bess.* My mind suggests me that this prating fellow
Is some notorious coward. If he persist,
I have a trick to try what metal's in him. [*To* CLEM.
What news with you?

*Clem.* I am now going to carry the captains a reckoning.

*Bess.* And what's the sum?

*Clem.* Let me see—eight shillings and sixpence.

*Bess.* How can you make that good? Write them a bill.

*Clem.* I'll watch them for that; 'tis no time of night to use our bills. The gentlemen are no dwarfs; and with one word of my mouth I can tell them what is to be-tall.

*Bess.* How comes it so much?

*Clem.* Imprimis, six quarts of wine, at sevenpence the quart, seven sixpences.

*Bess.* Why doest thou reckon it so?

*Clem.* Because, as they came in by hab nab, so I will bring them in a reckoning at six and at sevens.

*Bess.* Well, wine, three shillings and sixpence.

*Clem.* And what wants that of ten groats?

*Bess.* 'Tis twopence over.

*Clem.* Then put sixpence more to it, and make it four shillings wine, though you bate it them in their meat.

*Bess.* Why so, I prithee?

*Clem.* Because of the old proverb, "What they want in meat, let them take out in drink." Then, for twelve pennyworth of anchoves, eighteenpence.

*Bess.* How can that be?

*Clem.* Marry, very well, mistress: twelvepence anchoves, and sixpence oil and vinegar. Nay, they shall have a saucy reckoning.

*Bess.* And what for the other half-crown?

*Clem.* Bread, beer, salt, napkins, trenchers, one thing with another; so the *summa totalis* is eight shillings and sixpence.

*Bess.* Well, take the reckoning from the bar.

*Clem.* What needs that, forsooth? The gentlemen seem to be high-flown already. Send them in but another pottle of sack, and they will cast up the reckoning of themselves. Yes, I'll about it. [*Exit.*

*Bess.* Were I not with so many suitors pestered,
And might I enjoy my Spencer, what a sweet,
Contented life were this! for money flows,
And my gain's great. But to my Roughman next.
I have a trick to try what spirit's in him.
It shall be my next business; in this passion
For my dear Spencer, I propose me this:
'Mongst many sorrows, some mirth's not amiss. [*Exit.*

## SCENE V.

*Fayal.*

*Enter* SPENCER *and* CAPTAIN GOODLACK.

*Goodlack.* What were you thinking, sir?

*Spencer.* Troth, of the world: what any man should see in't to be in love with it.

*Goodlack.* The reason of your meditation?

*Spencer.* To imagine that in the same instant that one forfeits all his estate, another enters upon a rich possession. As one goes to the church to be married, another is hurried to the gallows to be hanged; the last having no feeling of the first man's joy, nor the first of the last man's misery. At the same time that one lies tortured upon the rack, another lies tumbling with his mistress over head and ears in down and feathers. This, when I truly consider, I cannot but wonder why any fortune should make a man ecstasied.

*Goodlack.* You give yourself too much to melancholy.

*Spencer.* These are my maxims; and were they as faithfully practised by others as truly apprehended by me, we should have less oppression, and more charity.

*Enter the two* CAPTAINS.

1*st Captain.* Make good thy words.

2*nd Captain.* I say, thou hast injured me.

1*st Captain.* Tell me wherein.

2*nd Captain.* When we assaulted Fayal,
And I had, by the general's command,
The onset, and with danger of my person
Enforced the Spaniard to a swift retreat,
And beat them from their fort, thou, when thou saw'st
All fear and danger past, madest up with me,
To share that honour which was sole mine own,
And never ventured shot for't, or e'er came where bullet grazed.

*Spencer.* See, captain, a fray towards;
Let's if we can, atone this difference.

*Goodlack.* Content.

1*st Captain.* I'll prove it with my sword,
That though thou hadst the foremost place in field,
And I the second, yet my company
Was equal in the entry of the fort.
My sword was that day drawn as soon as thine,
And that poor honour which I won that day
Was but my merit.

2*nd Captain.* Wrong me palpably
And justify the same!

*Spencer.* You shall not fight.

*1st Captain.* Why, sir, who made you first a justicer,
And taught you that word "shall?" You are no general;
Or, if you be, pray show us your commission.

*Spencer.* Sir, I have no commission but my counsel,
And that I'll show you freely.

*2nd Captain* 'Tis some chaplain.

*1st Captain.* I do not like his text.

*Goodlack.* Let's beat down their weapons.

*1st Captain.* I'll aim at him that offers to divide us!

[*They fight.*

*2nd Captain.* Pox of these part-frays! see I am wounded
By beating down my weapon.

*Goodlack.* How fares my friend?

*Spencer.* You sought for blood, and, gentlemen, you have it.
Let mine appease you: I am hurt to death.

*1st Captain.* My rage converts to pity, that this gentleman
Shall suffer for his goodness.

*Goodlack.* Noble friend,
I will revenge thy death.

*Spencer.* He is no friend
That murmurs such a thought.—Oh, gentlemen,
I killed a man in Plymouth, and by you
Am slain in Fayal. Carrol fell by me,
And I fall by Spencer. Heaven is just,
And will not suffer murder unrevenged.
Heaven pardon me, as I forgive you both!
Shift for yourselves: away!

*2nd Captain.* We saw him die,
But grieve you should so perish.

*Spencer.* Note Heaven's justice,
And henceforth make that use on't—I shall faint.

*1st Captain.* Short farewells now must serve. If thou survivest,
Live to thine honour; but if thou expirest
Heaven take thy soul to mercy! [*Exeunt* CAPTAINS.

*Spencer.* I bleed much;
I must go seek a surgeon.

*Goodlack.* Sir, how cheer you?

*Spencer.* Like one that's bound upon a new adventure
To the other world; yet thus much, worthy friend,

Let me entreat you: since I understand
The fleet is bound for England take your occasion
To ship yourself, and when you come to Foy,
Kindly commend me to my dearest Bess:
Thou shalt receive a will, in which I have
Possessed her of five hundred pounds a year.

*Goodlack.* A noble legacy.

*Spencer.* The rest I have bestowed amongst my friends,
Only reserving a bare hundred pounds,
To see me honestly and well interred.

*Goodlack.* I shall perform your trust as carefully
As to my father, breathed he.

*Spencer.* Mark me, captain;
Her legacy I give with this proviso:
If, at thy arrival where my Bess remains,
Thou find'st her well reported, free from scandal,
My will stands firm; but if thou hear'st her branded
For loose behaviour, or immodest life,
What she should have, I here bestow on thee;
It is thine own: but, as thou lovest thy soul,
Deal faithfully betwixt my Bess and me.

*Goodlack.* Else let me die a prodigy.

*Spencer.* This ring was hers; that, be she loose or chaste,
Being her own, restore her: she will know it;
And doubtless she deserves it. O my memory!
What had I quite forgot? She hath my picture.

*Goodlack.* And what of that?

*Spencer.* If she be ranked amongst the loose and lewd,
Take it away: I hold it much indecent
A whore should ha't in keeping; but if constant,
Let her enjoy it. This my will perform.

*Goodlack.* Sense else forsake me.

*Spencer.* Now lead me to my chamber. All's made even—
My peace with earth, and my atone with Heaven.

[*Exit.*

## SCENE VI.

*A Field near Foy.*

*Enter* Bess Bridges, *like a page, with a sword*; *and* Clem.

*Bess.* But that I know my mother to be chaste,
I'd swear some soldier got me.

*Clem.* It may be many a soldier's bluff jerkin came out of your father's tan-vat.

*Bess.* Methinks I have a manly spirit in me,
In this man's habit.

*Clem.* Now, am not I of many men's minds; for, if you should do me wrong, I should not kill you.

*Bess.* Methinks I could be valiant on the sudden,
And meet a man i' the field.
I could do all that I have heard discoursed.
Of Mary Ambree, or Westminster's Long Meg.

*Clem.* What Mary Ambree was I cannot tell; but unless you were taller, you will come short of Long Meg.

*Bess.* Of all thy fellows, thee I only trust,
And charge thee to be secret.

*Clem.* I am bound in my indentures to keep my master's secrets; and should I find a man in bed with you, I would not tell.

*Bess.* Begone, sir; but no words, as you esteem my favour.

*Clem.* But, mistress, I could wish you to look to your long seams; fights are dangerous. But am not I in a sweet taking, think you?

*Bess.* I prithee, why?

*Clem.* Why, if you should swagger and kill anybody,
I, being a vintner, should be called to the bar.

[*Exit.*

*Bess.* Let none condemn me of immodesty,
Because I try the courage of a man,
Who on my soul's a coward, beats my servants,
Cuffs them, and, as they pass by him, kicks my maids;
Nay, domineers over me, making himself
Lord o'er my house and household. Yesternight
I heard him make appointment on some business
To pass along this way. I'll venture fair,
But I will try what's in him.

*Enter* Roughman *and* Fawcett.

*Fawcett.* Sir, I can now no further, weighty business calls me away.

*Roughman.* Why, at your pleasure, then.
Yet I could wish that ere I passed this field,

That I could meet some Hector, so your eyes
Might witness what myself have oft repeated,
Namely, that I am valiant.

*Fawcett*. No doubt;
But now I am in haste. Farewell. [*Exit*.

*Roughman*. How many times brave words bear out a man!
For if he can but make a noise, he's feard.
To talk of frays, although he ne'er had heart
To face a man in the field, that's a brave fellow.
I have been valiant, I must needs confess,
In street and tavern, where there have been men
Ready to part the fray; but for the fields,
They are too cold to fight in.

*Bess*. You are a villain, a coward; and you lie
[*Strikes him*.

*Roughman*. You wrong me, I protest. Sweet, courteous gentleman, I never did you wrong.

*Bess*. Wilt tell me that?
Draw forth thy coward sword, and suddenly,
Or, as I am a man, I'll run thee through,
And leave thee dead i' the field.

*Roughman*. Hold! as you are a gentleman.
I have ta'en an oath I will not fight to-day.

*Bess*. Th'ast took a blow already, and the lie:
Will not both these enrage thee?

*Roughman*. No; would you give the bastinado too,
I will not break mine oath.

*Bess*. Oh! your name's Roughman:
No day doth pass you but you hurt or kill!
Is this out of your calender?

*Roughman*. I! you are deceived.
I ne'er drew sword in anger, I protest,
Unless it were upon some poor, weak fellow,
That ne'er wore steel about him.

*Bess*. Throw your sword.

*Roughman*. Here, sweet young sir;
[*Gives up his sword*.
But as you are a gentleman,
Do not impair mine honour.

*Bess*. Tie that shoe.

*Roughman*. I shall, sir.

*Bess.* Untruss that point.

*Roughman.* Anything, this day, to save mine oath.

*Bess.* Enough;—yet not enough. Lie down,
'Till I stride o'er thee.

*Roughman.* Sweet sir, anything.

*Bess.* Rise, thou hast leave. Now, Roughman, thou art blest:
This day thy life is saved; look to the rest.
Take back thy sword.

*Roughman.* Oh! you are generous: honour me so much
As let me know to whom I owe my life.

*Bess.* I am Bess Bridge's brother.

*Roughman.* Still methought
That you were something like her.

*Bess.* And I have heard
You domineer and revel in her house,
Control her servants, and abuse her guests,
Which if I ever shall hereafter hear,
Thou art but a dead man.

*Roughman.* She never told me of a brother living;
But you have power to sway me.

*Bess.* But for I see you are a gentleman,
I am content this once to let you pass;
But if I find you fall into relapse
The second's far more dangerous.

*Roughman.* I shall fear it.
Sir, will you take the wine?

*Bess.* I am for London,
And for these two terms cannot make return;
But if you see my sister, you may say
I was in health.

*Roughman.* Too well: the devil take you! [*Aside.*

*Bess.* Pray, use her well, and at my coming back
I'll ask for your acquaintance. Now farewell. [*Exit.*

*Roughman.* None saw't: he's gone for London; I am unhurt;
Then who shall publish this disgrace abroad?
One man's no slander, should he speak his worst.
My tongue's as loud as his; but in this country
Both of more fame and credit. Should we contest,
I can outface the proudest. This is, then, my comfort.

Roughman, thou art still the same, For a disgrace not seen is held no shame. [*Exit.*

## SCENE VII.

*Fayal.*

*Enter two* SAILORS.

*1st Sailor.* Aboard, aboard! the wind stands fair for England;
The ships have all weighed anchor.
*2nd Sailor.* A stiff gale
Blows from the shore.

*Enter* CAPTAIN GOODLACK.

*Goodlack.* The sailors call aboard, and I am forced
To leave my friend now at the point of death,
And cannot close his eyes. Here is the will.
Now may I find yon tanner's daughter turned
Unchaste or wanton, I shall gain by it.
Five hundred pounds a year. Here is good evidence.
*1st Sailor.* Sir, will you take the long-boat and aboard?

*Enter a third* SAILOR.

*Goodlack.* With all my heart.
*3rd Sailor.* What, are you ready, mates?
*1st Sailor.* We stayed for you. Thou canst not tell who's dead?
The great bell rung out now.
*3rd Sailor.* They say 'twas for one Spencer, who this night
Died of a mortal wound.
*Goodlack.* My worthy friend:
Unhappy man, that cannot stay behind,
To do him his last rites!—Was his name Spencer?
*3rd Sailor.* Yes, sir, a gentleman of good account,
And well known in the Navy.
*Goodlack.* This is the end of all mortality.
It will be news unpleasing to his Bess.
I cannot fare amiss, but long to see
Whether these lands belong to her or me.

*Enter* Spencer *and* Surgeon.

*Surgeon.* Nay, fear not, sir: now you have escaped this dressing,
My life for yours.

*Spencer.* I thank thee, honest friend.

*Surgeon.* Sir, I can tell you news.

*Spencer.* What is't, I prithee?

*Surgeon.* There is a gentleman, one of your name,
That died within this hour.

*Spencer.* My name! What was he? Of what sickness died he?

*Surgeon.* No sickness, but a slight hurt in the body,
Which showed at first no danger, but, being searched,
He died at the third dressing.

*Spencer.* At my third search I am in hope of life.
The Heavens are merciful.

*Surgeon.* Sir, doubt not your recovery.

*Spencer.* That hundred pound I had prepared to expend
Upon mine own expected funeral,
I for name's-sake will now bestow on his.

*Surgeon.* A noble resolution.

*Spencer.* What ships are bound for England? I would gladly venture to sea, though weak.

*Surgeon.* All bound that way are under sail already.

*Spencer.* Here's no security;
For when the beaten Spaniards shall return,
They'll spoil whom they can find.

*Surgeon.* We have a ship,
A London merchant, now bound for Mamorah,
A town in Barbary; please you to use that,
You shall command a free passage: ten months hence,
We hope to visit England.

*Spencer.* Friend, I thank thee.

*Surgeon.* I'll bring you to the master, who I know will entertain you gladly.

*Spencer.* When I have seen the funeral rites performed
To the dead body of my countryman
And kinsman, I will take your courteous offer
England, I no doubt, will hear news of my death;
How Bess will take it is to me unknown

On her behaviour I will build my fate,
There raise my love, or thence erect my hate. [*Exeunt.*

## SCENE VIII.

*Foy. The Windmill Tavern.*

*Enter* ROUGHMAN *and* FAWCETT.

*Roughman.* Oh! you're well met. Just as I prophesied,
So it fell out.

*Fawcett.* As how, I pray?

*Roughman.* Had you but stayed the crossing of one field,
You had beheld a Hector, the boldest Trojan
That ever Roughman met with.

*Fawcett.* Pray, what was he?

*Roughman.* You talk of Little Davy, Cutting Dick,
And divers such; but tush! this hath no fellow.

*Fawcett.* Of what stature and years was he?

*Roughman.* Indeed, I must confess he was no giant,
Nor above fifty; but he did bestir him—
Was here, and there, and everywhere, at once,
That I was ne'er so put to't since the midwife
First wrapped my head in linen. Where is Bess?
Where be these drawers—rascals, I should say—
That will give no attendance.

*Enter* CLEM.

*Clem.* Anon, anon, sir: please you see a room? What, you here, again! Now we shall have such roaring!

*Roughman.* You, sirrah, call your mistress.

*Clem.* Yes, sir, I know it is my duty to call her mistress.

*Roughman.* See an the slave will stir!

*Clem.* Yes, I do stir.

*Roughman.* Shall we have humours, sauce-box? You have ears;
I'll teach you prick-song.

*Clem.* But you have now a wrong sow by the ear. I will call her.

*Roughman.* Do, sir; you had best.

*Clem.* If you were twenty Roughmans, if you lug me by the ears again, I'll draw!

*Roughman.* Ha! what will you draw?

*Clem.* The best wine in the house for your worship; and I would call her, but I can assure you that she is either not stirring, or else not in case.

*Roughman.* How not in case?

*Clem.* I think she hath not her smock on; for I think I saw it lie at her bed's head.

*Roughman.* What! drawers grow capricious?

*Clem.* Help! Help!

*Enter* BESS BRIDGES.

*Bess.* What uproar's this? Shall we be never rid
From these disturbances?
*Roughman.* Why, how now, Bess?
Is this your housewifery? When you are mine,
I'll have you rise as early as the lark.
Look to the bar yourself; these lazy rascals
Will bring your state behind hand.
*Clem.* You lie, sir.
*Roughman.* How! lie.

*Clem.* Yes, sir, at the Raven in the High Street. I was at your lodging this morning for a pottle-pot.

*Roughman.* You will about your business: must you here stand gaping and idle? [*Strikes him.*

*Bess.* You wrong me, sir,
And tyrannize too much over my servants.
I will have no man touch them but myself.

*Clem.* If I do not put ratsbane into his wine, instead of sugar, say I am no true baker. [*Exit.*

*Roughman.* What! rise at noon?
A man may fight a tall fray in a morning,
And one of your best friends, too, be hacked and mangled,
And almost cut to pieces, and you fast,
Close in your bed, ne'er dream on't.
*Bess.* Fought you this day?
*Roughman.* And ne'er was better put to't in my days.
*Bess.* I pray, how was't?
*Roughman.* Thus. As I passed yon fields——

*Enter* KITCHENMAID.

*Maid.* I pray, forsooth, what shall I reckon for the jowl of ling in the portcullis?

*Roughman.* A pox upon your jowls, you kitchen-stuff!
Go, scour your skillets, pots, and dripping-pans,
And interrupt not us. [*Kicks at her.*

*Maid.* The devil take your ox-heels, you foul cod's-head! must you be kicking?

*Roughman.* Minion! dare you scold?

*Maid.* Yes, sir; and lay my ladle over your coxcomb. [*Exit.*

*Bess.* I do not think that thou darest strike a man
That swagger'st thus o'er women.

*Roughman.* How now, Bess?

*Bess.* Shall we be never quiet?

*Fawcett.* You are too rude.

*Roughman.* Now I profess all patience.

*Bess.* Then proceed.

*Roughman.* Rising up early, minion, whilst you slept,
To cross yon field, I had but newly parted
With this my friend, but that I soon espied
A gallant fellow, and most strongly armed:
In the mid-field we met, and, both being resolute,
We justled for the wall.

*Bess.* Why, did there stand a wall in the mid-field?

*Roughman.* I meant, strove for the way.
Two such brave spirits meeting, straight both drew.

*Re-enter* CLEM.

*Clem.* The maid, forsooth, sent me to know whether you would have the shoulder of mutton roasted or sod?

*Roughman.* A mischief on your shoulders! [*Strikes him.*

*Clem.* That's the way to make me never prove good porter.

*Bess.* You heap wrongs on wrongs.

*Roughman.* I was in fury,
To think upon the violence of that fight,
And could not stay my rage.

*Fawcett.* Once more proceed.

*Roughman.* Oh! had you seen two tilting meteors justle
In the mid-region, with like fear and fury
We too encountered.
Blows came about my head,—I took them still;

Thrusts by my sides, 'twixt body and my arms,—
Yet still I put them by.

*Bess.* When they were past, he put them by.—Go on.
But in this fury, what happened of him?

*Roughman.* I think I paid him home: he's soundly mauled.
I bosomed him at every second thrust.

*Bess.* Scaped he with life?

*Roughman.* Ay, that's my fear. If he recover this,
I'll never trust my sword more.

*Bess.* Why fly you not, if he be in such danger?

*Roughman.* Because a witch once told me
I ne'er should die for murder.

*Bess.* I believe thee.
But tell me, pray, was not this gallant fellow
A pretty, fair, young youth, about my years?

*Roughman.* Even thereabout.

*Clem.* He was not fifty, then?

*Bess.* Much of my stature?

*Roughman.* Much about your pitch.

*Clem.* He was no giant, then?

*Bess.* And wore a suit like this?

*Roughman.* I half suspect.

*Bess.* That a gallant fellow,
So mangled and wounded, was myself.
You base, white-livered slave! it was this shoe
That you stooped to untie; untrussed those points;
And, like a beastly coward, lay along
Till I strid over thee. Speak; was't not so?

*Roughman.* It cannot be denied.

*Bess.* Hare-hearted fellow! milksop! Dost not blush?
Give me that rapier: I will make thee swear
Thou shalt redeem this scorn thou hast incurred,
Or in this woman shape I'll cudgel thee,
And beat thee through the streets. As I am Bess, I'll do't

*Roughman.* Hold, hold! I swear.

*Bess.* Dare not to enter at my door till then.

*Roughman.* Shame confounds me quite.

*Bess.* That shame redeem, perhaps we'll do thee grace;
I love the valiant, but despise the base. [*Exit.*

*Clem.* Will you be kicked, sir?

*Roughman.* She hath wakened me,
And kindled that dead fire of courage in me
Which all this while hath slept. To spare my flesh,
And wound my fame, what is't? I will not rest,
Till by some valiant deed I have made, good
All my disgraces past. I'll cross the street,
And strike the next brave fellow that I meet.
*Fawcett.* I am bound to see the end on't.
*Roughman.* Are you sir?
[*Beats off* FAWCETT. *Exeunt.*

## SCENE IX.

*A Street in Foy.*

*Enter the* MAYOR OF FOY, *an* ALDERMAN, *and* SERVANT.

*Mayor.* Believe me sir, she bears herself so well,
No man can justly blame her; and I wonder,
Being a single woman as she is,
And living in a house of such resort,
She is no more distasted.
*Alderman.* The best gentlemen
The country yields become her daily guests.
Sure, sir, I think she's rich.
*Mayor.* Thus much I know: would I could buy her state,
Were't for a brace of thousands!
[*A shot within.*
*Alderman.* 'Twas said a ship is now put into harbour:
Know whence she is.
*Servant.* I'll bring news from the quay.
[*Exit.*
*Mayor.* To tell you true, sir, I could wish a match
Betwixt her and mine own and only son;
And stretch my purse, too, upon that condition.
*Alderman.* Please you, I'll motion it.

*Re-enter* SERVANT.

*Servant.* One of the ships is new come from the Islands;
The greatest man of note's one Captain Goodlack.
It is but a small vessel.

*Enter* CAPTAIN GOODLACK *and* SAILORS.

*Goodlack.* I'll meet you straight at the Windmill.
Not one word of my name.

*1st Sailor.* We understand you.

*Mayor.* Pray, sir, the news from thence?

*Goodlack.* The best is, that the general is in health,
And Fayal won from the Spaniards; but the fleet,
Extremely weather-beaten. You, sir, I take it,
Are mayor o' the town.

*Mayor.* I am the King's lieutenant.

*Goodlack.* I have some letters of import from one,
A gentleman of very good account,
That died late in the Islands, to a maid
That keeps a tavern here.

*Mayor.* Her name Bess Bridges?

*Goodlack.* The same. I was desired to make inquiry
What fame she bears, and what reports she's of.
Now, you, sir, being here chief magistrate,
Can best resolve me.

*Mayor.* To our understanding
She's without stain or blemish, well reputed;
And, by her modesty and fair demeanour,
Hath won the love of all.

*Goodlack* [*Aside.*] The worse for me.

*Alderman.* I can assure you, many narrow eyes
Have looked on her and her condition;
But those that with most envy have endeavoured
To entrap her, have returned, won by her virtues.

*Goodlack.* So all that I inquire to make report.
I am glad to hear't. Sir, I have now some business,
And I of force must leave you.

*Mayor.* I entreat you to sup with me to-night.

*Goodlack.* Sir, I may trouble you..

[*Exeunt* MAYOR *and* ALDERMAN.

*Goodlack.* Five hundred pound a year out of my way,
Is there no flaw that I can tax her with,
To forfeit this revenue? Is she such a saint,
None can missay her? Why, then, I myself
Will undertake it. If in her demeanour

I can find but one blemish, stain or spot,
It is five hundred pound a year well got. [*Exeunt.*

## SCENE X.

*The Windmill Tavern.*

*Enter* CLEM *and* SAILORS *on one side: on the other,* ROUGHMAN, *who draws and beats them off; then re-enter* CLEM, *and the* SAILORS *with* BESS.

*Bess.* But did he fight it bravely?

*Clem.* I assure you, mistress, most dissolutely: he hath run this sailor three times through the body, and yet never touched his skin.

*Bess.* How can that be?

*Clem.* Through the body of his doublet, I meant.

*Bess.* How shame, base impultation, and disgrace,
Can make a coward valiant! Sirrah, you look to the bar.

*Clem.* I'll hold up my hand there presently. [*Exit.*

*Bess.* I understand you came now from the Islands?

*1st Sailor.* We did so.

*Bess.* If you can tell me tidings of one gentleman,
I shall requite you largely.

*1st Sailor.* Of what name?

*Bess.* One Spencer.

*1st Sailor.* We both saw and knew the man.

*Bess.* Only for that, call for what wine you please.
Pray tell me where you left him?

*2nd Sailor.* In Fayal.

*Bess.* Was he in health? How did he fare?

*2nd Sailor.* Why, well.

*Bess.* For that good news, spend, revel, and carouse;
Your reckoning's paid beforehand.—I am ecstasied.
And my delight's unbounded.

*1st Sailor.* Did you love him?

*Bess.* Next to my hopes in Heaven.

*1st Sailor.* Then change your mirth.

*Bess.* Why, as I take it, you told me he was well;
And shall I not rejoice?

*1st Sailor.* He's well, in Heaven; for, mistress, he is dead.

*Bess.* Ha! dead! was't so you said? Th' hast given me, friend,
But one wound yet: speak but that word again,
And kill me outright.

*2nd Sailor.* He lives not.

*Bess.* And shall I?—Wilt thou not break, heart?
Are these my ribs wrought out of brass or steel,
Thou canst not craze their bars?

*1st Sailor.* Mistress, use patience,
Which conquers all despair.

*Bess.* You advise well.
I did but jest with sorrow: you may see
I am now in gentle temper.

*2nd Sailor.* True; we see't.

*Bess.* Pray take the best room in the house, and there call for what wine best tastes you: at my leisure, I'll visit you myself.

*1st Sailor.* I'll use your kindness. [*Exeunt* SAILORS.

*Bess.* That it should be my fate! Poor sweet-heart!
I do but think how thou becom'st thy grave,
In which would I lay by thee. What's my wealth,
To enjoy't without my Spencer? I will now
Study to die, that I may live with him.

*Enter* CAPTAIN GOODLACK.

*Goodlack.* [*Aside.*] The further I inquire, the more I hear to my discomfort. If my discontinuance
And change at sea disguise me from her knowledge,
I shall have scope enough to prove her fully.
This sadness argues she hath heard some news
Of my friend's death.

*Bess.* [*Aside.*] It cannot, sure, be true
That he is dead: Death could not be so envious,
To snatch him in his prime. I study to forget
Thate'er was such a man.

*Goodlack.* [*Aside.*] If not impeach her,
My purpose is to seek to marry her.
If she deny me, I'll conceal the will,
Or, at the least, make her compound for half—
Save you, [*to Bess*], fair gentlewoman.

*Bess.* You are welcome, sir.

*Goodlack*. I hear say there's a whore here, that draws wine.
I am sharp set, and newly come from sea,
And I would see the trash.

*Bess*. Sure, you mistake, sir.
If you desire attendance, and some wine,
I can command you both.—Where be these boys?

*Goodlack*. Are you the mistress?

*Bess*. I command the house.

*Goodlack*. Of what birth are you, pray?

*Bess*. A tanner's daughter.

*Goodlack*. Where born?

*Bess*. In Somersetshire.

*Goodlack*. A trade-fallen tanner's daughter go so brave!
Oh! you have tricks to compass these gay clothes.

*Bess*. None, sir, but what are honest.

*Goodlack*. What's your name?

*Bess*. Bess Bridges most men call me.

*Goodlack*. Y'are a whore.

*Bess*. Sir, I will fetch you wine, to wash your mouth;
It is so foul, I fear't may fester, else:
There may be danger in't.

*Goodlack*. [*Aside*.] Not all this move her patience!

*Bess*. Good, sir, at this time I am scarce myself,
By reason of a great and weighty loss
That troubles me. [*Notices the ring given to him by* SPENCER.] But I should know that ring.

*Goodlack*. How! this, you baggage? It was never made to grace a strumpet's finger.

*Bess*. Pardon, sir!
I both must and will leave you. [*Exit*.

*Goodlack*. Did not this well? This will stick in my stomach.
I could repent my wrongs done to this maid;
But I'll not leave her thus; if she still love him,
I'll break her heart-strings with some false report
Of his unkindness.

*Re-enter* CLEM.

*Clem*. You are welcome, gentleman. What wine will you drink? Claret, metheglin, or muscadine? Cider, or perry, to make you merry? Aragoosa, or peter-see-me? Canary, or charnica? But, by your nose, sir, you should love a cup of malmsey: you shall have a cup of the best in Cornwall.

*Goodlack.* Here's a brave drawer, will quarrel with his wine.

*Clem.* But if you prefer the Frenchman before the Spaniard, you shall either here of the deep red grape, or the pallid white. You are a pretty tall gentleman; you should love high country wine: none but clerks and sextons love Graves wine. Or, are you a married man, I'll furnish you with bastard, white or brown, according to the complexion of your bedfellow.

*Goodlack.* You rogue, how many years of your apprenticeship have you spent in studying this set speech?

*Clem.* The first line of my part was "Anon, anon, sir;" and the first question I answered to, was loggerhead, or blockhead—I know not whither.

*Goodlack.* Speak: where's your mistress?

*Clem.* Gone up to her chamber.

*Goodlack.* Set a pottle of sack in the fire, and carry it into the next room. [*Exit.*

*Clem.* Score a pottle of sack in the Crown, and see at the bar for some rotten eggs, to burn it; we must have one trick or other, to vent away our bad commodities.

[*Exit.*

## SCENE XI.

*A bedroom in the tavern.*

*Enter* BESS, *with* SPENCER'S *picture.*

*Bess.* To die, and not vouchsafe some few commends
Before his death, was most unkindly done.
This picture is more courteous: 'twill not shrink
For twenty thousand kisses; no, nor blush,
Then thou shalt be my husband; and I vow
Never to marry other.

*Enter* CAPTAIN GOODLACK.

*Goodlack.* Where's this harlot?

*Bess.* You are immodest, sir, to press thus rudely into my private chamber.

*Goodlack.* Pox of modesty,
When punks must have it mincing in their mouths!—
And have I found thee? Thou shalt hence with me.
[*Seizes the picture.*

*Bess.* Rob me not of the chiefest wealth I have;
Search all my trunks; take the best jewels there;
Deprive me not that treasure: I'll redeem it
With plate, and all the little coin I have,
So I may keep that still.

*Goodlack.* Think'st thou that bribes
Can make me leave my friend's will unperformed?

*Bess.* What was that friend?

*Goodlack.* One Spencer, dead i' the Islands,
Whose very last words, uttered at his death,
Were these: "If ever thou shalt come to Foy,
Take thence my picture, and deface it quite;
For let it not be said, my portraiture
Shall grace a strumpet's chamber."

*Bess.* 'Twas not so:
You lie! You are a villain! 'twas not so.
'Tis more than sin thus to belie the dead.
He knew, if ever I would have transgressed,
'T had been with him: he durst have sworn me chaste,
And died in that belief.

*Goodlack.* Are you so brief?
Nay, I'll not trouble you. God be wi' you!

*Bess.* Yet leave me still that picture, and I'll swear
You are a gentleman, and cannot lie.

*Goodlack.* I am inexorable.

*Bess.* Are you a Christian?
Have you any name that ever good man gave you?
'Twas no saint you were called after. What's thy name?

*Goodlack.* My name is Captain Thomas Good——

*Bess.* I see no good in thee: rase that syllable out of thy name.

*Goodlack.* Goodlack's my name.

*Bess.* I cry you mercy, sir: I now remember you;
You were my Spencer's friend; and I am sorry,
Because he loved you, I have been so harsh:
For whose sake I entreat, ere you take't hence,
I may but take my leave on't.

*Goodlack.* You'll return it?
*Bess.* As I am chaste, I will.
*Goodlack.* For once I'll trust you. [*Returns the picture.*
*Bess.* O thou, the perfect semblance of my love,
And all that's left of him, take one sweet kiss,
As my last farewell! Thou resemblest him
For whose sweet safety I was every morning
Down on my knees, and with the lark's sweet tunes
I did begin my prayers; and when sad sleep
Had charmed all eyes, when none save the bright stars
Were up and waking, I remembered thee;
But all, all to no purpose.
*Goodlack.* [*Aside.*] Sure, most sure,
This cannot be dissembled.
*Bess.* To thee I have been constant in thine absence;
And, when I looked upon this painted piece,
Remembered thy last rules and principles;
For thee I have given alms, visited prisons,
To gentlemen and passengers lent coin,
That, if they ever had the ability,
They might repay't to Spencer; yet for this,
All this, and more, I cannot have so much
As this poor table.
*Goodlack.* [*Aside.*] I should question truth,
If I should wrong this creature.
*Bess.* I am resolved.—
See, sir, this picture I restore you back;
Which since it was his will you should take hence,
I will not wrong the dead.
*Goodlack.* God be wi' you!
*Bess.* One word more.
Spencer, you say, was so unkind in death.
*Goodlack.* I tell you true.
*Bess.* I do entreat you, even for goodness' sake.
Since you were one that he entirely loved,
If you some few days hence hear me expired,
You will, 'mongst other good men, and poor people
That haply may miss Bess, grace me so much
As follow me to the grave. This, if you promise,
You shall not be the least of all my friends
Remembered in my will. Now, fare you well!

*Goodlack.* [*Aside.*] Had I had heart of flint or adamant,
It would relent at this. [*Aloud.*] My Mistress Bess,
I have better tidings for you.

*Bess.* You will restore my picture? Will you?

*Goodlack.* Yes, and more than that:
This ring from my friend's finger, sent to you
With infinite commends.

*Bess.* You change my blood.

*Goodlack.* These writings are the evidence of lands:
Five hundred pound a year's bequeathed to you,
Of which I here possess you: all is yours.

*Bess.* This surplusage of love hath made my loss,
That was but great before, now infinite.—
It may be compassed there's in this my purpose
No impossibility. [*Aside.*]

*Goodlack.* What study you?

*Bess.* Four thousand pound, besides this legacy,
In jewels, gold, and silver, I can make,
And every man discharged. I am resolved
To be a pattern to all maids hereafter
Of constancy in love.

*Goodlack.* Sweet Mistress Bess, will you command my service?
If to succeed your Spencer in his love,
I would expose me wholly to your wishes.

*Bess.* Alas! my love sleeps with him in his grave,
And cannot thence be wakened: yet for his sake
I will impart a secret to your trust,
Which, saving you, no mortal should partake.

*Goodlack.* Both for his love and yours, command my service.

*Bess.* There's a prize
Brought into Falmouth road, a good tight vessel;
The bottom will but cost eight hundred pound;
You shall have money: buy it.

*Goodlack.* To what end?

*Bess.* That you shall know hereafter. Furnish her
With all provision needful: spare no cost;
And join with you a ging of lusty lads,
Such as will bravely man her. All the charge
I will commit to you; and when she's fitted,
Captain, she is thine own.

*Goodlack.* I sound it not.

*Bess.* Spare me the rest.—This voyage I intend,
Though some may blame, all lovers will commend.

[*Exeunt.*

## SCENE XII.

*On board a Spanish vessel.*

*After an alarum, enter a* SPANISH CAPTAIN *with* SAILORS, *bringing in an* ENGLISH MERCHANT, SPENCER, *and the* SURGEON, prisoners.

*Spanish Captain.* For Fayal's loss and spoil, by the English done,
We are in part revenged. There's not a vessel
That bears upon her top St. George's cross,
But for that act shall suffer.

*Merchant.* Insult not, Spaniard,
Nor be too proud, that thou by odds of ships,
Provision, men, and powder, madest us yield.
Had you come one to one, or made assault
With reasonable advantage, we by this
Had made the carcase of your ship your graves,
Low sunk to the seas' bottom.

*Spanish Capt.* Englishman, thy ship shall yield us pillage.
These prisoners we will keep in strongest hold,
To pay no other ransom than their lives.

*Spencer.* Degenerate Spaniard, there's no nobless in thee,
To threaten men unarmed and miserable.
Thou mightest as well tread o'er a field of slaughter,
And kill them o'er that are already slain,
And brag thy manhood.

*Spanish Capt.* Sirrah, what are you?

*Spencer.* Thy equal, as I am a prisoner;
But once, to stay a better man than thou,
A gentleman in my country.

*Spanish Capt.* Wert thou not so, we have strappados, bolts,
And engines, to the mainmast fastened,
Can make you gentle.

*Spencer*. Spaniard, do thy worst:
Thou canst not act more tortures than my courage
Is able to endure.

*Spanish Capt.* These Englishmen, nothing can daunt them. Even in misery, they'll not regard their masters.

*Spencer*. Master! Insulting, bragging Thrasos!

*Spanish Capt.* His sauciness we'll punish 'bove the rest;
About their censures we will next devise.
And now towards Spain, with our brave English prize.

[*Flourish. Exeunt.*

## SCENE XIII.

*The Windmill Tavern*

*Enter* BESS, *the* MAYOR OF FOY, ALDERMAN, and CLEM

*Bess*. A table and some stools!

*Clem*. I shall give you occasion to ease your tails presently. [*Tables and stools set out.*

*Bess*. Will't please you sit?

*Mayor*. With all our hearts, and thank you.

*Bess*. Fetch me that parchment in my closet window.

*Clem*. The three sheepskins with the wrong side outward?

*Bess*. That with the seal.

*Clem*. I hope it is my indenture, and now she means to give me my time. [*Exit.*

*Alderman*. And now you are alone, fair Mistress Elzabeth
I think it good to taste you with a motion
That no way can displease you.

*Bess*. Pray, speak on.

*Alderman*. 'T hath pleased here Master Mayor so far to look
Into your fair demeanour, that he thinks you a fit match for his son.

*Re-enter* CLEM, *with the parchment.*

*Clem*. Here's the parchment; but if it be the lease of your house, I can assure you 'tis out.

*Bess*. The years are not expired.

*Clem*. No; but it is out of your closet.

*Bess.* About your business.

*Clem.* Here's even Susannah betwixt the two wicked elders. [*Exit.*

*Alderman.* What think you, Mistress Elzabeth?

*Bess.* Sir, I thank you;
And how much I esteem this goodness from you,
The trust I shall commit unto your charge
Will truly witness. Marry, gentle sir!
'Las, I have sadder business now in hand
Than sprightly marriage; witness these my tears.
Pray read there.

*Mayor.* [*Reads*] "The last will and testament of Elzabeth Bridges;
To be committed to the trust of the mayor and aldermen of Foy, and their successors for ever.
To set up young beginners in their trade, a thousand pound.
To relieve such as have had loss by sea, five hundred pound.
To every maid that's married out of Foy, whose name's Elzabeth, ten pound.
To relieve maimed soldiers, by the year, ten pound.
To Captain Goodlack, if he shall perform the business
He's employed in, five hundred pound.
The legacies for Spencer thus to stand:
To number all the poorest of his kin,
And to bestow on them—Item, to——"

*Bess.* Enough! You see, sir, I am now too poor
To bring a dowry with me fit for your son.

*Mayor.* You want a precedent, you so abound in charity and goodness.

*Bess.* All my servants I leave at your discretions to dispose;
Not one but I have left some lagacy.
What shall become of me, or what I purpose;
Spare further to inquire.

*Mayor.* We'll take our leaves, and prove to you faithful executors in this bequest.

*Alderman.* Let never such despair,
As, dying rich, shall make the poor their heir.

[*Exeunt* MAYOR *and* ALDERMAN.

*Bess.* Why, what is all the wealth the world contains, without my Spencer?

*Enter* ROUGHMAN *and* FAWCETT.

*Roughman.* Where's my sweet Bess?
Shall I become a welcome suitor, now
That I have changed my copy?

*Bess.* I joy to hear it.
I'll find employment for you.

*Enter* CAPTAIN GOODLACK, SAILORS, *and* CLEM.

*Goodlack.* A gallant ship, and wondrous proudly trimmed;
Well caulked, well tackled, every way prepared.

*Bess.* Here, then, our mourning for a season end.

*Roughman.* Bess, shall I strike that captain? Say the word,
I'll have him by the ears.

*Bess.* Not for the world.

*Goodlack.* What saith that fellow?

*Bess.* He desires your love, good captain: let him ha' it.

*Goodlack.* Then change a hand.

*Bess.* Resolve me all. I am bound upon a voyage:
Will you, in this adventure, take such part
As I myself shall do?

*Roughman.* With my fair Bess.
To the world's end.

*Bess.* Then, captain and lieutenant both join hands;
Such are your places now.

*Goodlack.* We two are friends.

*Bess.* I next must swear you two, with all your ging,
True to some articles you must observe,
Reserving to myself a prime command,
Whilst I enjoin nothing unreasonable.

*Goodlack.* All this is granted.

*Bess.* Then, first you said your ship was trim and gay:
I'll have her pitched all o'er, no spot of white,
No colour to be seen; no sail but black;
No flag but sable.

*Goodlack.* 'Twill be ominous,
And bode disastrous fortune.

*Bess.* I will ha't so.

*Goodlack.* Why, then, she shall be pitched black as the devil.

*Bess.* She shall be called the *Negro.* When you know my conceit, captain, you will thank me for't.

*Roughman.* But whither are we bound?

*Bess.* Pardon me that:
When we are out at sea, I'll tell you all.
For mine own wearing I have rich apparel,
For man or woman, as occasion serves,

*Clem.* But, mistress, if you be going to sea, what shall become of me a-land?

*Bess.* I'll give thee thy full time.

*Clem.* And shall I take time, when time is, and let my mistress slip away? No; it shall be seen that my teeth are as strong to grind biscuit as the best sailor of them all, and my stomach as able to digest powdered beef and poor-john. Shall I stay here to score a pudding in the Half-Moon, and see my mistress at the mainyard, with her sails up and spread? No; it shall be seen that I, who have been brought up to draw wine, will see what water the ship draws, or I'll bewray the voyage.

*Bess.* If thou hast so much courage, the captain shall accept thee.

*Clem.* If I have so much courage! When did you see a black beard with a white liver, or a little fellow without a tall stomach? I doubt not but to prove an honour to all the drawers in Cornwall.

*Goodlack.* What now remains?

*Fawcett.* To make myself associate
In this bold enterprise.

*Goodlack.* Most gladly, sir.
And now our number's full, what's to be done?

*Bess.* First, at my charge, I'll feast the town of Foy;
Then set the cellars ope, that these my mates
May quaff unto the health of our boon voyage,
Our needful things being once conveyed abroad;
Then, casting up our caps, in sign of joy,
Our purpose is to bid farewell to Foy.

[*Exeunt. Hautboys long.*

## SCENE XIV.

*Morocco. The Court.*

*Enter* MULLISHEG, BASHAW ALCADE, *and* BASHAW JOFFER, *with other* ATTENDANTS

*Mullisheg.* Out of these bloody and intestine broils
We have at length attained a fortunate peace,
And now at last established in the throne
Of our great ancestors, and reign as King
Of Fez and great Morocco.
*Alcade.* Mighty Mullisheg,
Pride of our age and glory of the Moors,
By whose victorious hand all Barbary
Is conquered, awed, and swayed, behold thy vassals
With loud applauses greet thy victory. [*Shout; flourish.*
*Mullisheg.* Upon the slaughtered bodies of our foes
We mount our high tribunal; and being sole,
Without competitor, we now have leisure
To stablish laws, first for our kingdom's safety,
The enriching of our public treasury,
And last our state and pleasure; then give order
That all such Christian Merchants as have traffic
And freedom in our country, that conceal
The least part of our custom due to us,
Shall forfeit ship and goods.
*Joffer.* There are appointed.
Unto that purpose careful officers.
*Mullisheg.* Those forfeitures must help to furnish up
The exhausted treasure that our wars consumed;
Part of such profits as accrue that way
We have already tasted.
*Alcade.* 'Tis most fit
Those Christians that reap profit by our land
Should contribute unto so great a loss.
*Mullisheg.* Alcade, they shall.—But what's the style of king,
Without his pleasure? Find us concubines,
The fairest Christian damsels you can hire,
Or buy for gold; the loveliest of the Moors
We can command, and negroes everywhere;

Italians, French, and Dutch, choice Turkish girls,
Must fill our Alkedavy, the great palace
Where Mullisheg now deigns to keep his court.

*Joffer.* Who else are worthy to be libertines but such as bear the sword?

*Mullisheg.* Joffer, thou pleasest us.
If kings on earth be termed demigods,
Why should we not make here terrestrial Heaven?
We can, we will: our God shall be our pleasure;
For so our Meccan prophet warrants us.
And now the music of the drums surcease:
We'll learn to dance to the soft tunes of peace.

[*Hautboys. Exeunt*

## SCENE XV.

*On Board an English Ship.*

*Enter* Bess *as a Sea-captain*, Captain Goodlack, Roughman, *and others.*

*Bess.* Good morrow, captain. Oh, this last sea-fight
Was gallantly performed! It did me good
To see the Spanish carvel vail her top
Unto my maiden flag. Where ride we now?

*Goodlack.* Among the Islands.

*Bess.* What coast is this we now descry from far?

*Goodlack.* Yon fort's called Fayal.

*Bess.* Is that the place where Spencer's body lies?

*Goodlack.* Yes; in yon church he's buried.

*Bess.* Then know, to this place was my voyage bound,
To fetch the body of my Spencer thence;
In his own country to erect a tomb
And lasting monument, where, when I die,
In the same bed of earth my bones may lie.
Then, all that love me, arm and make for shore;
Yours be the spoil, he mine: I crave no more.

*Roughman.* May that man die derided and accursed
That will not follow where a woman leads.

*Goodlack.* Roughman, you are too rash, and counsel ill.
Have not the Spaniards fortified the town?
In all our ging we are but sixty-five.

*Roughman.* Come, I'll make one.

*Goodlack.* Attend me, good lieutenant;
And, sweet Bess, listen what I have devised.
With ten tall fellows I have manned our boat,
To what straggling Spaniards they can take.
And see where Fawcett is returned with prisoners.

*Enter* FAWCETT *with two* SPANIARDS.

*Fawcett.* These Spaniards we by break of day surprised,
As they were ready to take boat for fishing.
*Goodlack.* Spaniards, upon your lives, resolve us truly,
How strong's the town and fort?
1*st Spaniard.* Since English Raleigh won and spoiled it first,
The town's re-edified, and fort new built,
And four field-pieces in the block-house lie,
To keep the harbour's mouth.
*Goodlack.* And what's one ship to these?
*Bess.* Was there not, in the time of their abode,
A gentleman called Spencer buried there,
Within the church, whom some report was slain,
Or perished by a wound?
1*st Spaniard.* Indeed, there was,
And o'er him raised a goodly monument;
But when the English navy were sailed thence,
And that the Spaniards did possess the town,
Because they held him for a heretic,
They straight removed his body from the church.
*Bess.* And would the tyrants be so uncharitable
To wrong the dead! Where did they then bestow him?
1*st Spaniard.* They buried him i' the fields.
*Bess.* Oh, still more cruel!
1*st Spaniard.* The man that owned the field, doubtful his corn
Would never prosper whilst a heretic's body
Lay there, he made a petition to the church
To ha' it digged up and burnt; and so it was.
*Bess.* What's he, that loves me, would persuade me live,
Not rather leap o'er hatches into the sea?
Yet ere I die, I hope to be revenged
Upon some Spaniards, for my Spencer's wrong.
*Roughman.* Let's first begin with these.

*Bess.* 'Las, these poor slaves! Besides their pardoned lives,
One give them money.—And, Spaniards, where you come,
Pray for Bess Bridges, and speak well o' the English.

*1st and 2nd Spaniards.* We shall.

*Bess.* Our mourning we will turn into revenge.
And since the church hath censured so my Spencer,
Bestow upon the church some few cast pieces.—
Command the gunner do't.

*Goodlack.* And, if he can,
To batter it to the earth. [*A gun is discharged.*

*Enter* Clem, *falling through haste.*

*Clem.* A sail! A sail!

*Bess.* From whence?

*Clem.* A pox upon yon gunner! Could he not give warning before he had shot?

*Roughman.* Why, I prithee?

*Clem.* Why? I was sent to the top-mast, to watch, and there I fell fast asleep. Bounce! quoth the guns; down tumbles Clem; and, if by chance my feet had not hung in the tackles, you must have sent to England for a bone-setter, for my neck had been in a pitiful taking.

*Roughman.* Thou told'st us of a sail.

*Enter* Sailor, *above.*

*Sailor.* Arm, gentlemen! a gallant ship of war
Makes with her full sails this way; who, it seems,
Hath took a bark of England.

*Bess.* Which we'll rescue,
Or perish in the adventure. You have sworn
That, whosoe'er we conquer or miscarry,
Not to reveal my sex.

*All.* We have.

*Bess.* Then, for your country's honour, my revenge,
For your own fame, and hope of golden spoil,
Stand bravely to't.—The manage of the fight we leave to you.

*Goodlack.* Then, now up with your fights, and let your ensigns,
Blest with St. George's cross, play with the winds.—
Fair Bess, keep you your cabin.

*Bess*. Captain, you wrong me: I will face the fight;
And where the bullets sing loud'st 'bout mine ears,
There shall you find me cheering up my men.

*Roughman*. This wench would of a coward make a Hercules.

*Bess*. Trumpets, a charge! and with your whistles shrill,
Sound, boatswains, an alarum to your mates.
With music cheer up their astonished souls,
The whilst the thundering ordnance bear the bass.

*Goodlack*. To fight against the Spaniards we desire.
Alarum, trumpets! [*Alarum.*

*Roughman*. Gunners, straight give fire!

[*A shot is fired.*

[*Exeunt* GOODLACK, *and* BESS, *etc.*

*Re-enter* CAPTAIN GOODLACK, *wounded*, BESS, ROUGHMAN, FAWCETT *and* CLEM.

*Goodlack*. I am shot, and can no longer man the deck:
Yet let not my wound daunt your courage, mates.

*Bess*. For every drop of blood that thou hast shed,
I'll have a Spaniard's life—Advance your targets,
And now cry all, "Board! Board! Amain for England!"

[*Alarum; Exeunt* GOODLACK, BESS, *etc.*

*Re-enter* BESS, ROUGHMAN, FAWCETT, CLEM, *etc.*, *victorious. The* SPANIARDS *prisoners.*

*Bess*. How is it with the captain?

*Roughman*. Nothing dangerous;
But, being shot i' the thigh, he keeps his cabin,
And cannot rise to greet your victory.

*Bess*. He stood it bravely out, whilst he could stand.

*Clem*. But for these Spaniards, now, you Don Diegos, You that made Paul's to stink.

*Roughman*. Before we further censure them, let's know what English prisoners they have here aboard.

[*Exit.*

1*st Spaniard*. You may command them all. We that were now Lords over them, fortune hath made slaves.
Release our prisoners.

*Bess*. Had my captain died,
Not one proud Spaniard had escaped with life.

Your ship is forfeit to us, and your goods:
So live.—Give him his long boat: him and his
Set safe ashore; and pray for English Bess.

1*st Spaniard*. I know not whom you mean; but be't your queen,
Famous Elizabeth, I shall report She and her subjects both are merciful. [*Exeunt* SPANIARDS.

*Re-enter* ROUGHMAN, *with a* MERCHANT, SPENCER, *and* English Prisoners.

*Bess*. Whence are you sir, and whither were you bound?

*Merchant*. I am a London merchant, bound for Barbary: but by this Spanish man-of-war surprised,
Pillaged and captived.

*Bess*. We much pity you.
What loss have you sustained, this Spanish prey
Shall make good to you, to the utmost farthing.

*Merchant*. Our lives, and all our fortunes whatsoever,
Are wholly at your service.

*Bess*. These gentlemen have been dejected long.
Let me peruse them all, and give them money
To drink our health. And pray forget not, sirs,
To pray for—— (*She sees* SPENCER). Hold! support me or I faint.

*Roughman*. What sudden, unexpected ecstasy
Disturbs your conquest?

*Bess*. Interrupt me not;
But give me way, for Heaven's sake!

*Spencer*. I have seen a face, ere now, like that young gentleman, But not remember where.

*Bess*. But he was slain;
Lay buried in yon church; and thence removed,
Denied all Christian rites, and, like an infidel,
Confined unto the fields; and thence digged up,
His body, after death, had martyrdom.
All these assure me 'tis his shadow dogs me,
For some most just revenge, thus far to sea.—
Is it because the Spaniards 'scaped with life,
That were to thee so cruel after death,
Thou haunt'st me thus? Sweet ghost, thy rage forbear;
I will revenge thee on the next we seize.

I am amazed; this sight I'll not endure.
Sleep, sleep, fair ghost, for thy revenge is sure.

*Roughman.* Fawcett, convey the owner to his cabin.

[*Exit* FAWCETT *with* BESS.

*Spencer.* I pray, sir, what young gentleman is that?

*Roughman.* He's both the owner of the ship and goods,
That for some reasons hath his name concealed.

*Spencer.* Methinks he looks like Bess; for in his eyes
lives the first love that did in my heart surprise.

*Roughman.* Come, gentlemen, first make your losses good,
Out of this Spanish prize. Let's then divide both several
ways, and Heavens be our guide.

*Merchant.* We towards Mamorah.

*Roughman.* We where the Fates do please,
'Till we have tracked a wilderness of seas.

[*Flourish. Exeunt.*

*Enter* CHORUS.

*Chorus.* Our stage so lamely can express a sea,
That we are forced by Chorus to discourse
What should have been in action. Now, imagine,
Her passion o'er, and Goodlack well recovered;
Who, had he not been wounded, and seen Spencer,
Had sure descried him. Much prize they have ta'en:
The French and Dutch she spares; only makes spoil
Of the Rich Spaniard and the barbarous Turk.
And now her fame grows great in all these seas.
Suppose her rich, and forced, for want of water,
To put into Mamorah, in Barbary,
Where, wearied by the habit of man,
She was discovered by the Moors aboard,
Which told it to the amorous King of Fez,
That ne'er before had English lady seen.
He sends for her on shore. How he receives her,
How she and Spencer meet, must next succeed.
Sit patient, then: when these are fully told,
Some may hap say, "Ay, there's a girl worth gold."

[*Exit* CHORUS.

## SCENE XVI.

*Morocco. The Court.*

*Enter* MULLISHEG, BASHAW ALCADE, BASHAW JOFFER, Attendants, *etc.*

*Mullisheg.* But was she of such presence?
*Alcade.* To describe her were to make eloquence dumb.
*Mullisheg.* Well habited?
*Alcade*: I ne'er beheld a beauty more complete.
*Mullisheg*: Thou hast inflamed our spirits.
In England born?
*Alcade.* The captain so reported.
*Mullisheg.* How her ship?
*Alcade.* I never saw a braver vessel sail.
And she is called the *Negro*.
*Mullisheg.* Ominous, perhaps, to our good fate: she in a *Negro*
Hath sailed thus far, to bosom with a Moor.
But for the motion made to come ashore,
How did she relish that?
*Alcade.* I promised to the captain large reward,
To win him to it, and this day he hath promised
To bring me her free answer.
*Mullisheg.* When he comes,
Give him the entertainment of a prince.

*Enter a* MOOR.

The news with thee?
*Moor.* The Captain of the *Negro* craves admittance
Unto your Highness' presence.
*Mullisheg.* A guard attend him, and our noblest bashaws
Conduct him safe where we will parley him. [*Flourish.*

*Enter* CAPTAIN GOODLACK *and* ROUGHMAN.

*Goodlack.* Long live the high and mighty King of Fez!
*Mullisheg.* If thou bring'st her, then dost thou bring me life.
Say, will she come.
*Goodlack.* She will, my lord; but yet conditionally, she may be free from violence.

*Mullisheg.* Now, by the mighty prophet we adore:
She shall live lady of her free desires:
'Tis love, not force, must quench our amorous fires.
*Roughman.* We will conduct her to your presence straight.
*Exit* ROUGHMAN *and* GOODLACK.
*Mullisheg.* We will have banquets, revels, and what not,
To entertain this stranger. [*Hautboys.*

*Re-enter* CAPTAIN GOODLACK *and* ROUGHMAN, *with* BESS BRIDGES, veiled, FAWCETT *and* MOORS.

A goodly presence!—Why's that beauty veiled?
*Bess.* Long live the King of Fez.
*Mullisheg.* I am amazed!
This is no mortal creature I behold,
But some bright angel, that is dropped from Heaven,
Sent by our prophet.—Captain, let me thus
Embrace thee in my arms.—Load him with gold,
For this great favour.
*Bess.* Captain, touch it not.—
Know, King of Fez, my followers want no gold.
I only came to see thee for my pleasure,
And show thee, what these say thou never saw'st,
A woman born in England.
*Mullisheg.* That English earth may well be termed a Heaven,
That breeds such divine beauties. Make me sure
That thou art mortal by one friendly touch.
*Bess.* Keep off: for, 'till thou swear'st to my demands,
I will have no commerce with Mullisheg.
But leave thee as I came.
*Mullisheg.* Were't half my kingdom,
That, beauteous English virgin, thou shalt have.
*Bess.* [*Hands* GOODLACK *a paper*]. Captain, read.
*Goodlack.* [*Reading*]. "First, liberty for her and hers to leave the land at her pleasure. Next, safe-conduct to and from her ship, at her own discretion. Thirdly, to be free from all violence, either by the King or any of his people. Fourthly, to allow her mariners fresh victuals aboard. Fifthly, to offer no further violence to her person than what he seeks by kindly usage and free entreaty."

*Mullisheg*. To these I vow and seal.

*Bess*. These being assured.
Your courtship's free, and henceforth we secured.

*Mullisheg*. Say, gentlemen of England, what's your fashion and garb of entertainment?

*Goodlack*. Our first greeting
Begins still on the lips.

*Mullisheg*. Fair creature, shall I be immortalized with that high favour?

*Bess*. 'Tis no immodest thing
You ask, nor shame for Bess to kiss a king. [*Kisses him.*

*Mullisheg*. This kiss hath all my vitals ecstasied.

*Roughman*. Captain,
This king is mightily in love. Well, let her
Do as she list, I'll make use of his bounty.

*Goodlack*. We should be madmen else.

*Mullisheg*. Grace me so much as take your seat by me.

*Bess*. I'll be so far commanded.

*Mullisheg*. Sweet, your age?

*Bess*. Not fully yet seventeen.

*Mullisheg*. But how your birth? How came you to this wealth?
To have such gentlemen at your command, and what your cause to travel?

*Bess*. Mighty prince,
If you desire to see me beat my breast,
Pour forth a river of increasing tears,
Then you may urge me to that sad discourse.

*Mullisheg*. Not for Mamorah's wealth, nor all the gold
Coined in rich Barbary. Nay, sweet, arise,
And ask of me, be't half this kingdom's treasure,
And thou art lady on't.

*Bess*. If I shall ask, 't must be, you will not give.
Our country breeds no beggars; for our hearts
Are of more noble temper.

*Mullisheg*. Sweet, your name?

*Bess*. Elizabeth.

*Mullisheg*. There's virtue in that name.
The virgin queen, so famous through the world,
The mighty Empress of the maiden isle,
Whose predecessors have o'er-run great France,

Whose powerful hand doth still support the Dutch,
And keeps the potent king of Spain in awe,
Is not she titled so?

*Bess.* She is.

*Mullisheg.* Hath she herself a face so fair as yours,
When she appears for wonder?

*Bess*: Mighty Fez,
You cast a blush upon my maiden cheek,
To pattern me with her. Why, England's queen,
She is the only phœnix of her age,
The pride and glory of the Western Isles.
Had I a thousand tongues, they all would tire,
And fail me in her true description.

*Mullisheg.* Grant me this:
To-morrow we supply our judgment seat,
And sentence causes; sit with us in state,
And let your presence beautify our throne.

*Bess.* In that I am your servant.

*Mullisheg.* And we thine.
Set on in state, attendants, and full train.
But find to ask, we vow thou shalt obtain.

[*Exeunt all except* GOODLACK.

*Enter* CLEM.

*Clem.* It is not now as when Andrea lived, or rather Andrew, our elder journeyman. What, drawers become courtiers! Now may I speak with the old ghost in Jeronimo—
When this eternal substance of my soul did live imprisoned in this wanton flesh, I was a courtier in the court of Fez.

*Goodlack.* Oh, well done, Clem! It is your mistress' pleasure,
None come ashore that's not well habited.

*Clem.* Nay; for mine own part, I hold myself as good a Christian in these clothes, as the proudest infidel of them all.

*Re-enter* ALCADE *and* JOFFER.

*Alcade.* Sir, by your leave, you're of the English train?

*Clem.* I am so, thou great monarch of the Mauritanians.

*Joffer*. Then, 'tis the king's command we give you all attendance.

*Clem*. Great Signior of the Saracens, I thank thee.

*Alcade*. Will you walk in to banquet?

*Clem*. I will make bold to march in towards your banquet, and there comfit myself, and cast all caraways down my throat, the best way I have to conserve myself in health; and for your country's sake, which is called Barbary, I will love all barbers and barberries the better. And for you Moors, thus much I mean to say, I'll see if more I eat, the more I may.

*Enter two* MERCHANTS.

1*st Merchant*. I pray, sir, are you of the English train?

*Clem*. Why, what art thou, my friend?

1*st Merchant*. Sir, a French merchant, run into relapse,
And forfeit of the law. Here's for you, sir,
Forty good Barbary pieces, to deliver
Your lady this petition, who, I hear,
Can all things with the king.

*Clem*. Your gold doth bind me to you.—You may see what it is to be a sudden courtier: I no sooner put my nose into the court, but my hand itches for a bribe already.—What's your business, my friend?

2*nd Merchant*. Some of my men, for a little outrage done,
Are sentenced to the galleys.

*Clem*. To the gallows?

2*nd Merchant*. No; to the galleys. Now, could your lady purchase
Their pardon from the king, here's twenty angels.

*Clem*. What are you, sir?

2*nd Merchant*. A Florentine merchant.

*Clem*. Then you are, as they say, a Christian?

2*nd Merchant*. Heaven forbid, else!

*Clem*. I should not have the faith to take your gold, else.
Attend on me: I'll speak in your behalf.—
Where be my bashaws? Usher us in state:
And when we sit to banquet, see you wait.

[*Flourish. Exeunt.*

## SCENE XVII.

*The same as before.*

*Enter* SPENCER.

*Spencer*. This day the king ascends his royal throne.
The honest merchant, in whose ship I came,
Hath, by a cunning quiddit in the law,
Both ship and goods made forfeit to the king,
To whom I will petition. But no more;
He's now upon his entrance. [*Hautboys*.

*Enter* MULLISHEG, BESS, CAPTAIN GOODLACK, ROUGHMAN, ALCADE JOFFER, *with all the other train.*

*Mullisheg*. Here seat thee, maid of England, like a queen
The style we'll give thee, wilt thou deign us love.
*Bess*. Bless me, you holy angels!
*Mullisheg*. What is't offends you, sweet?
*Spencer*. I am amazed, and know not what to think on't.
*Bess*. Captain, dost not see? Is not that Spencer's ghost?
*Goodlack*. I see, and, like you, am ecstasied.
*Spencer*. If mine eyes mistake not,
That should be Captain Goodlack, and that Bess.
But oh! I cannot be so happy.
*Goodlack*. 'Tis he, and I'll salute him.
*Bess*. Captain, stay.
You shall be swayed by me.
*Spencer*. Him I well know; but how should she come hither?
*Mullisheg*. What is't that troubles you?
*Bess*. Most mighty King,
Spare me no longer time but to bestow
My captain on a message.
*Mullisheg*. Thou shalt command my silence, and his ear.
*Bess*. [*To* GOODLACK]. Go wind about, and when you see least eyes
Are fixed on you, single him out, and see
If we mistake not. If he be the man,
Give me some private note.
*Goodlack*. This. [*Making a sign.*]
*Bess*. Enough.—What said your highness?

*Mullisheg.* Hark what I proffer thee. Continue here,
And grant me full fruition of thy love.—

*Bess.* Good.

*Mullisheg.* Thou shalt have all my peers to honour thee,
Next our great prophet.

*Bess.* Well.

*Mullisheg.* And when thou'rt weary of our sun-burnt clime,
Thy *Negro* shall be ballast home with gold.

*Bess.* I am eternized ever!
Now, all you sad disasters, dare your worst;
I neither care nor fear: my Spencer lives!

*Mullisheg.* You mind me not, sweet virgin.

*Bess.* You talk of love:
My lord, I'll tell you more of that hereafter;
But now to your state-business.—Bid him do thus
No more, and not to be seen till then.

*Goodlack.* Enough.—Come, sir, you must along with me.

[*Exeunt* GOODLACK *and* SPENCER.

*Bess.* Now, stood a thousand deaths before my face, I would not change my cheer, since Spencer's safe.

*Enter* CLEM with the French and Italian MERCHANTS; *and a* PREACHER.

*Clem.* By your leave, my masters; room for generosity.

1*st Merchant.* Pray, sir, remember me.

2*nd Merchant.* Good sir, my suit.

*Clem.* I am perfect in both your parts, without prompting. Mistress, here are two Christen friends of mine have forfeited ships and men to the black-a-morian king: now, one sweet word from your lips might get their release. I have had a feeling of the business already.

*Mullisheg.* For dealing in commodities forbid,
You're fined a thousand ducats.

*Bess.* Cast off the burden of your heavy doom.
A follower of my train petitions for him.

*Mullisheg.* One of thy train, sweet Bess?

*Clem.* And no worse man than myself, sir.

*Mullisheg.* Well, sirrah, for your lady's sake
His ship and goods shall be restored again.

*1st Merchant*. Long live the king of Fez!

*Clem*. Mayst thou never want sweet water to wash thy black face in, most mighty monarch of Morocco.—Mistress, another friend; ay, and paid beforehand.

*Mullisheg*. Sirrah, your men, for outrage and contempt,
Are doomed to the galleys.

*Bess*. A censure too severe for Christians.
Great King, I'll pay their ransom.

*Mullisheg*. Thou, my Bess!
Thy word shall be their ransom: they're discharged.
What grave old man is that?

*Joffer*. A Christian preacher; one that would convert your Moors, and turn them to a new belief.

*Mullisheg*. Then he shall die, as we are King of Fez.

*Bess*. For these I only spake; for him I kneel,
If I have any grace with mighty Fez.

*Mullisheg*. We can deny thee nothing, beauteous maid.
A kiss shall be his pardon.

*Bess*. Thus I pay't.

*Clem*. Must your black face be smouching my mistress' white lips with a moorian! I would you had kissed her a——

*Alcade*. Hah! how is that, sir?

*Clem*. I know what I say, sir; I would he had kissed her a——

*Alcade*. A—what?

*Clem*. A thousand times, to have done him a pleasure!

*Re-enter* SPENCER *and* CAPTAIN GOODLACK.

*Mullisheg*. That kiss was worth the ransom of a king.—
What's he, of that brave presence?

*Bess*. A gentleman of England, and my friend.
Do him some grace, for my sake.

*Mullisheg*. For thy sake what would not I perform?
He shall have grace and honour [*He goes to* JOFFER].
Joffer, go see him prepared to attend on us:
He shall be our chief eunuch.

[*They seize* SPENCER. *Coming down to them.*

*Bess*. Not for ten worlds. Behold, great king, I stand
Betwixt him and all danger.—Have I found thee?—
Seize what I have; take both my ship and goods;

Leave nought that's mine unrifled: spare me him.—
And have I found my Spencer?

*Clem.* Please your majesty, I see all men are not capable of honour: what he refuseth, may it please you to bestow on me.

*Mullisheg.* With all my heart. Go bear him hence, Alcade,
Into our Alkedavy: honour him.
And let him taste the razor.

*Clem.* There's honour for me!

*Alcade.* Come, follow.

*Clem.* No, sir; I'll go before you, for mine honour.

[*Exeunt* CLEM *and* ALCADE.

*Spencer.* Oh! show yourself, renowned king, the same
Fame blazons you. Bestow this maid on me:
'Tis such a gift as kingdoms cannot buy.
She is a precedent of all true love,
And shall be registered to aftertimes,
That ne'er shall pattern her.

*Goodlack.* Heard you the story of their constant love,
'Twould move in you compassion.

*Roughman.* Let not intemperate love sway you 'bove pity.
That foreign nations, that ne'er heard your name,
May chronicle your virtues.

*Mullisheg.* You have wakened in me an heroic spirit:
Lust shall not conquer virtue.—Till this hour,
We graced thee for thy beauty, English woman;
But now we wonder at thy constancy.

*Bess.* Oh! were you of our faith, I'd swear great Mullisheg
To be a god on earth.—And lives my Spencer?
In troth I thought thee dead.

*Spencer.* In hope of thee,
I lived to gain both life and liberty.

*Re-enter* CLEM, *running.*

*Clem.* No more of your honour, sir, if you love me! Is this your Moorish preferment, to rob a man of his best jewels?

*Mullisheg.* Hast thou seen our Alkedavy?

*Clem.* Davy do you call him? he may be called shavy;
No more of your cutting honour, if you love me.

*Mullisheg* [*To* SPENCER]. All your strange fortunes we will hear discoursed,
And after that your fair espousals grace,
If you can find a man of your belief
To do that grateful office.
*Spencer*. None more fit
Than this religious and brave gentleman,
Late rescued from death's sentence.
*Preacher*. None more proud.
To do you that poor service.
*Mullisheg*. Noble Englishman,
I cannot fasten bounty to my will
Worthy thy merit: move some suit to us.
*Spencer*. To make you more renowned, great king, and us the more indebted, there's an Englishman
Hath forfeited his ship for goods uncustomed.—
*Mullisheg*. Thy suit is granted ere it be half begged:
Dispose them at thy pleasure.
*Spencer*. Mighty king,
We are your highness' servants.
*Mullisheg*. Come, beauteous maid; we'll see thee crowned a bride.
At all our pompous banquets these shall wait
Thy followers and thy servants press with gold;
And not the mean'st that to thy train belongs,
But shall approve our bounty. Lead in state,
And, wheresoe'er thy fame shall be enrolled,
The world report thou art a Girl worth gold.

[*Exeunt*.

# WEDNESDAY

## ALL FOR LOVE
(1678)

By

JOHN DRYDEN

## DRAMATIS PERSONÆ

MARK ANTONY ........................................

VENTIDIUS, his General ........................................

DOLABELLA, his Friend ........................................

ALEXAS, the Queen's Eunuch........................................

SERAPION, Priest of Isis ........................................

MYRIS, another Priest ........................................

Servants to Antony ........................................

CLEOPATRA, Queen of Egypt ........................................

OCTAVIA, Antony's Wife ........................................

CHARMION, } Cleopatra's Maids ........................................
IRAS, }

# PROLOGUE

WHAT flocks of critics hover here to-day,
As vultures wait on armies for their prey,
All gaping for the carcase of a play!
With croaking notes they bode some dire event,
And follow dying poets by the scent.
Ours gives himself for gone; y' have watched your time:
He fights this day unarmed,—without his rhyme;—
And brings a tale which often has been told;
As sad as Dido's; and almost as old.
His hero, whom you wits his bully call,
Bates of his mettle, and scarce rants at all:
He's somewhat lewd; but a well-meaning mind;
Weeps much; fights little; but is wond'rous kind.
In short, a pattern, and companion fit,
For all the keeping Tonies of the pit.
I could name more: a wife, and mistress too;
Both (to be plain) too good for most of you:
The wife well-natured, and the mistress true.
  Now, poets, if your fame has been his care,
Allow him all the candour you can spare.
A brave man scorns to quarrel once a-day;
Like Hectors in at every petty fray.
Let those find fault whose wit's so very small,
They've need to show that they can think at all;
Errors, like straws, upon the surface flow;
He who would search for pearls, must dive below.
Fops may have leave to level all they can;
As pigmies would be glad to lop a man.
Half-wits are fleas; so little and so light,
We scarce could know they live, but that they bite.
But, as the rich, when tired with daily feasts,
For change, become their next poor tenant's guests;
Drink hearty draughts of ale from plain brown bowls,
And snatch the homely rasher from the coals:
So you, retiring from much better cheer,

For once, may venture to do penance here.
And since that plenteous autumn now is past,
Whose grapes and peaches have indulged your taste,
Take in good part, from our poor poet's board,
Such rivelled fruits as winter can afford.

SCENE—*Alexandria.*

# ACT I

## SCENE I.

*The Temple of Isis.*

*Enter* Serapion, Myris, Priests of Isis.

*Serapion.* Portents and prodigies have grown so frequent,
That they have lost their name. Our fruitful Nile
Flowed ere the wonted season, with a torrent
So unexpected, and so wondrous fierce,
That the wild deluge overtook the haste
Even of the hinds that watched it: Men and beasts
Were borne above the tops of trees, that grew
On the utmost margin of the water-mark.
Then, with so swift an ebb the flood drove backward,
It slipt from underneath the scaly herd:
Here monstrous phocæ panted on the shore;
Forsaken dolphins there with their broad tails,
Lay lashing the departing waves: hard by them,
Sea horses floundering in the slimy mud,
Tossed up their heads, and dashed the ooze about them.

*Enter* Alexas *behind them.*

*Myris.* Avert these omens, Heaven!

*Serapion.* Last night, between the hours of twelve and one,
In a lone aisle of the temple while I walked,
A whirlwind rose, that, with a violent blast,
Shook all the dome: the doors around me clapt;
The iron wicket, that defends the vault,
Where the long race of Ptolemies is laid,
Burst open, and disclosed the mighty dead.

From out each monument, in order placed,
An armed ghost starts up: the boy-king last
Reared his inglorious head. A peal of groans
Then followed, and a lamentable voice
Cried, Egypt is no more! My blood ran back,
My shaking knees against each other knocked;
On the cold pavement down I fell entranced,
And so unfinished left the horrid scene.

*Alexas.* And dreamed you this? or did invent the story,
To frighten our Egyptian boys withal, [*Showing himself.*
And train them up, betimes, in fear of priesthood?

*Serapion.* My lord, I saw you not,
Nor meant my words should reach your ears; but what
I uttered was most true.

*Alexas.* A foolish dream,
Bred from the fumes of indigested feasts,
And holy luxury.

*Serapion.* I know my duty:
This goes no further.

*Alexas.* 'Tis not fit it should;
Nor would the times now bear it, were it true.
All southern, from yon hills, the Roman camp
Hangs o'er us black and threatening, like a storm
Just breaking on our heads.

*Serapion.* Our faint Egyptians pray for Antony;
But in their servile hearts they own Octavius.

*Myris.* Why then does Antony dream out his hours,
And tempts not fortune for a noble day,
Which might redeem what Actium lost?

*Alexas.* He thinks 'tis past recovery.

*Serapion.* Yet the foe
Seems not to press the siege.

*Alexas.* Oh, there's the wonder.
Mæcenas and Agrippa, who can most
With Cæsar, are his foes. His wife Octavia,
Driven from his house, solicits her revenge;
And Dolabella, who was once his friend,
Upon some private grudge, now seeks his ruin:
Yet still war seems on either side to sleep.

*Serapion.* 'Tis strange that Antony, for some days past,
Has not beheld the face of Cleopatra;

But here, in Isis' temple, lives retired,
And makes his heart a prey to black despair.
*Alexas.* 'Tis true; and we much fear he hopes by absence
To cure his mind of love.
*Serapion.* If he be vanquished,
Or make his peace, Egypt is doomed to be
A Roman province; and our plenteous harvests
Must then redeem the scarceness of their soil.
While Antony stood firm, our Alexandria
Rivalled proud Rome (dominion's other seat),
And Fortune striding, like a vast Colossus,
Could fix an equal foot of empire here.
*Alexas.* Had I my wish, these tyrants of all nature,
Who lord it o'er mankind, should perish,—perish,
Each by the other's sword; but, since our will
Is lamely followed by our power, we must
Depend on one; with him to rise or fall.
*Serapion.* How stands the queen affected?
*Alexas.* Oh, she dotes,
She dotes, Serapion, on this vanquished man,
And winds herself about his mighty ruins;
Whom would she yet forsake, yet yield him up,
This hunted prey, to his pursuer's hands,
She might preserve us all: but 'tis in vain—
This changes my designs, this blasts my counsels,
And makes me use all means to keep him here,
Whom I could wish divided from her arms,
Far as the earth's deep centre. Well, you know
The state of things; no more of your ill omens
And black prognostics; labour to confirm
The people's hearts.

*Enter* VENTIDIUS, *talking aside with a* Gentleman of ANTONY'S.

*Serapion.* These Romans will o'erhear us.
But, who's that stranger? By his warlike port,
His fierce demeanour, and erected look,
He's of no vulgar note.
*Alexas.* Oh 'tis Ventidius,
Our emperor's great lieutenant in the East,
Who first showed Rome that Parthia could be conquered.

When Antony returned from Syria last,
He left this man to guard the Roman frontiers.

*Serapion.* You seem to know him well.

*Alexas.* Too well. I saw him at Cilicia first,
When Cleopatra there met Antony:
A mortal foe he was to us, and Egypt.
But,—let me witness to the worth I hate,—
A braver Roman never drew a sword;
Firm to his prince, but as a friend, not slave.
He ne'er was of his pleasures; but presides
O'er all his cooler hours, and morning counsels:
In short the plainness, fierceness, rugged virtue,
Of an old true-stampt Roman lives in him.
His coming bodes I know not what of ill
To our affairs. Withdraw to mark him better;
And I'll acquaint you why I sought you here,
And what's our present work.

[*They withdraw to a corner of the stage; and* VENTIDIUS, *with the other, comes forward to the front.*

*Ventidius.* Not see him, say you?
I say, I must, and will.

*Gentleman.* He has commanded,
On pain of death, none should approach his presence.

*Ventidius.* I bring him news will raise his drooping spirits,
Give him new life.

*Gentleman.* He sees not Cleopatra.

*Ventidius.* Would he had never seen her!

*Gentleman.* He eats not, drinks not, sleeps not, has no use
Of anything, but thought; or if he talks,
'Tis to himself, and then 'tis perfect raving:
Then he defies the world, and bids it pass;
Sometimes he gnaws his lip, and curses loud
The boy Octavius; then he draws his mouth
Into a scornful smile, and cries, "Take all,
The world's not worth my care."

*Ventidius.* Just, just his nature.
Virtue's his path; but sometimes 'tis too narrow
For his vast soul; and then he starts out wide,
And bounds into a vice, that bears him far
From his first course, and plunges him in ills:

But, when his danger makes him find his fault,
Quick to observe, and full of sharp remorse,
He censures eagerly his own misdeeds,
Judging himself with malice to himself,
And not forgiving what as man he did,
Because his other parts are more than man.—
He must not thus be lost.

[ALEXAS *and the* Priests *come forward.*

*Alexas.* You have your full instructions, now advance;
Proclaim your orders loudly.

*Serapion.* Romans, Egyptians, hear the queen's command.
Thus Cleopatra bids: Let labour cease;
To pomp and triumphs give this happy day,
That gave the world a lord: 'tis Antony's.
Live, Antony; and Cleopatra live!
Be this the general voice sent up to heaven,
And every public place repeat this echo.

*Ventidius.* Fine pageantry! [*Aside.*

*Serapion.* Set out before your doors
The images of all your sleeping fathers,
With laurels crowned; with laurels wreathe your posts,
And strew with flowers the pavement; let the priests
Do present sacrifice; pour out the wine,
And call the gods to join with you in gladness.

*Ventidius.* Curse on the tongue that bids this general joy!
Can they be friends of Antony, who revel
When Antony's in danger? Hide, for shame,
You Romans, your great grandsires' images,
For fear their souls should animate their marbles,
To blush at their degenerate progeny.

*Alexas.* A love, which knows no bounds, to Antony,
Would mark the day with honours, when all heaven
Laboured for him, when each propitious star
Stood wakeful in his orb, to watch that hour,
And shed his better influence. Her own birthday
Our queen neglected like a vulgar fate,
That passed obscurely by.

*Ventidius.* Would it had slept,
Divided far from this; till some remote
And future age had called it out, to ruin
Some other prince, not him!

*Alexas.* Your emperor,
Though grown unkind, would be more gentle, than
To upbraid my queen for loving him too well.

*Ventidius.* Does the mute sacrifice upbraid the priest?
He knows him not his executioner.
Oh, she has decked his ruin with her love,
Led him in golden bands to gaudy slaughter,
And made perdition pleasing: She has left him
The blank of what he was.
I tell thee, eunuch, she has quite unmanned him.
Can any Roman see, and know him now,
Thus altered from the lord of half mankind,
Unbent, unsinewed, made a woman's toy,
Shrunk from the vast extent of all his honours,
And crampt within a corner of the world?
O Antony!
Thou bravest soldier, and thou best of friends!
Bounteous as nature; next to nature's God!
Couldst thou but make new worlds, so wouldst thou give them,
As bounty were thy being! rough in battle,
As the first Romans when they went to war;
Yet after victory more pitiful
Than all their praying virgins left at home!

*Alexas.* Would you could add, to those more shining virtues,
His truth to her who loves him.

*Ventidius.* Would I could not!
But wherefore waste I precious hours with thee!
Thou art her darling mischief, her chief engine,
Antony's other fate. Go, tell thy queen,
Ventidius is arrived, to end her charms.
Let your Egyptian timbrels play alone,
Nor mix effeminate sounds with Roman trumpets.
You dare not fight for Antony; go pray
And keep your cowards' holiday in temples.

[*Exuent* ALEXAS, SERAPION.

*Re-enter the* Gentleman *of* M. ANTONY.

*2nd Gentleman.* The emperor approaches, and commands.
On pain of death, that none presume to stay.

*1st Gentleman.* I dare not disobey him.
[*Going out with the other.*

*Ventidius.* Well, I dare.
But I'll observe him first unseen, and find
Which way his humour drives: The rest I'll venture.
[*Withdraws.*

*Enter* ANTONY, *walking with a disturbed motion before he speaks.*

*Antony.* They tell me, 'tis my birthday, and I'll keep it
With double pomp of sadness.
'Tis what the day deserves, which gave me breath.
Why was I raised the meteor of the world,
Hung in the skies, and blazing as I travelled,
Till all my fires were spent; and then cast downward,
To be trod out by Cæsar?

*Ventidius* [*Aside.*] On my soul,
'Tis mournful, wondrous mournful!

*Antony.* Count thy gains.
Now, Antony, wouldst thou be born for this?
Glutton of fortune, thy devouring youth
Has starved thy wanting age.

*Ventidius.* How sorrow shakes him! [*Aside.*
So, now the tempest tears him up by the roots,
And on the ground extends the noble ruin.
[ANTONY *having thrown himself down.*
Lie there, thou shadow of an emperor;
The place thou pressest on thy mother earth
Is all thy empire now: now it contains thee;
Some few days hence, and then 'twill be too large,
When thou'rt contracted in thy narrow urn,
Shrunk to a few cold ashes; then Octavia
(For Cleopatra will not live to see it),
Octavia then will have thee all her own,
And bear thee in her widowed hand to Cæsar;
Cæsar will weep, the crocodile will weep,
To see his rival of the universe
Lie still and peaceful there. I'll think no more on't.

*Antony.* Give me some music: look that it be sad:
I'll soothe my melancholy, till I swell,
And burst myself with sighing.— [*Soft music.*

'Tis somewhat to my humour: stay, I fancy
I'm now turned wild, a commoner of nature;
Of all forsaken, and forsaking all;
Live in a shady forest's sylvan scene,
Stretched at my length beneath some blasted oak,
I lean my head upon the mossy bark,
And look just of a piece as I grew from it;
My uncombed locks, matted like mistletoe,
Hang o'er my hoary face; a murmuring brook
Runs at my foot.

*Ventidius.* Methinks I fancy
Myself there too.

*Antony.* The herd come jumping by me,
And, fearless, quench their thirst, while I look on,
And take me for their fellow-citizen.
More of this image, more; it lulls my thoughts.

[*Soft music again.*

*Ventidius.* I must disturb him; I can hold no longer.

[*Stands before him.*

*Antony* [*starting up*]. Art thou Ventidius?

*Ventidius.* Are you Antony?
I'm liker what I was, than you to him
I left you last.

*Antony.* I'm angry.

*Ventidius.* So am I.

*Antony.* I would be private: leave me.

*Ventidius.* Sir, I love you,
And therefore will not leave you.

*Antony.* Will not leave me!
Where have you learnt that answer? Who am I?

*Ventidius.* My emperor; the man I love next Heaven:
If I said more, I think 'twere scarce a sin:
You're all that's good, and god-like.

*Antony.* All that's wretched.
You will not leave me then?

*Ventidius.* 'Twas too presuming
To say I would not; but I dare not leave you:
And, 'tis unkind in you to chide me hence
So soon, when I so far have come to see you.

*Antony.* Now thou hast seen me, art thou satisfied?
For, if a friend, thou hast beheld enough;
And, if a foe, too much.

*Ventidius.* Look, emperor, this is no common dew. [*Weeping.*
I have not wept this forty years; but now
My mother comes afresh into my eyes;
I cannot help her softness.

*Antony.* By heaven, he weeps! poor good old man, he weeps!
The big round drops course one another down
The furrows of his cheeks.—Stop them, Ventidius,
Or I shall blush to death: they set my shame,
That caused them, full before me.

*Ventidius.* I'll do my best.

*Antony.* Sure there's contagion in the tears of friends:
See, I have caught it too. Believe me, 'tis not
For my own griefs, but thine.—Nay, father!

*Ventidius.* Emperor.

*Antony.* Emperor! Why, that's the style of victory;
The conqu'ring soldier, red with unfelt wounds,
Salutes his general so: but never more
Shall that sound reach my ears.

*Ventidius.* I warrant you.

*Antony.* Actium, Actium! Oh——

*Ventidius.* It sits too near you.

*Antony.* Here, here it lies; a lump of lead by day,
And, in my short, distracted, nightly slumbers,
The hag that rides my dreams.——

*Ventidius.* Out with it; give it vent.

*Antony.* Urge not my shame.
I lost a battle,——

*Ventidius.* So has Julius done.

*Antony.* Thou favour'st me, and speak'st not half thou think'st;
For Julius fought it out, and lost it fairly:
But Antony——

*Ventidius.* Nay, stop not.

*Antony.* Antony,—
Well, thou wilt have it—like a coward, fled,
Fled while his soldiers fought; fled first, Ventidius.

Thou long'st to curse me, and I give thee leave.
I know thou cam'st prepared to rail.

*Ventidius.* I did.

*Antony.* I'll help thee.—I have been a man, Ventidius.

*Ventidius.* Yes, and a brave one; but——

*Antony.* I know thy meaning.
But I have lost my reason, have disgraced
The name of soldier, with inglorious ease.
In the full vintage of my flowing honours,
Sat still, and saw it prest by other hands.
Fortune came smiling to my youth, and wooed it,
And purple greatness met my ripened years.
When first I came to empire, I was borne
On tides of people, crowding to my triumphs;
The wish of nations, and the willing world
Received me as its pledge of future peace;
I was so great, so happy, so beloved,
Fate could not ruin me; till I took pains,
And worked against my fortune, chid her from me,
And turned her loose; yet still she came again.
My careless days, and my luxurious nights,
At length have wearied her, and now she's gone,
Gone, gone, divorced for ever. Help me, soldier,
To curse this madman, this industrious fool,
Who laboured to be wretched: Pr'ythee, curse me.

*Ventidius.* No.

*Antony.* Why?

*Ventidius.* You are too sensible already
Of what you've done, too conscious of your failings;
And, like a scorpion, whipt by others first
To fury, sting yourself in mad revenge.
I would bring balm, and pour it in your wounds,
Cure your distempered mind, and heal your fortunes.

*Antony.* I know thou would'st.

*Ventidius.* I will.

*Antony.* Ha, ha, ha, ha!

*Ventidius.* You laugh.

*Antony.* I do, to see officious love
Give cordials to the dead.

*Ventidius.* You would be lost, then?

*Antony.* I am.

*Ventidius*. I say you are not. Try your fortune.
*Antony*. I have, to the utmost. Dost thou think me desperate,
Without just cause? No, when I found all lost
Beyond repair, I hid me from the world,
And learnt to scorn it here; which now I do
So heartily, I think it is not worth
The cost of keeping.
*Ventidius*. Cæsar thinks not so;
He'll thank you for the gift he could not take.
You would be killed like Tully, would you? do,
Hold out your throat to Cæsar, and die tamely.
*Antony*. No, I can kill myself; and so resolve.
*Ventidius*. I can die with you too, when time shall serve;
But fortune calls upon us now to live,
To fight, to conquer.
*Antony*. Sure thou dream'st, Ventidius.
*Ventidius*. No; 'tis you dream; you sleep away your hours
In desperate sloth, miscalled philosophy.
Up, up, for honour's sake; twelve legions wait you,
And long to call you chief: By painful journeys
I led them, patient both of heat and hunger,
Down from the Parthian marches to the Nile.
'Twill do you good to see their sunburnt faces,
Their scarred cheeks, and chopt hands: there's virtue in them.
They'll sell those mangled limbs at dearer rates
Than yon trim bands can buy.
*Antony*. Where left you them?
*Ventidius*. I said in Lower Syria.
*Antony*. Bring them hither;
There may be life in these.
*Ventidius*. They will not come.
*Antony*. Why didst thou mock my hopes with promised aids,
To double my despair? They're mutinous.
*Ventidius*. Most firm and loyal.
*Antony*. Yet they will not march
To succour me. O trifler!
*Ventidius*. They petition
You would make haste to head them.

*Antony*. I'm besieged.

*Ventidius*. There's but one way shut up: How came I hither?

*Antony*. I will not stir.

*Ventidius*. They would perhaps desire
A better reason.

*Antony*. I have never used
My soldiers to demand a reason of
My actions. Why did they refuse to march?

*Ventidius*. They said they would not fight for Cleopatra.

*Antony*. What was't they said?

*Ventidius*. They said they would not fight for Cleopatra.
Why should they fight indeed, to make her conquer,
And make you more a slave? to gain you kingdoms,
Which, for a kiss, at your next midnight feast,
You'll sell to her? Then she new-names her jewels,
And calls this diamond such or such a tax;
Each pendant in her ear shall be a province.

*Antony*. Ventidius, I allow your tongue free licence
On all my other faults; but, on your life,
No word of Cleopatra: she deserves
More worlds than I can lose.

*Ventidius*. Behold, you Powers,
To whom you have instrusted humankind!
See Europe, Afric, Asia, put in balance,
And all weighed down by one light, worthless woman!
I think the gods are Antonies, and give,
Like prodigals, this nether world away
To none but wasteful hands.

*Antony*. You grow presumptuous.

*Ventidius*. I take the privilege of plain love to speak.

*Antony*. Plain love! plain arrogance, plain insolence!
Thy men are cowards; thou, an envious traitor;
Who, under seeming honesty, hast vented
The burden of thy rank, o'erflowing gall.
O that thou wert my equal; great in arms
As the first Cæsar was, that I might kill thee
Without a stain to honour!

*Ventidius*. You may kill me;
You have done more already,—called me traitor.

*Antony*. Art thou not one?

*Ventidius.* For showing you yourself,
Which none else durst have done? but had I been
That name, which I disdain to speak again,
I needed not have sought your abject fortunes,
Come to partake your fate, to die with you.
What hindered me to have led my conquering eagles
To fill Octavius' bands? I could have been
A traitor then, a glorious, happy traitor,
And not have been so called.
*Antony.* Forgive me, soldier;
I've been too passionate.
*Ventidius.* You thought me false;
Thought my old age betrayed you: Kill me, sir,
Pray, kill me; yet you need not, your unkindness
Has left your sword no work.
*Antony.* I did not think so;
I said it in my rage: Pr'ythee, forgive me.
Why didst thou tempt my anger, by discovery
Of what I would not hear?
*Ventidius.* No prince but you
Could merit that sincerity I used,
Nor durst another man have ventured it;
But you, ere love misled your wandering eyes,
Were sure the chief and best of human race,
Framed in the very pride and boast of nature;
So perfect, that the gods, who formed you, wondered
At their own skill, and cried—A lucky hit
Has mended our design. Their envy hindered,
Else you had been immortal, and a pattern,
When Heaven would work for ostentation's sake
To copy out again.
*Antony.* But Cleopatra—
Go on; for I can bear it now.
*Ventidius.* No more.
*Antony.* Thou dar'st not trust my passion, but thou may'st;
Thou only lov'st, the rest have flattered me.
*Ventidius.* Heaven's blessing on your heart for that kind word!
May I believe you love me? Speak again.
*Antony.* Indeed I do. Speak this, and this, and this.
[*Hugging him.*

Thy praises were unjust; but, I'll deserve them,
And yet mend all. Do with me what thou wilt;
Lead me to victory! thou know'st the way.
*Ventidius*. And, will you leave this——
*Antony*. Pr'ythee, do not curse her,
And I will leave her; though, Heaven knows, I love
Beyond life, conquest, empire, all, but honour;
But I will leave her.
*Ventidius*. That's my royal master;
And, shall we fight?
*Antony*. I warrant thee, old soldier.
Thou shalt behold me once again in iron;
And at the head of our old troops, that beat
The Parthians, cry aloud—Come, follow me!
*Ventidius*. Oh, now I hear my emperor! in that word
Octavius fell. Gods, let me see that day,
And, if I have ten years behind, take all:
I'll thank you for the exchange.
*Antony*. O Cleopatra!
*Ventidius*. Again?
*Antony*. I've done: In that last sigh she went.
Cæsar shall know what 'tis to force a lover
From all he holds most dear.
*Ventidius*. Methinks, you breathe
Another soul: Your looks are more divine;
You speak a hero, and you move a god.
*Antony*. Oh, thou hast fired me; my soul's up in arms,
And mans each part about me: Once again,
That noble eagerness of fight has seized me;
That eagerness with which I darted upward
To Cassius' camp: In vain the steepy hill
Opposed my way; in vain a war of spears
Sung round my head, and planted on my shield;
I won the trenches, while my foremost men
Lagged on the plain below.
*Ventidius*. Ye gods, ye gods,
For such another honour!
*Antony*. Come on, my soldier!
Our hearts and arms are still the same: I long
Once more to meet our foes; that thou and I,
Like Time and Death, marching before our troops,

May taste fate to them; mow them out a passage,
And, entering where the foremost squadrons yield,
Begin the noble harvest of the field.
[*Exeunt.*

## ACT II

### SCENE I

*Enter* Cleopatra, Iras, *and* Alexas.

*Cleopatra.* What shall I do, or whither shall I turn?
Ventidius has o'ercome, and he will go.
*Alexas.* He goes to fight for you.
*Cleopatra.* Then he would see me, ere he went to fight:
Flatter me not: If once he goes, he's lost,
And all my hopes destroyed.
*Alexas.* Does this weak passion
Become a mighty queen?
*Cleopatra.* I am no queen:
Is this to be a queen, to be besieged
By yon insulting Roman, and to wait
Each hour the victor's chain? These ills are small:
For Antony is lost, and I can mourn
For nothing else but him. Now come, Octavius,
I have no more to lose! prepare thy bands;
I'm fit to be a captive: Antony
Has taught my mind the fortune of a slave.
*Iras.* Call reason to assist you.
*Cleopatra.* I have none,
And none would have: My love's a noble madness,
Which shows the cause deserved it. Moderate sorrow
Fits vulgar love, and for a vulgar man:
But I have loved with such transcendent passion,
I soared, at first, quite out of reason's view,
And now am lost above it. No, I'm proud
'Tis thus: Would Antony could see me now
Think you he would not sigh, though he must leave me?
Sure he would sigh; for he is noble-natured,

And bears a tender heart: I know him well.
Ah, no, I know him not; I knew him once,
But now 'tis past.
  *Iras.* Let it be past with you:
Forget him, madam.
  *Cleopatra.* Never, never, Iras.
He once was mine; and once, though now 'tis gone,
Leaves a faint image of possession still.
  *Alexas.* Think him inconstant, cruel, and ungrateful.
  *Cleopatra.* I cannot: If I could, those thoughts were vain.
Faithless, ungrateful, cruel, though he be,
I still must love him.

*Enter* CHARMION.

Now, what news, my Charmion?
Will he be kind? and will he not forsake me?
Am I to live, or die?—nay, do I live?
Or am I dead? for when he gave his answer,
Fate took the word, and then I lived or died.
  *Charmion.* I found him, madam——
  *Cleopatra.* A long speech preparing?
If thou bring'st comfort, haste, and give it me,
For never was more need.
  *Iras.* I know he loves you.
  *Cleopatra.* Had he been kind, her eyes had told me so,
Before her tongue could speak it: Now she studies,
To soften what he said; but give me death,
Just as he sent it, Charmion, undisguised,
And in the words he spoke.
  *Charmion.* I found him, then,
Encompassed round, I think, with iron statues;
So mute, so motionless his soldiers stood,
While awfully he cast his eyes about,
And every leader's hopes or fears surveyed:
Methought he looked resolved, and yet not pleased.
When he beheld me struggling in the crowd,
He blushed, and bade make way.
  *Alexas.* There's comfort yet.
  *Charmion.* Ventidius fixed his eyes upon my passage
Severely, as he meant to frown me back,
And sullenly gave place: I told my message,

Just as you gave it, broken and disordered;
I numbered in it all your sighs and tears,
And while I moved your pitiful request,
That you but only begged a last farewell,
He fetched an inward groan; and every time
I named you, sighed, as if his heart were breaking,
But, shunned my eyes, and guiltily looked down;
He seemed not now that awful Antony,
Who shook an armed assembly with his nod;
But, making show as he would rub his eyes,
Disguised and blotted out a falling tear.

*Cleopatra.* Did he then weep? And was I worth a tear?
If what thou hast to say be not as pleasing,
Tell me no more, but let me die contented.

*Charmion.* He bid me say,—He knew himself so well,
He could deny you nothing, if he saw you;
And therefore——

*Cleopatra.* Thou wouldst say, he would not see me?

*Charmion.* And therefore begged you not to use a power,
Which he could ill resist; yet he should ever
Respect you, as he ought.

*Cleopatra.* Is that a word
For Antony to use to Cleopatra?
O that faint word, *respect!* how I disdain it!
Disdain myself, for loving after it!
He should have kept that word for cold Octavia.
Respect is for a wife: Am I that thing,
That dull, insipid lump, without desires,
And without power to give them?

*Alexas.* You misjudge;
You see through love, and that deludes your sight;
As, what is straight, seems crooked through the water:
But I, who bear my reason undisturbed,
Can see this Antony, this dreaded man,
A fearful slave, who fain would run away,
And shuns his master's eyes: If you pursue him,
My life on't, he still drags a chain along
That needs must clog his flight.

*Cleopatra.* Could I believe thee!—

*Alexas.* By every circumstance I know he loves.
True, he's hard prest, by interest and by honour;

Yet he but doubts, and parleys, and casts out
Many a long look for succour.

*Cleopatra.* He sends word,
He fears to see my face.

*Alexas.* And would you more?
He shows his weakness who declines the combat,
And you must urge your fortune. Could he speak
More plainly? To my ears, the message sounds—
Come to my rescue, Cleopatra, come;
Come, free me from Ventidius; from my tyrant:
See me, and give me a pretence to leave him!—
I hear his trumpets. This way he must pass.
Please you, retire a while; I'll work him first,
That he may bend more easy.

*Cleopatra.* You shall rule me;
But all, I fear, in vain.

[*Exit with* CHARMION *and* IRAS.

*Alexas.* I fear so too;
Though I concealed my thoughts, to make her bold;
But 'tis our utmost means, and fate befriend it!

[*Withdraws*

*Enter* Lictors *with Fasces; one bearing the Eagle; then enter* ANTONY *with* VENTIDIUS, *followed by other* Commanders.

*Antony.* Octavius is the minion of blind chance,
But holds from virtue nothing.

*Ventidius.* Has he courage?

*Antony.* But just enough to season him from coward.
Oh, 'tis the coldest youth upon a charge,
The most deliberate fighter! if he ventures
(As in Illyria once, they say, he did,
To storm a town), 'tis when he cannot choose;
When all the world have fixt their eyes upon him;
And then he lives on that for seven years after;
But, at a close revenge he never fails.

*Ventidius.* I heard you challenged him.

*Antony.* I did, Ventidius.
What think'st thou was his answer? 'Twas so tame!—
He said, he had more ways than one to die;
I had not.

*Ventidius.* Poor!

*Antony.* He has more ways than one;
But he would choose them all before that one.
*Ventidius.* He first would choose an ague, or a fever.
*Antony.* No; it must be an ague, not a fever;
He has not warmth enough to die by that.
*Ventidius.* Or old age and a bed.
*Antony.* Ay, there's his choice,
He would live, like a lamp, to the last wink,
And crawl upon the utmost verge of life.
O Hercules! Why should a man like this,
Who dares not trust his fate for one great action,
Be all the care of Heaven? Why should he lord it
O'er fourscore thousand men, of whom each one
Is braver than himself?
*Ventidius.* You conquered for him:
Philippi knows it; there you shared with him
That empire, which your sword made all your own.
*Antony.* Fool that I was, upon my eagle's wings
I bore this wren, till I was tired with soaring,
And now he mounts above me.
Good heavens, is this—is this the man who braves me?
Who bids my age make way? Drives me before him,
To the world's ridge, and sweeps me off like rubbish?
*Ventidius.* Sir, we lose time; the troops are mounted all.
*Antony.* Then we give the word to march:
I long to leave this prison of a town,
To join thy legions; and, in open field,
Once more to show my face. Lead, my deliverer.

*Enter* ALEXAS.

*Alexas.* Great emperor,
In mighty arms renowned above mankind,
But, in soft pity to the opprest, a god;
This message sends the mournful Cleopatra
To her departing lord.
*Ventidius.* Smooth sycophant!
*Alexas.* A thousand wishes, and ten thousand prayers,
Millions of blessings wait you to the wars;
Millions of sighs and tears she sends you too,
And would have sent

As many dear embraces to your arms,
As many parting kisses to your lips;
But those, she fears, have wearied you already.

*Ventidius* [*Aside.*] False crocodile!

*Alexas.* And yet she begs not now, you would not leave her;
That were a wish too mighty for her hopes,
Too presuming
For her low fortune, and your ebbing love;
That were a wish for her more prosperous days,
Her blooming beauty, and your growing kindness.

*Antony.* [*Aside.*] Well, I must man it out:—What would the queen?

*Alexas.* First, to these noble warriors, who attend
Your daring courage in the chase of fame,—
Too daring, and too dangerous for her quiet,—
She humbly recommends all she holds dear,
All her own cares and fears,—the care of you.

*Ventidius.* Yes, witness Actium.

*Antony.* Let him speak, Ventidius.

*Alexas.* You, when his matchless valour bears him forward,
With ardour too heroic, on his foes,
Fall down, as she would do, before his feet;
Lie in his way, and stop the paths of death:
Tell him, this god is not invulnerable;
That absent Cleopatra bleeds in him;
And, that you may remember her petition,
She begs you wear these trifles, as a pawn,
Which, at your wished return, she will redeem

[*Gives jewels to the* Commanders.

With all the wealth of Egypt:
This to the great Ventidius she presents,
Whom she can never count her enemy,
Because he loves her lord.

*Ventidius.* Tell her, I'll none on't;
I'm not ashamed of honest poverty;
Not all the diamonds of the east can bribe
Ventidius from his faith. I hope to see
These and the rest of all her sparkling store,
Where they shall more deservingly be placed.

*Antony*. And who must wear them then?
*Ventidius*. The wronged Octavia.
*Antony*. You might have spared that word.
*Ventidius*. And he that bribe.
*Antony*. But have I no remembrance?
*Alexas*. Yes, a dear one;
Your slave the queen——
*Antony*. My mistress.
*Alexas*. Then your mistress;
Your mistress would, she says, have sent her soul,
But that you had long since; she humbly begs
This ruby bracelet, set with bleeding hearts,
The emblems of her own, may bind your arm.
[*Presenting a bracelet.*
*Ventidius*. Now, my best lord,—in honour's name, I ask you,
For manhood's sake, and for your own dear safety,—
Touch not these poisoned gifts,
Infected by the sender; touch them not;
Myriads of bluest plagues lie underneath them,
And more than aconite has dipt the silk.
*Antony*. Nay, now you grow too cynical, Ventidius:
A lady's favours may be worn with honour.
What, to refuse her bracelet! On my soul,
When I lie pensive in my tent alone,
'Twill pass the wakeful hours of winter nights,
To tell these pretty beads upon my arm,
To count for every one a soft embrace,
A melting kiss at such and such a time:
And now and then the fury of her love,
When—— And what harm's in this?
*Alexas*. None, none, my lord,
But what's to her, that now 'tis past for ever.
*Antony*. [*Going to tie it.*] We soldiers are so awkward—help me tie it.
*Alexas*. In faith, my lord, we courtiers too are awkward
In these affairs: so are all men indeed:
Even I, who am not one. But shall I speak?
*Antony*. Yes, freely.
*Alexas*. Then, my lord, fair hands alone
Are fit to tie it; she, who sent it can.

*Ventidius.* Hell, death! this eunuch pander ruins you.
You will not see her?

[ALEXAS *whispers an* Attendant, *who goes out.*

*Antony.* But to take my leave.

*Ventidius.* Then I have washed an Æthiop. You're undone;
Y' are in the toils; y' are taken; y' are destroyed:
Her eyes do Cæsar's work.

*Antony.* You fear too soon.
I'm constant to myself: I know my strength;
And yet she shall not think me barbarous neither,
Born in the depths of Afric: I am a Roman,
Bred in the rules of soft humanity.
A guest, and kindly used, should bid farewell.

*Ventidius.* You do not know
How weak you are to her, how much an infant:
You are not proof against a smile, or glance;
A sigh will quite disarm you.

*Antony.* See, she comes!
Now you shall find your error.—Gods, I thank you:
I formed the danger greater than it was,
And now 'tis near, 'tis lessened.

*Ventidius* Mark the end yet.

*Enter* CLEOPATRA, CHARMION, *and* IRAS.

*Antony.* Well, madam, we are met.

*Cleopatra.* Is this a meeting?
Then, we must part?

*Antony.* We must.

*Cleopatra.* Who says we must?

*Antony.* Our own hard fates.

*Cleopatra.* We make those fates ourselves.

*Antony.* Yes, we have made them; we have loved each other,
Into our mutual ruin.

*Cleopatra.* The gods have seen my joys with envious eyes;
I have no friends in heaven; and all the world,
As 'twere the business of mankind to part us,
Is armed against my love: even you yourself
Join with the rest; you, you are armed against me.

*Antony.* I will be justified in all I do
To late posterity, and therefore hear me.

If I mix a lie
With any truth, reproach me freely with it;
Else, favour me with silence.
*Cleopatra.* You command me
And I am dumb.
*Ventidius.* I like this well; he shows authority.
*Antony.* That I derive my ruin
From you alone——
*Cleopatra.* O heavens! I ruin you!
*Antony.* You promised me your silence, and you break it
Ere I have scarce begun
*Cleopatra.* Well, I obey you.
*Antony.* When I beheld you first, it was in Egypt.
Ere Cæsar saw your eyes, you gave me love,
And were too young to know it; that I settled
Your father in his throne, was for your sake;
I left the acknowledgment for time to ripen.
Cæsar stept in, and, with a greedy hand,
Plucked the green fruit, ere the first blush of red
Yet cleaving to the bough. He was my lord,
And was, beside, too great for me to rival;
But, I deserved you first, though he enjoyed you.
When, after, I beheld you in Cilicia,
An enemy to Rome, I pardoned you.
*Cleopatra.* I cleared myself——
*Antony.* Again you break your promise.
I loved you still, and took your weak excuses,
Took you into my bosom, stained by Cæsar,
And not half mine: I went to Egypt with you,
And hid me from the business of the world,
Shut out inquiring nations from my sight,
To give whole years to you.
*Ventidius.* Yes, to your shame be't spoken. [*Aside.*
*Antony.* How I loved.
Witness, ye days and nights, and all ye hours,
That danced away with down upon your feet,
As all your business were to count my passion!
One day passed by, and nothing saw but love;
Another came, and still 'twas only love:
The suns were wearied out with looking on,
And I untired with loving.

I saw you every day, and all the day;
And every day was still but as the first,
So eager was I still to see you more.
*Ventidius.* 'Tis all too true.
*Antony.* Fulvia, my wife, grew jealous
(As she indeed had reason), raised a war
In Italy, to call me back.
*Ventidius.* But yet
You went not.
*Antony.* While within your arms I lay,
The world fell mouldering from my hands each hour,
And left me scarce a grasp—I thank your love for't.
*Ventidius.* Well pushed: that last was home.
*Cleopatra.* Yet may I speak?
*Antony.* If I have urged a falsehood, yes; else, not.
Your silence says, I have not. Fulvia died
(Pardon, you gods, with my unkindness died);
To set the world at peace, I took Octavia,
This Cæsar's sister; in her pride of youth,
And flower of beauty, did I wed that lady,
Whom blushing I must praise, because I left her.
You called; my love obeyed the fatal summons:
This raised the Roman arms; the cause was yours.
I would have fought by land, where I was stronger;
You hindered it: yet, when I fought at sea,
Forsook me fighting; and (O stain to honour!
O lasting shame!) I knew not that I fled;
But fled to follow you.
*Ventidius.* What haste she made to hoist her purple sails!
And, to appear magnificent in flight,
Drew half our strength away.
*Antony.* All this you caused.
And, would you multiply more ruins on me?
This honest man, my best, my only friend,
Has gathered up the shipwreck of my fortunes;
Twelve legions I have left, my last recruits.
And you have watched the news, and bring your eyes
To seize them too. If you have aught to answer,
Now speak, you have free leave.
*Alexas* [*Aside.*] She stands confounded:
Despair is in her eyes.

*Ventidius.* Now lay a sigh in the way to stop his passage:
Prepare a tear, and bid it for his legions;
'Tis like they shall be sold.

*Cleopatra.* How shall I plead my cause, when you, my judge,
Already have condemned me? Shall I bring
The love you bore me for my advocate?
That now is turned against me, that destroys me;
For love, once past, is, at the best, forgotten;
But oftener sours to hate; 'twill please my lord
To ruin me, and therefore I'll be guilty.
But, could I once have thought it would have pleased you,
That you would pry, with narrow searching eyes,
Into my faults, severe to my destruction,
And watching all advantages with care,
That serve to make me wretched? Speak, my lord,
For I end here. Though I deserved this usage,
Was it like you to give it?

*Antony.* Oh, you wrong me,
To think I sought this parting, or desired
To accuse you more than what will clear myself,
And justify this breach.

*Cleopatra.* Thus low I thank you;
And, since my innocence will not offend,
I shall not blush to own it.

*Ventidius.* After this,
I think she'll blush at nothing.

*Cleopatra.* You seemed grieved
(And therein you are kind), that Cæsar first
Enjoyed my love, though you deserved it better:
I grieve for that, my lord, much more than you;
For, had I first been yours, it would have saved
My second choice: I never had been his,
And ne'er had been but yours. But Cæsar first,
You say, possessed my love. Not so, my lord:
He first possessed my person; you, my love:
Cæsar loved me; but I loved Antony.
If I endured him after, 'twas because
I judged it due to the first name of men;
And, half constrained, I gave, as to a tyrant,
What he would take by force.

*Ventidius.* O Syren! Syren!
Yet grant that all the love she boasts were true,
Has she not ruined you? I still urge that,
The fatal consequence.

*Cleopatra.* The consequence indeed,
For I dare challenge him, my greatest foe,
To say it was designed: 'tis true, I loved you
And kept you far from an uneasy wife,—
Such Fulvia was.
Yes, but he'll say, you left Octavia for me;—
And, can you blame me to receive that love,
Which quitted such desert, for worthless me?
How often have I wished some other Cæsar,
Great as the first, and as the second young,
Would court my love, to be refused for you!

*Ventidius.* Words, words; but Actium, sir; remember Actium.

*Cleopatra.* Even there, I dare his malice. True, I counselled
To fight at sea; but I betrayed you not.
I fled, but not to the enemy. 'Twas fear;
Would I had been a man, not to have feared!
For none would then have envied me your friendship,
Who envy me your love.

*Antony.* We are both unhappy:
If nothing else, yet our ill fortune parts us.
Speak: would you have me perish by my stay?

*Cleopatra.* If, as a friend, you ask my judgment, go;
If, as a lover, stay. If you must perish——
'Tis a hard word—but stay.

*Ventidius.* See now the effects of her so boasted love!
She strives to drag you down to ruin with her;
But, could she 'scape without you, oh, how soon
Would she let go her hold, and haste to shore,
And never look behind!

*Cleopatra.* Then judge my love by this.

[*Giving* ANTONY *a writing.*

Could I have borne
A life or death, a happiness or woe,
From yours divided, this had given me means.

*Antony.* By Hercules, the writing of Octavius!
I know it well: 'tis that proscribing hand,

Young as it was, that led the way to mine,
And left me but the second place in murder.—
See, see, Ventidius! here he offers Egypt,
And joins all Syria to it, as a present;
So, in requital, she forsake my fortunes,
And join her arms with his.

*Cleopatra.* And yet you leave me!
You leave me, Antony; and yet I love you,
Indeed I do: I have refused a kingdom;
That is a trifle;
For I could part with life, with anything,
But only you. Oh, let me die but with you!
Is that a hard request?

*Antony.* Next living with you,
'Tis all that Heaven can give.

*Alexas.* He melts: we conquer. [*Aside.*

*Cleopatra.* No; you shall go: your interest calls you hence;
Yes; your dear interest pulls too strong, for these
Weak arms to hold you here. [*Takes his hand.*
Go; leave me, soldier
(For you're no more a lover): leave me dying:
Push me, all pale and panting, from your bosom,
And, when your march begins, let one run after,
Breathless almost for joy, and cry—She's dead.
The soldiers shout; you then, perhaps, may sigh,
And muster all your Roman gravity:
Ventidius chides; and straight your brow clears up,
As I had never been.

*Antony.* Gods, 'tis too much; too much for man to bear.

*Cleopatra.* What is't for me then,
A weak, forsaken woman, and a lover?—
Here let me breathe my last: envy me not
This minute in your arms: I'll die apace,
As fast as e'er I can, and end your trouble.

*Antony.* Die! rather let me perish; loosened nature
Leap from its hinges, sink the props of heaven,
And fall the skies, to crush the nether world!
My eyes, my soul, my all!
[*Embraces her.*

*Ventidius.* And what's this toy,
In balance with your fortune, honour, fame?

*Antony.* What is't, Ventidius?—it outweighs them all;
Why, we have more than conquered Cæsar now:
My queen's not only innocent, but loves me.
This, this is she, who drags me down to ruin!
"But, could she 'scape without me, with what haste
Would she let slip her hold, and make to shore,
And never look behind!"
Down on thy knees, blasphemer as thou art,
And ask forgiveness of wronged innocence.

*Ventidius.* I'll rather die, than take it. Will you go?

*Antony.* Go! whither? Go from all that's excellent?
Faith, honour, virtue, all good things forbid,
That I should go from her, who sets my love
Above the price of kingdoms! Give, you gods,
Give to your boy, your Cæsar,
This rattle of a globe to play withal,
This gewgaw world, and put him cheaply off:
I'll not be pleased with less than Cleopatra.

*Cleopatra.* She's wholly yours. My heart's so full of joy,
That I shall do some wild extravagance
Of love, in public; and the foolish world,
Which knows not tenderness, will think me mad.

*Ventidius.* O women! women! women! all the gods
Have not such power of doing good to man,
As you of doing harm. [*Exit.*

*Antony.* Our men are armed:
Unbar the gate that looks to Cæsar's camp:
I would revenge the treachery he meant me;
And long security makes conquest easy.
I'm eager to return before I go;
For, all the pleasures I have known beat thick
On my remembrance.—How I long for night!
That both the sweets of mutual love may try,
And triumph once o'er Cæsar ere we die. [*Exeunt.*

# ACT III

## SCENE I.

*At one door enter* CLEOPATRA, CHARMION, IRAS, *and* ALEXAS, *a Train of* Egyptians: *at the other* ANTONY *and* Romans. *The entrance on both sides is prepared by music; the trumpets first sounding on* ANTONY'S *part: then answered by timbrels, etc., on* CLEOPATRA'S. CHARMION *and* IRAS *hold a laurel wreath betwixt them. A Dance of* Egyptians. *After the ceremony,* CLEOPATRA *crowns* ANTONY.

*Antony.* I thought how those white arms would fold me in,
And strain me close, and melt me into love;
So pleased with that sweet image, I sprung forwards,
And added all my strength to every blow.

*Cleopatra.* Come to me, come, my soldier, to my arms!
You've been too long away from my embraces;
But, when I have you fast, and all my own,
With broken murmurs, and with amorous sighs,
I'll say, you were unkind, and punish you,
And mark you red with many an eager kiss.

*Antony.* My brighter Venus!

*Cleopatra.* O my greater Mars!

*Antony.* Thou join'st us well, my love!
Suppose me come from the Phlegræan plains,
Where gasping giants lay, cleft by my sword,
And mountain-tops paired off each other blow,
To bury those I slew. Receive me, goddess!
Let Cæsar spread his subtle nets; like Vulcan,
In thy embraces I would be beheld
By heaven and earth at once;
And make their envy what they meant their sport.
Let those, who took us, blush; I would love on,
With awful state, regardless of their frowns,

As their superior gods.
There's no satiety of love in thee:
Enjoyed, thou still art new; perpetual spring
Is in thy arms; the ripened fruit but falls,
And blossoms rise to fill its empty place;
And I grow rich by giving.

*Enter* VENTIDIUS, *and stands apart.*

*Alexas.* Oh, now the danger's past, your general comes!
He joins not in your joys, nor minds your triumphs;
But, with contracted brows, looks frowning on,
As envying your success.

*Antony.* Now, on my soul, he loves me; truly loves me:
He never flattered me in any vice,
But awes me with his virtue: even this minute,
Methinks, he has a right of chiding me.
Lead to the temple: I'll avoid his presence;
It checks too strong upon me. [*Exeunt the rest.*

[*As* ANTONY *is going,* VENTIDIUS *pulls him by the robe.*

*Ventidius.* Emperor!

*Antony.* 'Tis the old argument; I pr'ythee, spare me. [*Looking back.*

*Ventidius.* But this one hearing, emperor.

*Antony.* Let go
My robe; or, by my father Hercules——

*Ventidius.* By Hercules' father, that's yet greater,
I bring you somewhat you would wish to know.

*Antony.* Thou see'st we are observed; attend me here,
And I'll return. [*Exit.*

*Ventidius.* I am waning in his favour, yet I love him;
I love this man, who runs to meet his ruin;
And sure the gods, like me, are fond of him:
His virtues lie so mingled with his crimes,
As would confound their choice to punish one,
And not reward the other.

*Enter* ANTONY.

*Antony.* We can conquer,
You see, without your aid.
We have dislodged their troops;
They look on us at distance, and, like curs

'Scaped from the lion's paws, they bay far off.
And lick their wounds, and faintly threaten war.
Five thousand Romans, with their faces upward,
Lie breathless on the plain.

*Ventidius.* 'Tis well; and he,
Who lost them, could have spared ten thousand more.
Yet if, by this advantage, you could gain
An easier peace, while Cæsar doubts the chance
Of arms——

*Antony.* Oh, think not on't, Ventidius!
The boy pursues my ruin, he'll no peace;
His malice is considerate in advantage.
Oh, he's the coolest murderer! so staunch,
He kills, and keeps his temper.

*Ventidius.* Have you no friend
In all his army, who has power to move him?
Mæcenas, or Agrippa, might do much.

*Antony.* They're both too deep in Cæsar's interests.
We'll work it out by dint of sword, or perish.

*Ventidius.* Fain I would find some other.

*Antony.* Thank thy love.
Some four or five such victories as this
Will save thy further pains.

*Ventidius.* Expect no more; Cæsar is on his guard:
I know, sir, you have conquered against odds;
But still you draw supplies from one poor town,
And of Egyptians: he has all the world,
And, at his beck, nations come pouring in,
To fill the gaps you make. Pray, think again.

*Anthony.* Why dost thou drive me from myself, to search
For foreign aids?—to hunt my memory,
And range all o'er a waste and barren place,
To find a friend? The wretched have no friends,
Yet I had one, the bravest youth of Rome,
Whom Cæsar loves beyond the love of women:
He could resolve his mind, as fire does wax,
From that hard rugged image melt him down,
And mould him in what softer form he pleased.

*Ventidius.* Him would I see; that man, of all the world;
Just such a one we want.

*Antony*. He loved me too;
I was his soul; he lived not but in me:
We were so closed within each other's breasts,
The rivets were not found, that joined us first.
That does not reach us yet: we were so mixt,
As meeting streams, both to ourselves were lost;
We were one mass; we could not give or take,
But from the same; for he was I, I he.
*Ventidius*. He moves as I would wish him. [*Aside*.
*Antony*. After this,
I need not tell his name;—'twas Dolabella.
*Ventidius*. He's now in Cæsar's camp.
*Antony*. No matter where,
Since he's no longer mine. He took unkindly,
That I forbade him Cleopatra's sight,
Because I feared he loved her: he confessed,
He had a warmth, which, for my sake, he stifled;
For 'twere impossible that two, so one,
Should not have loved the same. When he departed,
He took no leave; and that confirmed my thoughts.
*Ventidius*. It argues, that he loved you more than her,
Else he had stayed; but he perceived you jealous,
And would not grieve his friend; I know he loves you.
*Antony*. I should have seen him, then, ere now.
*Ventidius*. Perhaps
He has thus long been labouring for your peace.
*Antony*. Would he were here!
*Ventidius*. Would you believe he loved you?
I read your answer in your eyes, you would.
Not to conceal it longer, he has sent
A messenger from Cæsar's camp, with letters.
*Antony*. Let him appear.
*Ventidius*. I'll bring him instantly.

[*Exit* VENTIDIUS, *and re-enters immediately with* DOLABELLA

*Antony*. 'Tis he himself! himself, by holy friendship!
[*Runs to embrace him*.
Art thou returned at last, my better half?
Come, give me all myself!
Let me not live,

If the young bridegroom, longing for his night,
Was ever half so fond.

*Dolabella.* I must be silent, for my soul is busy
About a nobler work: she's new come home,
Like a long-absent man, and wanders o'er
Each room, a stranger to her own, to look
If all be safe.

*Antony.* Thou hast what's left of me;
For I am now so sunk from what I was,
Thou find'st me at my lowest water-mark.
The rivers that ran in, and raised my fortunes,
Are all dried up, or take another course:
What I have left is from my native spring;
I've still a heart that swells, in scorn of fate,
And lifts me to my banks.

*Dolabella.* Still you are lord of all the world to me.

*Antony.* Why, then I yet am so; for thou art all.
If I had any joy when thou were absent,
I grudged it to myself; methought I robbed
Thee of thy part. But, O my Dolabella!
Thou hast beheld me other than I am.
Hast thou not seen my morning chambers filled
With sceptred slaves, who waited to salute me?
With eastern monarchs, who forgot the sun,
To worship my uprising?—menial kings
Ran coursing up and down my palace-yard,
Stood silent in my presence, watched my eyes,
And, at my least command, all started out,
Like racers to the goal.

*Dolabella.* Slaves to your fortune.

*Antony.* Fortune is Cæsar's now; and what am I?

*Ventidius.* What you have made yourself; I will not flatter.

*Antony.* Is this friendly done?

*Dolabella.* Yes; when his end is so, I must join with him;
Indeed I must, and yet you must not chide;
Why am I else your friend?

*Antony.* Take heed, young man,
How thou upbraid'st my love: The queen has eyes,
And thou too hast a soul. Canst thou remember,
When, swelled with hatred, thou beheld'st her first,
As accessary to thy brother's death?

*Dolabella*. Spare my remembrance; 'twas a guilty day,
And still the blush hangs here.
*Antony*. To clear herself,
For sending him no aid, she came from Egypt.
Her galley down the silver Cydnus rowed,
The tackling silk, the streamers waved with gold;
The gentle winds were lodged in purple sails:
Her nymphs, like Nereids, round her couch were placed;
Where she, another sea-born Venus lay.
*Dolabella*. No more; I would not hear it.
*Antony*. Oh, you must!
She lay, and leant her cheek upon her hand,
And cast a look so languishingly sweet,
As if, secure of all beholders' hearts,
Neglecting, she could take them: boys, like Cupids,
Stood fanning, with their painted wings, the winds,
That played about her face. But if she smiled,
A darting glory seemed to blaze abroad,
That men's desiring eyes were never wearied,
But hung upon the object: To soft flutes
The silver oars kept time; and while they played,
The hearing gave new pleasure to the sight;
And both to thought. 'Twas heaven or, somewhat more:
For she so charmed all hearts, that gazing crowds
Stood panting on the shore, and wanted breath
To give their welcome voice.
Then, Dolabella, where was then thy soul?
Was not thy fury quite disarmed with wonder?
Didst thou not shrink behind me from those eyes
And whisper in my ear—Oh, tell her not
That I accused her with my brother's death?
*Dolabella*. And should my weakness be a plea for yours?
Mine was an age when love might be excused,
When kindly warmth, and when my springing youth
Made it a debt to nature. Yours——
*Ventidius*. Speak boldly.
Yours, he would say, in your declining age,
When no more heat was left but what you forced,
When all the sap was needful for the trunk,
When it went down, then you constrained the course,
And robbed from nature, to supply desire;

In you (I would not use so harsh a word)
'Tis but plain dotage.
*Antony*. Ha!
*Dolabella*. 'Twas urged too home.—
But yet the loss was private, that I made;
'Twas but myself I lost: I lost no legions;
I had no world to lose, no people's love.
*Antony*. This from a friend?
*Dolabella*. Yes, Antony, a true one;
A friend so tender, that each word I speak
Stabs my own heart, before it reach your ear.
Oh, judge me not less kind, because I chide!
To Cæsar I excuse you.
*Antony*. O ye gods!
Have I then lived to be excused to Cæsar?
*Dolabella*. As to your equal.
*Antony*. Well, he's but my equal:
While I wear this he never shall be more.
*Dolabella*. I bring conditions from him.
*Antony*. Are they noble?
Methinks thou shouldst not bring them else; yet he
Is full of deep dissembling; knows no honour
Divided from his interest. Fate mistook him;
For nature meant him for an usurer:
He's fit indeed to buy, not conquer kingdoms.
*Ventidius*. Then, granting this,
What power was theirs, who wrought so hard a temper
To honourable terms?
*Antony*. It was my Dolabella, or some god.
*Dolabella*. Nor I, nor yet Mæcenas, nor Agrippa:
They were your enemies; and I, a friend,
Too weak alone; yet 'twas a Roman's deed.
*Antony*. 'Twas like a Roman done: show me that man,
Who has preserved my life, my love, my honour;
Let me but see his face.
*Ventidius*. That task is mine,
And, Heaven, thou know'st how pleasing.
[*Exit* VENTIDIUS.
*Dolabella*. You'll remember
To whom you stand obliged?

*Antony*. When I forget it,
Be thou unkind, and that's my greatest curse.
My queen shall thank him too.
*Dolabella*. I fear she will not.
*Antony*. But she shall do it: The queen, my Dolabella!
Hast thou not still some grudgings of thy fever?
*Dolabella*. I would not see her lost.
*Antony*. When I forsake her,
Leave me my better stars! for she has truth
Beyond her beauty. Cæsar tempted her,
At no less price than kingdoms, to betray me;
But she resisted all: and yet thou chidest me
For loving her too well. Could I do so?
*Dolabella*. Yes; there's my reason.

*Re-enter* VENTIDIUS, *with* OCTAVIA.

*Antony*. Where?—Octavia there!
[*Starting back*.
*Ventidius*. What, is she poison to you?—a disease?
*Dolabella*. For shame, my lord, if not for love, receive her
With kinder eyes. If you confess a man
Meet her, embrace her, bid her welcome to you.
Your arms should open, even without your knowledge,
To clasp her in; your feet should turn to wings,
To bear you to her; and your eyes dart out
And aim a kiss, ere you could reach the lips.
*Antony*. I stood amazed, to think how she came hither.
*Ventidius*. I sent for her; I brought her in unknown
To Cleopatra's guards.
*Dolabella*. Yet, are you cold?
*Octavia*. Thus long I have attended for my welcome;
Which, as a stranger, sure I might expect.
Who am I?
*Antony*. Cæsar's sister.
*Octavia*. That's unkind.
Had I been nothing more than Cæsar's sister,
Know, I had still remained in Cæsar's camp:
But your Octavia, your much injured wife,
Though banished from your bed, driven from your house,
In spite of Cæsar's sister, still is yours.

'Tis true, I have a heart disdains your coldness,
And prompts me not to seek what you should offer;
But a wife's virtue still surmounts that pride.
I come to claim you as my own; to show
My duty first; to ask, nay beg, your kindness:
Your hand, my lord; 'tis mine, and I will have it.
[*Taking his hand.*

*Ventidius.* Do, take it; thou deserv'st it.

*Dolabella.* On my soul,
And so she does: she's neither too submissive,
Nor yet too haughty; but so just a mean
Shows, as it ought, a wife and Roman too.

*Antony.* I fear, Octavia, you have begged my life.

*Octavia.* Begged it, my lord?

*Antony.* Yes, begged it, my ambassadress!
Poorly and basely begged it of your brother.

*Octavia.* Poorly and basely I could never beg:
Nor could my brother grant.

*Antony.* Shall I, who, to my kneeling slave, could say,
Rise up, and be a king; shall I fall down
And cry,—Forgive me, Cæsar! Shall I set
A man, my equal, in the place of Jove,
As he could give me being? No; that word,
Forgive, would choke me up,
And die upon my tongue.

*Dolabella.* You shall not need it.

*Antony.* I will not need it. Come, you've all betrayed me,—
My friend too!—to receive some vile conditions.
My wife has bought me, with her prayers and tears;
And now I must become her branded slave.
In every peevish mood, she will upbraid
The life she gave: if I but look awry,
She cries—I'll tell my brother.

*Octavia.* My hard fortune
Subjects me still to your unkind mistakes.
But the conditions I have brought are such,
You need not blush to take: I love your honour,
Because 'tis mine; it never shall be said,
Octavia's husband was her brother's slave.

Sir, you are free; free, even from her you loathe;
For, though my brother bargains for your love,
Makes me the price and cement of your peace,
I have a soul like yours; I cannot take
Your love as alms, nor beg what I deserve.
I'll tell my brother we are reconciled;
He shall draw back his troops, and you shall march
To rule the East: I may be dropt at Athens;
No matter where. I never will complain,
But only keep the barren name of wife,
And rid you of the trouble.

*Ventidius.* Was ever such a strife of sullen honour!
Both scorn to be obliged.

*Dolabella.* Oh, she has touched him in the tenderest part;
See how he reddens with despite and shame,
To be outdone in generosity!

*Ventidius.* See how he winks! how he dries up a tear,
That fain would fall! *Apart*

*Antony.* Octavia, I have heard you, and must praise
The greatness of your soul;
But cannot yield to what you have proposed
For I can ne'er be conquered but by love;
And you do all for duty. You would free me,
And would be dropt at Athens; was't not so??

*Octavia.* It was, my lord.

*Antony.* Then I must be obliged
To one who loves me not; who, to herself,
May call me thankless and ungrateful man:—
I'll not endure it; no.

*Ventidius.* I am glad it pinches there. [*Aside.*

*Octavia.* Would you triumph o'er poor Octavia's virtue?
That pride was all I had to bear me up;
That you might think you owed me for your life,
And owed it to my duty, not my love.
I have been injured, and my haughty soul
Could brook but ill the man who slights my bed.

*Antony.* Therefore you love me not.

*Octavia.* Therefore, my lord,
I should not love you.
*Antony.* Therefore you would leave me?
*Octavia.* And therefore I should leave you—if I could.
*Dolabella.* Her soul's too great, after such injuries,
To say she loves; and yet she lets you see it.
Her modesty and silence plead her cause.
*Antony.* O Dolabella, which way shall I turn?
I find a secret yielding in my soul;
But Cleopatra, who would die with me,
Must she be left? Pity pleads for Octavia;
But does it not plead more for Cleopatra?
*Ventidius.* Justice and pity both plead for Octavia;
For Cleopatra, neither.
One would be ruined with you; but she first
Had ruined you: The other, you have ruined,
And yet she would preserve you.
In everything their merits are unequal.
*Antony.* O my distracted soul!
*Octavia.* Sweet Heaven compose it!—
Come, come, my lord, if I can pardon you,
Methinks you should accept it.
*Ventidius.* Was ever sight so moving?—Emperor!
*Dolabella.* Friend!
*Octavia.* Husband!
*Antony.* I am vanquished: take me,
Octavia; take me.
[*Embracing her*.
I've been a thriftless debtor to your love,
And run out much, in riot, from your stock;
But all shall be amended.
*Octavia.* O blest hour!
*Dolabella.* O happy change!
*Ventidius.* My joys stops at my tongue;
But it has found two channels here for one,
And bubbles out above.
*Antony.* [*to* OCTAVIA]. This is thy triumph; lead me where thou wilt;
Even to thy brother's camp.
*Octavia.* All there are yours.

*Enter* ALEXAS *hastily.*

*Alexas.* The queen, my mistress, sir, and yours——

*Antony.* 'Tis past.—
Octavia, you shall stay this night: To-morrow,
Cæsar and we are one.

[*Exit leading* OCTAVIA; DOLABELLA *follows.*

*Ventidius.* There's news for you; run, my officious eunuch,
Be sure to be the first; haste forward:
Haste, my dear eunuch, haste. [*Exit.*

*Alexas.* This downright fighting fool, this thick-skulled hero.
This blunt, unthinking instrument of death,
With plain dull virtue has outgone my wit.
Pleasure forsook my earliest infancy;
The luxury of others robbed my cradle,
And ravished thence the promise of a man.
Cast out from nature, disinherited
Of what her meanest children claim by kind,
Yet greatness kept me from contempt: that's gone.
Had Cleopatra followed my advice,
Then he had been betrayed who now forsakes.
She dies for love; but she has known its joys:
Gods, is this just, that I, who know no joys,
Must die, because she loves?

*Enter* CLEOPATRA, CHARMION, IRAS, *and Train.*

O madam, I have seen what blasts my eyes!
Octavia's here.

*Cleopatra.* Peace with that raven's note.
I know it too; and now am in
The pangs of death.

*Alexas.* You are no more a queen;
Egypt is lost.

*Cleopatra.* What tell'st thou me of Egypt?
My life, my soul is lost! Octavia has him!—
O fatal name to Cleopatra's love!
My kisses, my embraces now are hers;
While I——But thou hast seen my rival; speak,

Does she deserve this blessing? Is she fair?
Bright as a goddess? and is all perfection
Confined to her? It is. Poor I was made
Of that coarse matter, which, when she was finished,
The gods threw by for rubbish.

*Alexas.* She is indeed a very miracle.

*Cleopatra.* Death to my hopes, a miracle!

*Alexas.* A miracle. [*Bowing.*
I mean of goodness; for in beauty, madam,
You make all wonders cease.

*Cleopatra.* I was too rash:
Take this in part of recompense. But, oh! [*Giving a ring.*
I fear thou flatterest me.

*Charmion.* She comes! she's here!

*Iras.* Fly, madam, Cæsar's sister!

*Cleopatra.* Were she the sister of the thunderer Jove,
And bore her brother's lightning in her eyes,
Thus would I face my rival.

[*Meets* OCTAVIA *with* VENTIDIUS. OCTAVIA *bears up to her. Their Trains come up on either side.*

*Octavia.* I need not ask if you are Cleopatra;
Your haughty carriage——

*Cleopatra.* Shows I am a queen:
Nor need I ask you, who you are.

*Octavia.* A Roman:
A name, that makes and can unmake a queen.

*Cleopatra.* Your lord, the man who serves me, is a Roman.

*Octavia.* He was a Roman, till he lost that name,
To be a slave in Egypt; but I come
To free him thence.

*Cleopatra.* Peace, peace, my lover's Juno.
When he grew weary of that household clog,
He chose my easier bonds.

*Octavia.* I wonder not
Your bonds are easy: you have long been practised
In that lascivious art: He's not the first
For whom you spread your snares: Let Cæsar witness.

*Cleopatra.* I loved not Cæsar; 'twas but gratitude
I paid his love: The worst your malice can,
Is but to say the greatest of mankind

Has been my slave. The next, but far above him
In my esteem, is he whom law calls yours,
But whom his love made mine.

*Octavia.* I would view nearer [*Coming up close to her.*
That face, which has so long usurped my right,
To find the inevitable charms, that catch
Mankind so sure, that ruined my dear lord.

*Cleopatra.* Oh, you do well to search; for had you known
But half these charms, you had not lost his heart.

*Octavia.* Far be their knowledge from a Roman lady,
Far from a modest wife! Shame of our sex,
Dost thou not blush to own those black endearments,
That make sin pleasing?

*Cleopatra.* You may blush, who want them.
If bounteous nature, if indulgent Heaven
Have given me charms to please the bravest man,
Should I not thank them? Should I be ashamed,
And not be proud? I am, that he has loved me;
And, when I love not him, Heaven change this face
For one like that.

*Octavia.* Thou lov'st him not so well.

*Cleopatra.* I love him better, and deserve him more.

*Octavia.* You do not; cannot: You have been his ruin.
Who made him cheap at Rome, but Cleopatra?
Who made him scorned abroad, but Cleopatra?
At Actium, who betrayed him? Cleopatra.
Who made his children orphans, and poor me
A wretched widow? only Cleopatra.

*Cleopatra.* Yet she, who loves him best, is Cleopatra.
If you have suffered, I have suffered more.
You bear the specious title of a wife,
To gild your cause, and draw the pitying world
To favour it: the world condemns poor me.
For I have lost my honour, lost my fame,
And stained the glory of my royal house,
And all to bear the branded name of mistress.
There wants but life, and that too I would lose
For him I love.

*Octavia.* Be't so, then; take thy wish.
[*Exit with her Train.*

*Cleopatra.* And 'tis my wish,
Now he is lost for whom alone I lived.
My sight grows dim, and every object dances,
And swims before me, in the maze of death.
My spirits, while they were opposed, kept up;
They could not sink beneath a rival's scorn!
But now she's gone, they faint.

*Alexas.* Mine have had leisure
To recollect their strength, and furnish counsel,
To ruin her, who else must ruin you.

*Cleopatra.* Vain promiser!
Lead me, my Charmion; nay, your hand too, Iras.
My grief has weight enough to sink you both.
Conduct me to some solitary chamber,
And draw the curtains round;
Then leave me to myself, to take alone
My fill of grief:
There I till death will his unkindness weep;
As harmless infants moan themselves asleep. [*Exeunt.*

## ACT IV

### SCENE I.

*Enter* ANTONY *and* DOLABELLA.

*Dolabella.* Why would you shift it from yourself on me?
Can you not tell her, you must part?
*Antony.* I cannot.
I could pull out an eye, and bid it go,
And t'other should not weep. O Dolabella,
How many deaths are in this word, *Depart!*
I dare not trust my tongue to tell her so:
One look of hers would thaw me into tears,
And I should melt, till I were lost again.
*Dolabella.* Then let Ventidius;
He's rough by nature.
*Antony.* Oh, he'll speak too harshly;
He'll kill her with the news: Thou, only thou.
*Dolabella.* Nature has cast me in so soft a mould,
That but to hear a story, feigned for pleasure,
Of some sad lover's death, moistens my eyes,
And robs me of my manhood. I should speak
So faintly, with such fear to grieve her heart,
She'd not believe it earnest.
*Antony.* Therefore,—therefore
Thou only, thou art fit: Think thyself me:
And when thou speak'st (but let it first be long),
Take off the edge from every sharper sound,
And let our parting be as gently made,
As other loves begin: Wilt thou do this?
*Dolabella.* What you have said so sinks into my soul,
That, if I must speak, I shall speak just so.
*Antony.* I leave you then to your sad task: Farewell.
I sent her word to meet you.
[*Goes to the door, and comes back.*

I forgot;
Let her be told, I'll make her peace with mine:
Her crown and dignity shall be preserved,
If I have power with Cæsar.——Oh, be sure
To think on that.

*Dolabella.* Fear not, I will remember.

[ANTONY *goes again to the door, and comes back.*

*Antony.* And tell her, too, how much I was constrained;
I did not this, but with extremest force:
Desire her not to hate my memory,
For I still cherish hers;—insist on that.

*Dolabella.* Trust me, I'll not forget it.

*Antony.* Then that's all. [*Goes out, and returns again.*
Wilt thou forgive my fondness this once more?
Tell her, though we shall never meet again,
If I should hear she took another love,
The news would break my heart.—Now I must go;
For every time I have returned, I feel
My soul more tender; and my next command
Would be, to bid her stay, and ruin both. [*Exit.*

*Dolabella.* Men are but children of a larger growth;
Our appetites as apt to change as theirs,
And full as craving too, and full as vain;
And yet the soul, shut up in her dark room,
Viewing so clear abroad, at home sees nothing;
But, like a mole in earth, busy and blind,
Works all her folly up, and casts it outward
To the world's open view: Thus I discovered,
And blamed the love of ruined Antony;
Yet wish that I were he, to be so ruined.

*Enter* VENTIDIUS *above.*

*Ventidius.* Alone, and talking to himself? concerned too?
Perhaps my guess is right; he loved her once,
And may pursue it still.

*Dolabella.* O friendship! friendship!
Ill canst thou answer this; and reason, worse:
Unfaithful in the attempt; hopeless to win;
And if I win, undone: mere madness all.
And yet the occasion's fair. What injury
To him, to wear the robe which he throws by!

*Ventidius*. None, none at all. This happens as I wish,
To ruin her yet more with Antony.

*Enter* CLEOPATRA, *talking with* ALEXAS; CHARMION, IRAS *on the other side.*

*Dolabella*. She comes! What charms have sorrow on that face!
Sorrow seems pleased to dwell with so much sweetness;
Yet, now and then, a melancholy smile
Breaks loose, like lightning in a winter's night,
And shows a moment's day.

*Ventidius*. If she should love him too! her eunuch there?
That porc'pisce bodes ill weather. Draw, draw nearer,
Sweet devil, that I may hear.

*Alexas*. Believe me; try

DOLABELLA *goes over to* CHARMION *and* IRAS; *seems to talk with them.*

To make him jealous; jealousy is like
A polished glass held to the lips when life's in doubt;
If there be breath, 'twill catch the damp, and show it.

*Cleopatra*. I grant you, jealousy's a proof of love,
But 'tis a weak and unavailing medicine;
It puts out the disease, and makes it show,
But has no power to cure.

*Alexas*. 'Tis your last remedy, and strongest too:
And then this Dolabella, who so fit
To practise on? He's handsome, valiant, young,
And looks as he were laid for nature's bait,
To catch weak women's eyes.
He stands already more than half suspected
Of loving you: the least kind word or glance
You give this youth, will kindle him with love:
Then, like a burning vessel set adrift,
You'll send him down amain before the wind,
To fire the heart of jealous Antony.

*Cleopatra*. Can I do this? Ah, no; my love's so true,
That I can neither hide it where it is,
Nor show it where it is not. Nature meant me
A wife; a silly, harmless, household dove,
Fond without art, and kind without deceit;
But Fortune, that has made a mistress of me,

Has thrust me out to the wide world, unfurnished
Of falsehood to be happy.

*Alexas.* Force yourself.
The event will be, your lover will return,
Doubly desirous to possess the good
Which once he feared to lose.

*Cleopatra.* I must attempt it;
But oh, with what regret!

[*Exit* ALEXAS. *She comes up to* DOLABELLA.

*Ventidius.* So, now the scene draws near; they're in my reach.

*Cleopatra.* [*To* DOLABELLA]. Discoursing with my women! might not I
Share in your entertainment?

*Charmion.* You have been
The subject of it, madam.

*Cleopatra.* How! and how?

*Iras.* Such praises of your beauty!

*Cleopatra.* Mere poetry.
Your Roman wits, your Gallus and Tibullus,
Have taught you this from Cytheris and Delia.

*Dolabella.* Those Roman wits have never been in Egypt;
Cytheris and Delia else had been unsung:
I, who have seen——had I been born a poet,
Should choose a nobler name.

*Cleopatra.* You flatter me.
But, 'tis your nation's vice: All of your country
Are flatterers, and all false. Your friend's like you.
I'm sure, he sent you not to speak these words.

*Dolabella.* No, madam; yet he sent me——

*Cleopatra.* Well, he sent you——

*Dolabella.* Of a less pleasing errand.

*Cleopatra.* How less pleasing?
Less to yourself, or me?

*Dolabella.* Madam, to both;
For you must mourn, and I must grieve to cause it.

*Cleopatra.* You, Charmion, and your fellow, stand at distance.—
Hold up, my spirits. [*Aside*]——Well, now your mournful matter!
For I'm prepared, perhaps can guess it too.

*Dolabella.* I wish you would; for 'tis a thankless office,
To tell ill news: And I, of all your sex,
Most fear displeasing you.

*Cleopatra.* Of all your sex,
I soonest could forgive you, if you should.

*Ventidius.* Most delicate advances! Women! women!
Dear, damned, inconstant sex!

*Cleopatra.* In the first place,
I am to be forsaken; is't not so?

*Dolabella.* I wish I could not answer to that question.

*Cleopatra.* Then pass it o'er, because it troubles you:
I should have been more grieved another time.
Next, I'm to lose my kingdom——Farewell, Egypt!
Yet, is there any more?

*Dolabella.* Madam, I fear
Your too deep sense of grief has turned your reason.

*Cleopatra.* No, no, I'm not run mad; I can bear fortune:
And love may be expelled by other love,
As poisons are by poisons.

*Dolabella.* You o'erjoy me, madam,
To find your griefs so moderately borne.
You've heard the worst; all are not false like him.

*Cleopatra.* No; Heaven forbid they should.

*Dolabella.* Some men are constant.

*Cleopatra.* And constancy deserves reward, that's certain.

*Dolabella.* Deserves it not; but give it leave to hope.

*Ventidius.* I'll swear, thou hast my leave. I have enough:
But how to manage this! Well, I'll consider. [*Exit.*

*Dolabella.* I came prepared
To tell you heavy news; news, which I thought
Would fright the blood from your pale cheeks to hear:
But you have met it with a cheerfulness,
That makes my task more easy; and my tongue,
Which on another's message was employed,
Would gladly speak its own.

*Cleopatra.* Hold, Dolabella.
First tell me, were you chosen by my lord?
Or sought you this employment?

*Dolabella.* He picked me out; and, as his bosom friend,
He charged me with his words.

*Cleopatra.* The message then
I know was tender, and each accent smooth,
To mollify that rugged word, *Depart.*

*Dolabella.* Oh, you mistake: he chose the harshest words;
With fiery eyes, and with contracted brows,
He coined his face in the severest stamp;
And fury shook his fabric, like an earthquake;
He heaved for vent, and burst like bellowing Ætna,
In sounds scarce human—"Hence away for ever,
Let her begone, the blot of my renown,
And bane of all my hopes!"

[*All the time of the speech,* CLEOPATRA *seems more and more concerned, till she sinks quite down.*

"Let her be driven, as far as men can think,
From man's commerce! she'll poison to the centre."

*Cleopatra.* Oh, I can bear no more!

*Dolabella.* Help, help!—O wretch! O cursed, cursed wretch!
What have I done!

*Charmion.* Help, chafe her temples, Iras.

*Iras.* Bend, bend her forward quickly.

*Charmion.* Heaven be praised,
She comes again.

*Cleopatra.* Oh, let him not approach me.
Why have you brought me back to this loathed being,
The abode of falsehood, violated vows,
And injured love? For pity, let me go;
For, if there be a place of long repose,
I'm sure I want it. My disdainful lord
Can never break that quiet; nor awake
The sleeping soul, with hollowing in my tomb
Such words as fright her hence.—Unkind, unkind!

*Dolabella.* Believe me, 'tis against myself I speak; [*Kneeling.*
That sure desires belief; I injured him:
My friend ne'er spoke those words. Oh, had you seen
How often he came back, and every time
With something more obliging and more kind,
To add to what he said; what dear farewells;
How almost vanquished by his love he parted,

And leaned to what unwillingly he left!
I, traitor as I was, for love of you
(But what can you not do, who made me false?)
I forged that lie; for whose forgiveness kneels
This self-accused, self-punished criminal.

*Cleopatra.* With how much ease believe we what we wish!
Rise, Dolabella; if you have been guilty,
I have contributed, and too much love
Has made me guilty too.
The advance of kindness, which I made, was feigned.
To call back fleeting love by jealousy;
But 'twould not last. Oh, rather let me lose,
Than so ignobly trifle with his heart.

*Dolabella.* I find your breast fenced round from human reach,
Transparent as a rock of solid crystal;
Seen through, but never pierced. My friend, my friend,
What endless treasure hast thou thrown away;
And scattered, like an infant, in the ocean,
Vain sums of wealth, which none can gather thence!

*Cleopatra.* Could you not beg
An hour's admittance to his private ear?
Like one, who wanders through long barren wilds
And yet foreknows no hospitable inn
Is near to succour hunger, eats his fill,
Before his painful march;
So would I feed a while my famished eyes
Before we part; for I have far to go,
If death be far, and never must return.

VENTIDIUS *with* OCTAVIA, *behind.*

*Ventidius.* From hence you may discover—oh, sweet, sweet!
Would you indeed? The pretty hand in earnest?
[*Takes her hand.*

*Dolabella.* I will, for this reward.
Draw it not back.
'Tis all I e'er will beg.

*Ventidius.* They turn upon us.

*Octavia.* What quick eyes has guilt!

*Ventidius.* Seem not to have observed them, and go on.

*They enter.*

*Dolabella.* Saw you the emperor, Ventidius?
*Ventidius.* No.
I sought him; but I heard that he was private,
None with him but Hipparchus, his freedman.
*Dolabella.* Know you his business?
*Ventidius.* Giving him instructions,
And letters to his brother Cæsar.
*Dolabella.* Well,
He must be found. [*Exeunt* DOLABELLA *and* CLEOPATRA.
*Ocatavia.* Most glorious impudence!
*Ventidius.* She looked, methought,
As she would say—Take your old man, Octavia;
Thank you, I'm better here.—
Well, but what use
Make we of this discovery?
*Octavia.* Let it die.
*Ventidius.* I pity Dolabella; but she's dangerous;
Her eyes have power beyond Thessalian charms,
To draw the moon from heaven; for eloquence,
The sea-green Syrens taught her voice their flattery;
And, while she speaks, night steals upon the day,
Unmarked of those that hear: Then she's so charming,
Age buds at sight of her, and swells to youth:
The holy priests gaze on her when she smiles;
And with heaved hands, forgetting gravity,
They bless her wanton eyes: Even I, who hate her,
With a malignant joy behold such beauty;
And, while I curse, desire it. Antony
Must needs have some remains of passion still,
Which may ferment into a worse relapse,
If now not fully cured. I know, this minute,
With Cæsar he's endeavouring her peace.
*Octavia.* You have prevailed:——But for a further purpose. [*Walks off.*
I'll prove how he will relish this discovery.
What, make a strumpet's peace! it swells my heart:
It must not, shall not be.
*Ventidius.* His guards appear.
Let me begin, and you shall second me.

*Enter* ANTONY.

*Antony.* Octavia, I was looking for you, my love:
What, are your letters ready? I have given
My last instructions.

*Octavia.* Mine, my lord, are written.

*Antony.* Ventidius. [*Drawing him aside.*

*Ventidius.* My lord?

*Antony.* A word in private.—
When saw you Dolabella?

*Ventidius.* Now, my lord,
He parted hence; and Cleopatra with him.

*Antony.* Speak softly.—'Twas by my command he went,
To bear my last farewell.

*Ventidius.* It looked indeed [*Aloud.*
Like your farewell.

*Antony.* More softly.—My farewell?
What secret meaning have you in those words
Of—My farewell? He did it by my order.

*Ventidius.* Then he obeyed your order. I suppose [*Aloud.*
You bid him do it with all gentleness,
All kindness, and all——love.

*Antony.* How she mourned,
The poor forsaken creature!

*Ventidius.* She took it as she ought; she bore your parting
As she did Cæsar's, as she would another's,
Were a new love to come.

*Antony.* Thou dost belie her;
Most basely, and maliciously belie her. [*Aloud.*

*Ventidius.* I thought not to displease you; I have done.

*Octavia.* You seemed disturbed, my lord. [*Coming up.*

*Antony.* A very trifle.
Retire, my love.

*Ventidius.* It was indeed a trifle.
He sent——

*Antony.* No more. Look how thou disobey'st me; [*Angrily.*
Thy life shall answer it.

*Octavia.* Then 'tis no trifle.

*Ventidius.* [*To* OCTAVIA.] 'Tis less; a very nothing: You too saw it,
As well as I, and therefore 'tis no secret.

*Antony*. She saw it!
*Ventidius*. Yes: She saw young Dolabella——
*Antony*. Young Dolabella!
*Ventidius*. Young, I think him young,
And handsome too; and so do others think him.
But what of that? He went by your command,
Indeed 'tis probable, with some kind message;
For she received it graciously; she smiled;
And then he grew familiar with her hand,
Squeezed it, and worried it with ravenous kisses;
She blushed, and sighed, and smiled, and blushed again;
At last she took occasion to talk softly,
And brought her cheek up close, and leaned on his;
At which, he whispered kisses back on hers;
And then she cried aloud—That constancy
Should be rewarded.
*Octavia*. This I saw and heard.
*Antony*. What woman was it, whom you heard and saw
So playful with my friend?
Not Cleopatra?
*Ventidius*. Even she, my lord.
*Antony*. My Cleopatra?
*Ventidius*. Your Cleopatra;
Dolabella's Cleopatra; every man's Cleopatra.
*Antony*. Thou liest.
*Ventidius*. I do not lie, my lord.
Is this so strange? Should mistresses be left,
And not provide against a time of change?
You know she's not much used to lonely nights.
*Antony*. I'll think no more on't.
I know 'tis false, and see the plot betwixt you.—
You needed not have gone this way, Octavia.
What harms it you that Cleopatra's just?
She's mine no more. I see, and I forgive:
Urge it no further, love.
*Octavia*. Are you concerned,
That she's found false?
*Antony*. I should be, were it so;
For, though 'tis past, I would not that the world
Should tax my former choice, that I loved one
Of so light note; but I forgive you both.

*Ventidius.* What has my age deserved, that you should think
I would abuse your ears with perjury?
If Heaven be true, she's false.

*Antony.* Though heaven and earth
Should witness it, I'll not believe her tainted.

*Ventidius.* I'll bring you, then, a witness
From hell, to prove her so.—Nay, go not back;

[*Seeing* ALEXAS *just entering, and starting back.*

For stay you must and shall.

*Alexas.* What means my lord?

*Ventidius.* To make you do what most you hate,—speak truth.
You are of Cleopatra's private counsel,
Of her bed-counsel, her lascivious hours;
Are conscious of each nightly change she makes,
And watch her, as Chaldeans do the moon,
Can tell what signs she passes through, what day.

*Alexas.* My noble lord!

*Ventidius.* My most illustrious pander,
No fine set speech, no cadence, no turned periods,
But a plain homespun truth, is what I ask:
I did, myself, o'erhear your queen make love
To Dolabella. Speak; for I will know,
By your confession, what more passed betwixt them;
How near the business draws to your employment;
And when the happy hour.

*Antony.* Speak truth, Alexas; whether it offend
Or please Ventidius, care not: Justify
Thy injured queen from malice: Dare his worst.

*Octavia* [*Aside.*] See how he gives him courage! how he fears
To find her false! and shuts his eyes to truth,
Willing to be misled!

*Alexas.* As far as love may plead for woman's frailty,
Urged by desert and greatness of the lover,
So far, divine Octavia, may my queen
Stand even excused to you for loving him
Who is your lord: so far, from brave Ventidius,
May her past actions hope a fair report.

*Antony.* 'Tis well, and truly spoken; mark, Ventidius.

*Alexas.* To you, most noble emperor, her strong passion
Stands not excused, but wholly justified.

Her beauty's charms alone, without her crown,
From Ind and Meroe drew the distant vows
Of sighing kings; and at her feet were laid
The sceptres of the earth, exposed on heaps,
To choose where she would reign:
She thought a Roman only could deserve her,
And, of all Romans, only Antony;
And, to be less than wife to you, disdained
Their lawful passion.

*Antony*. 'Tis but truth.

*Alexas*. And yet, though love, and your unmatched desert,
Have drawn her from the due regard of honour
At last Heaven opened her unwilling eyes
To see the wrongs she offered fair Octavia,
Whose holy bed she lawlessly usurped.
The sad effects of this improsperous war
Confirmed those pious thoughts.

*Ventidius* [*Aside.*] Oh, wheel you there?
Observe him now; the man begins to mend,
And talk substantial reason.—Fear not, eunuch;
The emperor has given thee leave to speak.

*Alexas*. Else had I never dared to offend his ears
With what the last necessity has urged
On my forsaken mistress; yet I must not
Presume to say, her heart is wholly altered.

*Antony*. No, dare not for thy life, I charge thee dare not
Pronounce that fatal word!

*Octavia*. Must I bear this? Good Heaven, afford me patience. [*Aside*.

*Ventidius*. On, sweet eunuch; my dear half-man, proceed.

*Alexas*. Yet Dolabella
Has loved her long; he, next my god-like lord,
Deserves her best; and should she meet his passion,
Rejected, as she is, by him she loved——

*Antony*. Hence from my sight! for I can bear no more:
Let furies drag thee quick to hell; let all
The longer damned have rest; each torturing hand
Do thou employ, till Cleopatra comes;
Then join thou, too, and help to torture her!

[*Exit* ALEXAS, *thrust out by* ANTONY.

*Octavia*. 'Tis not well,
Indeed, my lord, 'tis much unkind to me,
To show this passion, this extreme concernment,
For an abandoned, faithless prostitute.

*Antony*. Octavia, leave me; I am much disordered:
Leave me, I say.

*Octavia*. My lord!

*Antony*. I bid you leave me.

*Ventidius*. Obey him, madam: best withdraw a while,
And see how this will work.

*Octavia*. Wherein have I offended you, my lord,
That I am bid to leave you? Am I false,
Or infamous? Am I a Cleopatra?
Were I she,
Base as she is, you would not bid me leave you;
But hang upon my neck, take slight excuses,
And fawn upon my falsehood.

*Antony*. 'Tis too much.
Too much, Octavia; I am pressed with sorrows
Too heavy to be borne; and you add more:
I would retire, and recollect what's left
Of man within, to aid me.

*Octavia*. You would mourn,
In private, for your love, who has betrayed you.
You did but half return to me: your kindness
Lingered behind with her. I hear, my lord,
You make conditions for her,
And would include her treaty. Wondrous proofs
Of love to me!

*Antony*. Are you my friend, Ventidius?
Or are you turned a Dolabella, too,
And let this fury loose?

*Ventidius*. Oh, be advised,
Sweet madam, and retire.

*Octavia*. Yes, I will go; but never to return.
You shall no more be haunted with this Fury.
My lord, my lord, love will not always last,
When urged with long unkindness and disdain:
Take her again, whom you prefer to me;
She stays but to be called. Poor cozened man!
Let a feigned parting give her back your heart,

Which a feigned love first got; for injured me,
Though my just sense of wrongs forbid my stay,
My duty shall be yours.
To the dear pledges of our former love
My tenderness and care shall be transferred,
And they shall cheer, by turns, my widowed nights:
So, take my last farewell; for I despair
To have you whole, and scorn to take you half. [*Exit.*

*Ventidius.* I combat Heaven, which blasts my best designs:
My last attempt must be to win her back;
But oh! I fear in vain. [*Exit.*

*Antony.* Why was I framed with this plain, honest heart,
Which knows not to disguise its griefs and weakness,
But bears its workings outward to the world?
I should have kept the mighty anguish in,
And forced a smile at Cleopatra's falsehood:
Octavia had believed it, and had stayed.
But I am made a shallow-forded stream,
Seen to the bottom: all my clearness scorned,
And all my faults exposed.—See where he comes,

*Enter* DOLABELLA.

Who has profaned the sacred name of friend,
And worn it into vileness!
With how secure a brow, and specious form
He gilds the secret villain! Sure that face
Was meant for honesty; but Heaven mismatched it,
And furnished treason out with nature's pomp,
To make its work more easy.

*Dolabella.* O my friend!

*Antony.* Well, Dolabella, you performed my message?

*Dolabella.* I did, unwillingly.

*Antony.* Unwillingly?
Was it so hard for you to bear our parting?
You should have wished it.

*Dolabella.* Why?

*Antony.* Because you love me.
And she received my message with as true,
With as unfeigned a sorrow as you brought it?

*Dolabella.* She loves you, even to madness.

*Antony*. Oh, I know it.
You, Dolabella, do not better know
How much she loves me. And should I
Forsake this beauty? This all-perfect creature?
*Dolabella*. I could not, were she mine.
*Antony*. And yet you first
Persuaded me: How come you altered since?
*Dolabella*. I said at first I was not fit to go:
I could not hear her sighs, and see her tears,
But pity must prevail: And so, perhaps,
It may again with you; for I have promised,
That she should take her last farewell: And see,
She comes to claim my word.

*Enter* CLEOPATRA.

*Antony*. False, Dolabella!
*Dolabella*. What's false, my lord?
*Antony*. Why, Dolabella's false,
And Cleopatra's false; both false and faithless.
Draw near, you well-joined wickedness, you serpents,
Whom I have in my kindly bosom warmed,
Till I am stung to death.
*Dolabella*. My lord, have I
Deserved to be thus used?
*Cleopatra*. Can Heaven prepare
A newer torment? Can it find a curse
Beyond our separation?
*Antony*. Yes, if fate
Be just, much greater: Heaven should be ingenious
In punishing such crimes. The rolling stone,
And gnawing vulture, were slight pains, invented
When Jove was young, and no examples known
Of mighty ills; but you have ripened sin,
To such a monstrous growth, 'twill pose the gods
To find an equal torture. Two, two such!—
Oh, there's no further name,—two such! to me,
To me, who locked my soul within your breasts,
Had no desires, no joys, no life, but you;
When half the globe was mine, I gave it you
In dowry with my heart; I had no use,
No fruit of all, but you: A friend and mistress

Was what the world could give. O Cleopatra!
O Dolabella! how could you betray
This tender heart, which with an infant fondness
Lay lulled betwixt your bosoms, and there slept,
Secure of injured faith?

*Dolabella.* If she has wronged you,
Heaven, hell, and you revenge it.

*Antony.* If she has wronged me!
Thou wouldst evade thy part of guilt; but swear
Thou lov'st not her.

*Dolabella.* Not so as I love you.

*Antony.* Not so? Swear, swear, I say, thou dost not love her.

*Dolabella.* No more than friendship will allow.

*Antony.* No more?
Friendship allows thee nothing: Thou art perjured—
And yet thou didst not swear thou lov'st her not;
But not so much, no more. O trifling hypocrite,
Who dar'st not own to her, thou dost not love,
Nor own to me, thou dost! Ventidius heard it;
Octavia saw it.

*Cleopatra.* They are enemies.

*Antony.* Alexas is not so: He, he confessed it;
He, who, next hell, best knew it, he avowed it.
Why do I seek a proof beyond yourself? [*To* DOLABELLA.
You, whom I sent to bear my last farewell,
Returned, to plead her stay.

*Dolabella.* What shall I answer?
If to have loved be guilt, then I have sinned;
But if to have repented of that love
Can wash away my crime, I have repented.
Yet, if I have offended past forgiveness,
Let not her suffer: She is innocent.

*Cleopatra.* Ah, what will not a woman do, who loves?
What means will she refuse, to keep that heart,
Where all her joys are placed? 'Twas I encouraged.
'Twas I blew up the fire that scorched his soul,
To make you jealous, and by that regain you.
But all in vain; I could not counterfeit:
In spite of all the dams my love broke o'er,
And drowned my heart again: fate took the occasion;

And thus one minute's feigning has destroyed
My whole life's truth.
*Antony*. Thin cobweb arts of falsehood;
Seen, and broke through at first.
*Dolabella*. Forgive your mistress.
*Cleopatra*. Forgive your friend.
*Antony*. You have convinced yourselves.
You plead each other's cause: What witness have you,
That you but meant to raise my jealousy?
*Cleopatra*. Ourselves, and Heaven.
*Antony*. Guilt witnesses for guilt. Hence, love and friendship!
You have no longer place in human breasts,
These two have driven you out: Avoid my sight!
I would not kill the man whom I have loved,
And cannot hurt the woman; but avoid me:
I do not know how long I can be tame;
For, if I stay one minute more, to think
How I am wronged, my justice and revenge
Will cry so loud within me, that my pity
Will not be heard for either.
*Dolabella*. Heaven has but
Our sorrow for our sins; and then delights
To pardon erring man: Sweet mercy seems
Its darling attribute, which limits justice;
As if there were degrees in infinite,
And infinite would rather want perfection
Than punish to extent.
*Antony*. I can forgive
A foe; but not a mistress and a friend.
Treason is there in its most horrid shape,
Where trust is greatest; and the soul resigned,
Is stabbed by its own guards: I'll hear no more;
Hence from my sight for ever!
*Cleopatra*. How? for ever!
I cannot go one moment from your sight,
And must I go for ever?
My joys, my only joys, are centred here:
What place have I to go to? My own kingdom?
That I have lost for you: Or to the Romans?
They hate me for your sake: Or must I wander

The wide world o'er, a helpless, banished woman,
Banished for love of you; banished from you?
Ay, there's the banishment! Oh, hear me; hear me,
With strictest justice: For I beg no favour;
And if I have offended you, then kill me,
But do not banish me.

*Antony.* I must not hear you.
I have a fool within me takes your part;
But honour stops my ears.

*Cleopatra.* For pity hear me!
Would you cast off a slave who followed you?
Who crouched beneath your spurn?—He has no pity!
See, if he gives one tear to my departure;
One look, one kind farewell: O iron heart!
Let all the gods look down, and judge betwixt us,
If he did ever love!

*Antony.* No more: Alexas!

*Dolabella.* A perjured villain!

*Antony* [*To* CLEOPATRA.] Your Alexas; yours.

*Cleopatra.* Oh, 'twas his plot; his ruinous deign,
To engage you in my love by jealousy.
Hear him; confront him with me; let him speak.

*Antony.* I have; I have.

*Cleopatra.* And if he clear me not——

*Antony.* Your creature! one, who hangs upon your smiles!
Watches your eye, to say or to unsay.
Whate'er you please! I am not to be moved.

*Cleopatra.* Then must we part? Farewell, my cruel lord!
The appearance is against me; and I go,
Unjustified, for ever from your sight.
How I have loved, you know; how yet I love,
My only comfort is, I know myself:
I love you more, even now you are unkind,
Than when you loved me most; so well, so truly
I'll never strive against it; but die pleased,
To think you once were mine.

*Antony.* Good heaven, they weep at parting!
Must I weep too? that calls them innocent.
I must not weep; and yet I must, to think
That I must not forgive.——
Live, but live wretched; 'tis but just you should,

Who made me so: Live from each other's sight:
Let me not hear you meet. Set all the earth,
And all the seas, betwixt your sundered loves:
View nothing common but the sun and skies.
Now, all take several ways;
And each your own sad fate, with mine, deplore;
That you were false, and I could trust no more.
[*Exeunt severally.*

## ACT V

### SCENE I.

*Enter* CLEOPATRA, CHARMION, *and* IRAS.

*Charmion.* Be juster, Heaven; such virtue punished thus,
Will make us think that chance rules all above,
And shuffles, with a random hand, the lots,
Which man is forced to draw.

*Cleopatra.* I could tear out these eyes, that gained his heart,
And had not power to keep it. O the curse
Of doting on, even when I find it dotage!
Bear witness, gods, you heard him bid me go;
You, whom he mocked with imprecating vows
Of promised faith!—I'll die; I will not bear it.
You may hold me——
[*She pulls out her dagger, and they hold her.*
But I can keep my breath; I can die inward,
And choke this love.

*Enter* ALEXAS.

*Iras.* Help, O Alexas, help!
The queen grows desperate; her soul struggles in her
With all the agonies of love and rage,
And strives to force its passage.

*Cleopatra.* Let me go.
Art thou there, traitor!—O,
O for a little breath, to vent my rage,
Give, give me way, and let me loose upon him.

*Alexas.* Yes, I deserve it, for my ill-timed truth.
Was it for me to prop

The ruins of a falling majesty?
To place myself beneath the mighty flaw,
Thus to be crushed, and pounded into atoms,
By its o'erwhelming weight? 'Tis too presuming
For subjects to preserve that wilful power,
Which courts its own destruction.

*Cleopatra.* I would reason
More calmly with you. Did not you o'errule,
And force my plain, direct, and open love,
Into these crooked paths of jealousy?
Now, what's the event? Octavia is removed;
But Cleopatra's banished. Thou, thou villain,
Hast pushed my boat to open sea; to prove,
At my sad cost, if thou canst steer it back.
It cannot be; I'm lost too far; I'm ruined:
Hence, thou impostor, traitor, monster, devil!—
I can no more: Thou, and my griefs, have sunk
Me down so low, that I want voice to curse thee.

*Alexas.* Suppose some shipwrecked seaman near the shore,
Dropping and faint with climbing up the cliff,
If, from above, some charitable hand
Pull him to safety, hazarding himself,
To draw the other's weight; would he look back,
And curse him for his pains? The case is yours;
But one step more, and you have gained the height.

*Cleopatra.* Sunk, never more to rise.

*Alexas.* Octavia's gone, and Dolabella banished.
Believe me, madam, Antony is yours.
His heart was never lost, but started off
To jealousy, love's last retreat and covert;
Where it lies hid in shades, watchful in silence,
And listening for the sound that calls it back.
Some other, any man ('tis so advanced),
May perfect this unfinished work, which I
(Unhappy only to myself) have left
So easy to his hand.

*Cleopatra.* Look well thou do't; else——

*Alexas.* Else, what your silence threatens.—Antony
Is mounted up the Pharos; from whose turret,
He stands surveying our Egyptian galleys,
Engaged with Cæsar's fleet. Now death or conquest!

If the first happen, fate acquits my promise;
If we o'ercome, the conqueror is yours.
[*A distant shout within.*

*Charmion.* Have comfort, madam: Did you mark that shout? [*Second shout nearer.*

*Iras.* Hark! they redouble it.

*Alexas.* 'Tis from the port.
The loudness shows it near: Good news, kind heavens!

*Cleopatra.* Osiris make it so!

*Enter* SERAPION.

*Serapion.* Where, where's the queen?

*Alexas.* How frightfully the holy coward stares
As if not yet recovered of the assault,
When all his gods, and, what's more dear to him,
His offerings, were at stake.

*Serapion.* O horror, horror!
Egypt has been; our latest hour has come:
The queen of nations, from her ancient seat,
Is sunk for ever in the dark abyss:
Time has unrolled her glories to the last,
And now closed up the volume.

*Cleopatra.* Be more plain:
Say, whence thou comest; though fate is in thy face,
Which from thy haggard eyes looks wildly out,
And threatens ere thou speakest.

*Serapion.* I came from Pharos;
From viewing (spare me, and imagine it)
Our land's last hope, your navy—

*Cleopatra.* Vanquished?

*Serapion.* No:
They fought not.

*Cleopatra.* Then they fled.

*Serapion.* Nor that. I saw,
With Antony, your well-appointed fleet
Row out; and thrice he waved his hand on high,
And thrice with cheerful cries they shouted back:
'Twas then false Fortune, like a fawning strumpet,
About to leave the bankrupt prodigal,
With a dissembled smile would kiss at parting,
And flatter to the last; the well-timed oars,

Now dipt from every bank, now smoothly run
To meet the foe; and soon indeed they met,
But not as foes. In few, we saw their caps
On either side thrown up; the Egyptian galleys,
Received like friends, passed through, and fell behind
The Roman rear: And now, they all come forward,
And ride within the port.
*Cleopatra* Enough, Serapion:
I've heard my doom.—This needed not, you gods:
When I lost Antony, your work was done;
'Tis but superfluous malice.—Where's my lord?
How bears he this last blow?
*Serapion.* His fury cannot be expressed by words:
Thrice he attempted headlong to have fallen
Full on his foes, and aimed at Cæsar's galley:
Withheld, he raves on you; cries,—He's betrayed.
Should he now find you——
*Alexas.* Shun him; seek your safety,
Till you can clear your innocence.
*Cleopatra.* I'll stay.
*Alexas.* You must not; haste you to your monument,
While I make speed to Cæsar.
*Cleopatra.* Cæsar! No,
I have no business with him.
*Alexas.* I can work him
To spare your life, and let this madman perish.
*Cleopatra.* Base fawning wretch! wouldst thou betray him too?
Hence from my sight! I will not hear a traitor;
'Twas thy design brought all this ruin on us.—
Serapion, thou art honest; counsel me:
But haste, each moment's precious.
*Serapion.* Retire; you must not yet see Antony.
He who began this mischief,
'Tis just he tempt the danger; let him clear you:
And, since he offered you his servile tongue,
To gain a poor precarious life from Cæsar,
Let him expose that fawning eloquence,
And speak to Antony.
*Alexas.* O heavens! I dare not;
I meet my certain death.

*Cleopatra*. Slave, thou deservest it.—
Not that I fear my lord, will I avoid him;
I know him noble: when he banished me,
And thought me false, he scorned to take my life;
But I'll be justified, and then die with him.

*Alexas*. O pity me, and let me follow you.

*Cleopatra*. To death, if thou stir hence. Speak, if thou canst,
Now for thy life, which basely thou wouldst save;
While mine I prize at—this! Come, good Serapion.

[*Exeunt* CLEOPATRA, SERAPION, CHARMION, *and* IRAS.

*Alexas*. O that I less could fear to lose this being,
Which, like a snowball in my coward hand,
The more 'tis grasped, the faster melts away.
Poor reason! what a wretched aid art thou!
For still, in spite of thee,
These two long lovers, soul and body, dread
Their final separation. Let me think:
What can I say, to save myself from death?
No matter what becomes of Cleopatra.

*Antony*. Which way? where? [*Within.*

*Ventidius*. This leads to the monument. [*Within.*

*Alexas*. Ah me! I hear him; yet I'm unprepared:
My gift of lying's gone;
And this court-devil, which I so oft have raised,
Forsakes me at my need. I dare not stay;
Yet cannot far so hence. [*Exit.*

*Enter* ANTONY *and* VENTIDIUS.

*Antony*. O happy Cæsar! thou hast men to lead:
Think not 'tis thou hast conquered Antony;
But Rome has conquered Egypt. I'm betrayed.

*Ventidius*. Curse on this treacherous train!
Their soil and heaven infect them all with baseness:
And their young souls come tainted to the world
With the first breath they draw.

*Antony*. The original villain sure no god created;
He was a bastard of the sun, by Nile,
Aped into man; with all his mother's mud
Crusted about his soul.

*Ventidius*. The nation is
One universal traitor; and their queen

The very spirit and extract of them all.
*Antony*. Is there yet left
A possibility of aid from valour?
Is there one god unsworn to my destruction?
The least unmortgaged hope? for, if there be,
Methinks I cannot fall beneath the fate
Of such a boy as Cæsar.
The world's one half is yet in Antony;
And from each limb of it, that's hewed away,
The soul comes back to me.
*Ventidius*. There yet remain
Three legions in the town. The last assault
Lopt off the rest; if death be your design,—
As I must wish it now,—these are sufficient
To make a heap about us of dead foes,
An honest pile for burial.
*Antony*. They are enough.
We'll not divide our stars; but, side by side,
Fight emulous, and with malicious eyes
Survey each other's acts: So every death
Thou giv'st, I'll take on me, as a just debt,
And pay thee back a soul.
*Ventidius*. Now you shall see I love you. Not a word
Of chiding more. By my few hours of life,
I am so pleased with this brave Roman fate,
That I would not be Cæsar, to outlive you.
When we put off this flesh, and mount together,
I shall be shown to all the ethereal crowd,—
Lo, this is he who died with Antony!
*Antony*. Who knows, but we may pierce through all their troops,
And reach my veterans yet? 'tis worth the 'tempting,
To o'erleap this gulf of fate,
And leave our wandering destinies behind.

*Enter* ALEXAS, *trembling*.

*Ventidius*. See, see, that villain!
See Cleopatra stamped upon that face,
With all her cunning, all her arts of falsehood!
How she looks out through those dissembling eyes!
How he sets his countenance for deceit,

And promises a lie, before he speaks!
Let me despatch him first. [*Drawing.*

*Alexas.* O spare me, spare me!

*Antony.* Hold; he's not worth your killing.—On thy life
Which thou may'st keep, because I scorn to take it,
No syllable to justify thy queen;
Save thy base tongue its office.

*Alexas.* Sir, she is gone,
Where she shall never be molested more
By love, or you.

*Antony.* Fled to her Dolabella!
Die, traitor! I revoke my promise! die! [*Going to kill him.*

*Alexas.* O hold! she is not fled.

*Antony.* She is: my eyes
Are open to her falsehood; my whole life
Has been a golden dream of love and friendship:
But, now I wake, I'm like a merchant, roused
From soft repose, to see his vessel sinking,
And all his wealth cast over. Ungrateful woman!
Who followed me, but as the swallow summer,
Hatching her young ones in my kindly beams,
Singing her flatteries to my morning wake:
But, now my winter comes, she spreads her wings,
And seeks the spring of Cæsar.

*Alexas.* Think not so:
Her fortunes have, in all things, mixed with yours.
Had she betrayed her naval force to Rome,
How easily might she have gone to Cæsar,
Secure by such a bribe!

*Ventidius.* She sent it first,
To be more welcome after.

*Antony.* 'Tis too plain;
Else would she have appeared, to clear herself.

*Alexas.* Too fatally she has: she could not bear
To be accused by you; but shut herself
Within her monument; looked down and sighed;
While, from her unchanged face, the silent tears
Dropt, as they had not leave, but stole their parting.
Some indistinguished words she inly murmured;
At last, she raised her eyes; and, with such looks
As dying Lucrece cast——

*Antony.* My heart forebodes——

*Ventidius.* All for the best:—Go on.

*Alexas.* She snatched her poniard,
And, ere we could prevent the fatal blow,
Plunged it within her breast; then turned to me:
Go, bear my lord, said she, my last farewell;
And ask him, if he yet suspect my faith.
More she was saying, but death rushed betwixt.
She half pronounced your name with her last breath,
And buried half within her.

*Ventidius.* Heaven be praised!

*Antony.* Then art thou innocent, my poor dear love,
And art thou dead?
O those two words! their sound should be divided:
Hadst thou been false, and died; or hadst thou lived,
And hadst been true—But innocence and death!
This shows not well above. Then what am I,
The murderer of this truth, this innocence!
Thoughts cannot form themselves in words so horrid
As can express my guilt!

*Ventidius.* Is't come to this? The gods have been too gracious;
And thus you thank them for it!

*Antony.* [*To* ALEXAS.] Why stayest thou here?
Is it for thee to spy upon my soul,
And see its inward mourning? Get thee hence;
Thou art not worthy to behold, what now
Becomes a Roman emperor to perform.

*Alexas.* He loves her still:
His grief betrays it. Good! the joy to find
She's yet alive, completes the reconcilement.
I've saved myself, and her. But, oh! the Romans!
Fate comes too fast upon my wit,
Hunts me too hard, and meets me at each double.
[*Aside. Exit.*

*Ventidius.* Would she had died a little sooner, though!
Before Octavia went, you might have treated:
Now 'twill look tame, and would not be received.
Come, rouse yourself, and let's die warm together.

*Antony.* I will not fight: there's no more work for war.
The business of my angry hours is done.

*Ventidius.* Cæsar is at your gates.

*Antony.* Why, let him enter;
He's welcome now.

*Ventidius.* What lethargy has crept into your soul?

*Antony.* 'Tis but a scorn of life, and just desire
To free myself from bondage.

*Ventidius.* Do it bravely.

*Antony.* I will; but not by fighting. O Ventidius!
What should I fight for now?—my queen is dead.
I was but great for her; my power, my empire,
Were but my merchandise to buy her love;
And conquered kings, my factors. Now she's dead,
Let Cæsar take the world,—
An empty circle, since the jewel's gone
Which made it worth my strife: my being's nauseous;
For all the bribes of life are gone away.

*Ventidius.* Would you be taken?

*Antony.* Yes, I would be taken;
But, as a Roman ought,—dead, my Ventidius:
For I'll convey my soul from Cæsar's reach,
And lay down life myself. 'Tis time the world
Should have a lord, and know whom to obey.
We two have kept its homage in suspense,
And bent the globe, on whose each side we trod,
Till it was dented inwards. Let him walk
Alone upon't: I'm weary of my part.
My torch is out; and the world stands before me,
Like a black desert at the approach of night:
I'll lay me down, and stray no farther on.

*Ventidius.* I could be grieved,
But that I'll not outlive you: choose your death;
For, I have seen him in such various shapes,
I care not which I take: I'm only troubled,
The life I bear is worn to such a rag,
'Tis scarce worth giving. I could wish, indeed,
We threw it from us with a better grace;
That, like two lions taken in the toils,
We might at last thrust out our paws, and wound
The hunters that inclose us.

*Antony.* I have thought on it.
Ventidius, you must live.

*Ventidius.* I must not, sir.

*Antony.* Wilt thou not live, to speak some good of me?
To stand by my fair fame, and guard the approaches
From the ill tongues of men?

*Ventidius.* Who shall guard mine,
For living after you?

*Antony.* Say, I command it.

*Ventidius.* If we die well, our deaths will speak themselves
And need no living witness.

*Antony.* Thou hast loved me,
And fain I would reward thee. I must die;
Kill me, and take the merit of my death,
To make thee friends with Cæsar.

*Ventidius.* Thank your kindness.
You said I loved you; and in recompense,
You bid me turn a traitor: Did I think
You would have used me thus?—that I should die
With a hard thought of you?

*Antony.* Forgive me, Roman.
Since I have heard of Cleopatra's death,
My reason bears no rule upon my tongue,
But lets my thoughts break all at random out.
I've thought better; do not deny me twice.

*Ventidius.* By Heaven I will not.
Let it not be to outlive you.

*Antony.* Kill me first,
And then die thou; for 'tis but just thou serve
Thy friend before thyself.

*Ventidius.* Give me your hand.
We soon shall meet again. Now farewell, emperor!— [*Embrace.*
Methinks that word's too cold to be my last:
Since death sweeps all distinctions, farewell, friend!
That's all——
I will not make a business of a trifle;
And yet I cannot look on you, and kill you;
Pray turn your face.

*Antony.* I do: strike home, be sure.

*Ventidius.* Home as my sword will reach. [*Kills himself.*

*Antony.* Oh, thou mistak'st;
That wound was not of thine; give it me back;
Thou robb'st me of my death.
*Ventidius.* I do indeed;
But think 'tis the first time I e'er deceived you,
If that may plead my pardon.—And you, gods,
Forgive me, if you will; for I die perjured,
Rather than kill my friend. [*Dies*
*Antony.* Farewell! Ever my leader, even in death!
My queen and thou have got the start of me,
And I'm the lag of honour.—Gone so soon?
Is Death no more? he used him carelessly,
With a familiar kindness: ere he knocked,
Ran to the door, and took him in his arms,
As who should say—You're welcome at all hours,
A friend need give no warning. Books had spoiled him;
For all the learned are cowards by profession.
'Tis not worth
My further thought; for death, for aught I know,
Is but to think no more. Here's to be satisfied.
[*Falls on his sword.*
I've missed my heart. O unperforming hand!
Thou never couldst have erred in a worse time.
My fortune jades me to the last; and death,
Like a great man, takes state, and makes me wait
For my admittance.—— [*Trampling within.*
Some, perhaps, from Cæsar:
If he should find me living, and suspect
That I played booty with my life! I'll mend
My work, ere they can reach me. [*Rises upon his knees.*

*Enter* CLEOPATRA, CHARMION, *and* IRAS.

*Cleopatra.* Where is my lord? where is he?
*Charmion.* There he lies,
And dead Ventidius by him.
*Cleopatra.* My fears were prophets; I am come too late.
[*Runs to him.*
O that accursed Alexas!
*Antony.* Art thou living?
Or am I dead before I knew, and thou
The first kind ghost that meets me?

*Cleopatra.* Help me seat him.
Send quickly, send for help! [*They place him in a chair.*

*Antony.* I am answered.
We live both. Sit thee down, my Cleopatra:
I'll make the most I can of life, to stay
A moment more with thee.

*Cleopatra.* How is it with you?

*Antony.* 'Tis as with a man
Removing in a hurry; all packed up,
But one dear jewel that his haste forgot;
And he, for that, returns upon the spur:
So I come back for thee.

*Cleopatra.* Too long, ye heavens, you have been cruel to me:
Now show your mended faith, and give me back
His fleeting life!

*Antony.* It will not be, my love;
I keep my soul by force.
Say but, thou art not false.

*Cleopatra.* 'Tis now too late
To say I'm true: I'll prove it, and die with you.
Unknown to me, Alexas feigned my death:
Which, when I knew, I hasted to prevent
This fatal consequence. My fleet betrayed
Both you and me.

*Antony.* And Dolabella——

*Cleopatra.* Scarce
Esteemed before he loved; but hated now.

*Antony.* Enough: my life's not long enough for more.
Thou say'st, thou wilt come after: I believe thee;
For I can now believe whate'er thou sayest,
That we may part more kindly.

*Cleopatra.* I will come:
Doubt not, my life, I'll come, and quickly too:
Cæsar shall triumph o'er no part of thee.

*Antony.* But grieve not, while thou stayest,
My last disastrous times:
Think we have had a clear and glorious day
And Heaven did kindly to delay the storm,
Just till our close of evening. Ten years' love,
And not a moment lost, but all improved

To the utmost joys,—what ages have we lived?
And now to die each other's; and, so dying,
While hand in hand we walk in groves below,
Whole troops of lovers' ghosts shall flock about us,
And all the train be ours.

*Cleopatra.* Your words are like the notes of dying swans,
Too sweet to last. Were there so many hours
For your unkindness, and not one for love?

*Antony.* No, not a minute.—This one kiss—more worth
Than all I leave to Cæsar. [*Dies.*

*Cleopatra.* O tell me so again,
And take ten thousand kisses for that word.
My lord, my lord! speak, if you yet have being;
Sign to me, if you cannot speak; or cast
One look! Do anything that shows you live.

*Iras.* He's gone too far to hear you;
And this you see, a lump of senseless clay,
The leavings of a soul.

*Charmion.* Remember, madam,
He charged you not to grieve.

*Cleopatra.* And I'll obey him.
I have not loved a Roman, not to know
What should become his wife; his wife, my Charmion!
For 'tis to that high title I aspire;
And now I'll not die less. Let dull Octavia
Survive, to mourn him dead: My nobler fate
Shall knit our spousals with a tie, too strong
For Roman laws to break.

*Iras.* Will you then die?

*Cleopatra.* Why shouldst thou make that question?

*Iras.* Cæsar is merciful.

*Cleopatra.* Let him be so
To those that want his mercy: My poor lord
Made no such covenant with him, to spare me
When he was dead. Yield me to Cæsar's pride?
What! to be led in triumph through the streets,
A spectacle to base plebeian eyes;
While some dejected friend of Antony's,
Close in a corner, shakes his head, and mutters
A secret curse on her who ruined him!
I'll none of that.

*Charmion.* Whatever you resolve,
I'll follow, even to death.
*Iras.* I only feared
For you; but more should fear to live without you.
*Cleopatra.* Why, now, 'tis as it should be. Quick, my friends,
Despatch; ere this, the town's in Cæsar's hands:
My lord looks down concerned, and fears my stay,
Lest I should be surprised;
Keep him not waiting for his love too long.
You, Charmion, bring my crown and richest jewels:
With them, the wreath of victory I made
(Vain augury!) for him, who now lies dead:
You, Iras, bring the cure of all our ills.
*Iras.* The aspics, madam?
*Cleopatra.* Must I bid you twice?
[*Exit* CHARMION *and* IRAS.
'Tis sweet to die, when they would force life on me,
To rush into the dark abode of death,
And seize him first; if he be like my love,
He is not frightful, sure.
We're now alone, in secrecy and silence;
And is not this like lovers? I may kiss
These pale, cold lips; Octavia does not see me:
And, oh! 'tis better far to have him thus,
Than see him in her arms.—Oh, welcome, welcome!

*Enter* CHARMION *and* IRAS.

*Charmion.* What must be done?
*Cleopatra.* Short ceremony, friends;
But yet it must be decent. First, this laurel
Shall crown my hero's head: he fell not basely,
Nor left his shield behind him.—Only thou
Couldst triumph o'er thyself; and thou alone
Wert worthy so to triumph.
*Charmion.* To what end
These ensigns of your pomp and royalty?
*Cleopatra.* Dull, that thou art! why 'tis to meet my love;
As when I saw him first, on Cydnus' bank,
All sparkling, like a goddess: so adorned,
I'll find him once again; my second spousals

Shall match my first in glory. Haste, haste, both,
And dress the bride of Antony.

*Charmion*. 'Tis done.

*Cleopatra*. Now seat me by my lord. I claim this place;
For I must conquer Cæsar too, like him,
And win my share of the world.—Hail, you dear relics
Of my immortal love!
O let no impious hand remove you hence:
But rest for ever here! Let Egypt give
His death that peace, which it denied his life.—
Reach me the casket.

*Iras*. Underneath the fruit
The aspic lies.

*Cleopatra*. Welcome, thou kind deceiver!
[*Putting aside the leaves*.
Thou best of thieves; who, with an easy key,
Dost open life, and, unperceived by us,
Even steal us from ourselves; discharging so
Death's dreadful office, better than himself;
Touching our limbs so gently into slumber,
That Death stands by, deceived by his own image,
And thinks himself but sleep.

*Serapion*. The queen, where is she? [*Within*.
The town is yielded, Cæsar's at the gates.

*Cleopatra*. He comes too late to invade the rights of death.
Haste, bare my arm, and rouse the serpent's fury.
[*Holds out her arm, and draws it back*.
Coward flesh,
Wouldst thou conspire with Cæsar to betray me,
As thou wert none of mine? I'll force thee to it,
And not be sent by him,
But bring, myself, my soul to Antony.
[*Turns aside, and then shows her arm bloody*.
Take hence; the work is done.

*Serapion*. Break ope the door, [*Within*.
And guard the traitor well.

*Charmion*. The next is ours.

*Iras*. Now, Charmion, to be worthy
Of our great queen and mistress. [*They apply the aspics*.

*Cleopatra*. Already, death, I feel thee in my veins:
I go with such a will to find my lord,

That we shall quickly meet.
A heavy numbness creeps through every limb,
And now 'tis at my head: My eyelids fall
And my dear love is vanquished in a mist.
Where shall I find him, where? O turn me to him,
And lay me on his breast!—Cæsar, thy worst;
Now part us, if thou canst. [*Dies.*

[IRAS *sinks down at her feet, and dies;* CHARMION *stands behind her chair, as dressing her head.*

*Enter* SERAPION, *two* Priests, ALEXAS *bound*, Egyptians.

*Priest.* Behold, Serapion,
What havoc death has made!

*Serapion.* 'Twas what I feard.—
Charmion, is this well done?

*Charmion.* Yes, 'tis well done, and like a queen, the last
Of her great race: I follow her. [*Sinks down : dies.*

*Alexas.* 'Tis true,
She has done well: Much better thus to die,
Than live to make a holiday in Rome.

*Serapion.* See how the lovers sit in state together,
As they were giving laws to half mankind!
The impression of a smile, left in her face,
Shows she died pleased with him for whom she lived,
And went to charm him in another world.
Cæsar's just entering: grief has now no leisure.
Secure that villain, as our pledge of safety,
To grace the imperial triumph.—Sleep, blest pair,
Secure from human chance, long ages out,
While all the storms of fate fly o'er your tomb;
And fame to late posterity shall tell,
No lovers lived so great, or died so well. [*Exeunt.*

# EPILOGUE

Poets, like disputants, when reasons fail,
Have one sure refuge left—and that's to rail.
Fop, coxcomb, fool, are thundered through the pit;
And this is all their equipage of wit.
We wonder how the devil this difference grows,
Betwixt our fools in verse, and yours in prose:
For, 'faith, the quarrel rightly understood,
'Tis civil war with their own flesh and blood.
The threadbare author hates the gaudy coat;
And swears at the gilt coach, but swears afoot:
For 'tis observed of every scribbling man,
He grows a fop as fast as e'er he can;
Prunes up, and asks his oracle, the glass,
If pink or purple best become his face.
For our poor wretch, he neither rails nor prays;
Nor likes your wit just as you like his plays;
He has not yet so much of Mr. Bayes.
He does his best; and if he cannot please,
Would quietly sue out his *writ of ease.*
Yet, if he might his own grand jury call,
By the fair sex he begs to stand or fall.
Let Cæsar's power the men's ambition move,
But grace you him who lost the world for love!
Yet if some antiquated lady say,
The last age is not copied in his play;
Heaven help the man who for that face must drudge,
Which only has the wrinkles of a judge.
Let not the young and beauteous join with those;
For should you raise such numerous hosts of foes,
Young wits and sparks he to his aid must call;
'Tis more than one man's work to please you all.

# THURSDAY

## THE LOVE-CHASE
(1837)

*A Comedy in Five Acts*

By

JAMES SHERIDAN KNOWLES

## CAST OF CHARACTERS.

SIR WILLIAM FONDLOVE (an old Baronet) ........................

WALLER (in love with Lydia) ........................

WILDRAKE (a Sportsman) ........................

TRUEWORTH (a friend of Sir William) ........................

NEVILLE, HUMPHREYS, } Friends to Waller ........................

LASH ........................

CHARGEWELL ........................

GEORGE ........................

SERVANT ........................

LAWYER ........................

WIDOW GREEN ........................

CONSTANCE (daughter to Sir William) ........................

LYDIA ........................

ALICE ........................

PHŒBE ........................

AMELIA ........................

Four Bridesmen, Three Bridesmaids, and Three Servants.

# ACT I

## SCENE I.—*The Lobby of an Inn.*

*Enter* CHARGEWELL, *hurriedly*, L.

*Chargewell.* What, hoa, there! Hoa, Sirrahs! More wine. Are the knaves asleep? Let not our guests cool, or we shall starve the till! Good waiting, more than viands and wine, doth help to make the Inn! George!—Richard! —Ralph!—Where are you?

*Enter* GEORGE, R.

*George.* Here am I, Sir.

*Chargewell.* Have they taken in more wine to that company?

*George.* Yes, Sir.

*Chargewell.* That's right. Serve them as quick as they order! A fair company! I have seen them here before. Take care they come again. A choice company! That Master Waller, I hear, is a fine spirit—leads the town. Pay him much duty. A deep purse, and easy strings!

*George.* And there is another, Sir;—a capital gentleman, though from the country. A gentleman most learned in dogs and horses! He doth talk wondrous edification:— one Master Wildrake. I wish you could hear him, Sir.

*Chargewell.* Well, well!—attend to them. Let them not cool o'er the liquor, or their calls will grow slack. Keep feeding the fire while it blazes, and the blaze will continue. Look to it well!

*George.* I will, Sir.

*Chargewell.* And be careful, above all, that you please Master Waller. He is a guest worth pleasing; he is a gentleman.—Free order, quick pay!

*George.* And such, I'll dare be sworn, is the other. A man of mighty stores of knowledge—most learned in dogs and horses! Never was I so edified by the discourse of mortal man. [*Exeunt*, CHARGEWELL, L., GEORGE, R.

## SCENE II.—*A Room in an Inn*,

MASTERS WALLER, WILDRAKE, TRUEWORTH, NEVILLE, *and* HUMPHREYS, *sitting round a table*, C.

*Waller*. Well, Master Wildrake, speak you of the chase!
To hear you, one doth feel the bounding steed;
You bring the hounds, and game, and all to view—
All scudding to the jovial huntsman's cheer!
And yet I pity the poor crownéd deer,
And always fancy 'tis by Fortune's spite,
That lordly head of his, he bears so high—
Like Virtue, stately in calamity,
And hunted by the human, worldly hound—
Is made to fly before the pack, that straight
Burst into song at prospect of his death.
You say their cry is harmony; and yet
The chorus scarce is music to my ear,
When I bethink me what it sounds to his;
Nor deem I sweet the note that rings the knell
Of the once merry forester!

*Neville*. The same things
Do please or pain, according to the thought
We take of them. Some smile at their own death,
Which most do shrink from, as a beast of prey
It kills to look upon. But you, who take
Such pity of the deer, whence follows it
You hunt more costly game?—The comely maid,
To wit, that waits on buxom Widow Green?

*Humphreys*. The comely maid!—Such term not half the sum
Of her rich beauty gives! Were rule to go
By loveliness, I know not in the court,
Or city, lady might not fitly serve
That lady serving-maid!

*Trueworth*. Come! your defence!
Why show you ruth where there's least argument,
Deny it where there's most? You will not plead?

Oh, Master Waller, where we use to hunt,
We think the sport no crime.
*Humphreys.* I give you joy,
You prosper in your chase.
*Waller.* Not so! The maid
In simple honesty I must pronounce
A miracle of virtue, well as beauty.
*Neville.* And well do I believe you, Master Waller;
Those know I who have ventured gift and promise
But for a minute of her ear—the boon
Of a poor dozen words spoke through a chink—
And come off bootless, save the haughty scorn
That cast their bounties back to them again.
*Trueworth.* That warrants her what Master Waller speaks
her. Is she so very fair?
*Neville.* Yes, Master Trueworth;
And I believe indeed an honest maid;
But love's the coin to market with for love,
And that knows Master Waller. On pretence
Of sneaking kindness for gay Widow Green,
He visits her for sake of her fair maid!
To whom a glance or word avails to hint
His proper errand: and—as glimpses only
Do only serve to whet the wish to see—
Awakens interest to hear the tale
So stintingly that's told. I know his practice—
Luck to you, Master Waller! If you win,
You merit it, who take the way to win!
*Waller.* Good, Master Neville!
*Trueworth.* I should laugh to see
The poacher snared!—the maid, for mistress sought,
Turn out a wife.
*Neville.* How say you, Master Waller?
Things quite as strange have fallen!
*Waller.* Impossible!
*Trueworth.* Impossible! Most possible of things—
If thou'rt in love! Where merit lies itself,
What matters it to want the name, which, weighed,
Is not the worth of so much breath as it takes
To utter it! If but from Nature's hand.
She is all you could expect of gentle blood,

Face, form, mien, speech; with these, what to belong
To lady more behoves—thoughts delicate,
Affections generous, and modesty—
Perfectionating brightening, crown of all!—
If she hath these—true titles to thy heart—
What doth she lack that's title to thy hand?
The name of lady, which is none of these,
But may belong without? Thou might'st do worse
Than marry her! Thou would'st, undoing her!
Yea, by my mother's name a shameful act,
Most shamefully performed!

*Waller.* [*Starting up and drawing,* R. C.] Sir!

*Neville.* [*And the others interposing,* C.] Gentlemen!

*Trueworth.* (L. C.) All's right! Sit down!—I will not draw again.

A word with you:—If—as a man—thou say'st,
Upon thy honour, I have spoken wrong,
I'll ask thy pardon—though I never hold
Communion with thee more!

*Waller.* [*After a pause, putting up his sword,* R. C.] My sword is sheathed!

Wilt let me take thy hand?

*Trueworth.* (L. C.) 'Tis thine, good Sir,
And faster than before—A fault confessed,
Is a new virtue added to a man!
Yet let me own some blame was mine. A truth
May be too harshly told—but 'tis a theme
I am tender on—I had a sister, Sir—
You understand me!—'Twas my happiness
To own her once—I would forget her now!—
I have forgotten!—I know not if she lives!—
Things of such strain as we were speaking of,
Spite of myself, remind me of her!—So!—

*Neville.* Sit down! Let's have more wine.

*Wildrake.* (L.) Not so, good Sirs.
Partaking of your hospitality,
I have overlooked good friends I came to visit,
And who have late become sojourners here—
Old country friends and neighbours, and with whom
I e'en take up my quarters. Master Trueworth,
Bear witness for me.

*Trueworth.* It is even so:
Sir William Fondlove and his charming daughter.

*Wildrake.* Ay, neighbour Constance. Charming, does he say?
Yes, neighbour Constance is a charming girl
To those that do not know her. If she plies me
As hard as was her custom in the country,
I should not wonder, though this very day
I seek the home I quitted for a month! [*Aside*, R.
Good even, gentlemen. [*Crosses*, L., *going out.*

*Humphreys.* Nay, if you go,
We all break up, and sally forth together.

*Waller.* (R. C.) Be it so—Your hand again, good Master Trueworth!
I am sorry I did pain you.

*Trueworth.* (C) It is thine, Sir. [*They go out*, L.

## SCENE III. *Sir William Fondlove's House.—A Room.*

*Enter* SIR WILLIAM, R.

*Sir William.* At sixty-two, to be in leading strings,
Is an old child—and with a daughter, too!
Her mother held me ne'er in check so strait
As she. I must not go but where she likes,
Nor see but whom she likes, do anything
But what she likes!—A slut, bare twenty-one!
Nor minces she commands!—A brigadier
More coolly doth not give his orders out
Than she! Her waiting maid is aide-de-camp;
My steward adjutant; my lacqueys sergeants;
That bring me her high pleasure how I march
And counter-march—when I'm on duty—when
I'm off—when suits it not to tell it me
Herself—"Sir William, thus my mistress says!"
As saying it were enough—no will of mine
Consulted! I will marry. Must I serve,
Better a wife, my mistress, than a daughter!
And yet the vixen says, if I do marry,
I'll find she'll rule my wife as well as me!

*Enter* TRUEWORTH, L.

Ah, Master Trueworth! Welcome, Master Trueworth!
*Trueworth.* Thanks Sir; I am glad to see you look so well!
*Sir William.* Ah, Master Trueworth, when one turns the hill,
'Tis rapid going down! We climb by steps;
By strides, we reach the bottom. Look at me,
And guess my age.
*Trueworth.* Turned fifty.
*Sir William.* Ten years more!
How marvellously well I wear! I think
You would not flatter me!—But scan me close,
And pryingly, as one who seeks a thing
He means to find—What signs of age dost see?
*Trueworth.* None!
*Sir William.* None about the corners of the eyes?
Lines that diverge like to the spider's joists,
Whereon he builds his airy fortalice?
They call them crow's feet—has the ugly bird
Been perching there?—Eh?—Well?
*Trueworth.* There's something like,
But not what one must see, unless he's blind
Like steeple on a hill.
*Sir William* [*After a pause.*] Your eyes are good!
I am certainly a wonder for my age;
I walk as well as ever! Do I stoop?
*Trueworth.* A plummet from your head would find your heel.
*Sir William.* It is my make—my make, good Master Trueworth;
I do not study it. Do you observe
The hollow in my back? That's natural.
As now I stand, so stood I when a child,
A rosy, chubby boy!—I am youthful to
A miracle! My arm is firm as 'twas
At twenty. Feel it!
*Trueworth.* [*Feeling his arm.*] It is deal!
*Sir William.* Oak—oak,
Isn't it, Master Trueworth? Thou hast known me
Ten years and upwards. Think'st my leg is shrunk?
*Trueworth.* No.

*Sir William.* No! not in the calf?
*Trueworth.* As big a calf
As ever.
*Sir William.* Thank you, thank you—I believe it!
When others waste 'tis growing time with me!
I feel it, Master Trueworth! Vigour, Sir,
In every joint of me!—could run! could leap!
Why shouldn't I marry? Knife and fork I play
Better than many a boy of twenty-five—
Why shouldn't I marry? If they come to wine,
My brace of bottles can I carry home,
And ne'er a headache. Death! why shouldn't I marry!
*Trueworth.* I see in nature no impediment.
*Sir William.* Impediment? she's all appliances!—
And fortune's with me, too! The Widow Green
Gives hints to me! The pleasant Widow Green!
Whose fortieth year, instead of autumn, brings
A second Summer in. Odds boddikins,
How young she looks! What life is in her eyes!
What ease is in her gait! while, as she walks,
Her waist, still tapering, takes it pliantly!
How lollingly she bears her head withal:
On this side now—now that! When enters she
A drawing-room, what worlds of gracious things
Her courtesy says!—she sinks with such a sway,
Greeting on either hand the company,
Then slowly rises to her state again!
She is the empress of the card-table!
Her hand and arm!—Gods, did you see her deal—
With curved and pliant wrist dispense the pack,
Which at the touch of her fair fingers fly!
How soft she speaks—how very soft! Her voice
Comes melting from her round and swelling throat,
Reminding you of sweetest, mellowest things—
Plums, peaches, apricots and nectarines—
Whose bloom is poor to paint her cheeks and lips.
By Jove, I'll marry! [*Crosses*, L.
*Trueworth.* You forget, Sir William,
I do not know the lady.
*Sir William.* Great your loss.
By all the Gods, I'll marry!—But my daughter

Must needs be married first. She rules my house
Would rule it still, and will not have me wed.
A clever, handsome, darling, forward minx!
When I became a widower, the reins
Her mother dropped she caught,—a hoyden girl;
Nor since would e'er give up, howe'er I strove
To coax or catch them from her. One way still
Or t'other, she would keep them—laugh, pout, plead;
Now vanquish me with water, now with fire;
Would box my face, and, ere I well could ope
My mouth to chide her, stop it with a kiss!
The monkey! what a plague she's to me!—How
I love her! how I love the Widow Green! [*Crosses*, R.

*Trueworth.* Then marry her!

*Sir William.* I tell thee, first of all
Must needs my daughter marry.—See I not
A hope of that; she naught affects the sex:
Comes suitor after suitor—all in vain.
Fast as they bow, she courtesies, and says "Nay!"
Or she, a woman, lacks a woman's heart,
Or hath a special taste which none can hit.

*Trueworth.* Or taste, perhaps, which is already hit.

*Sir William.* Eh!—how?

*Trueworth.* Remember you no country friend,
Companion of her walks—her squire to church,
Her beau whenever she went visiting—
Before she came to town?

*Sir William.* No!

*Trueworth.* None!—art sure?
No playmate when she was a girl?

*Sir William.* Oh! ay!
That Master Wildrake I did pray thee go
And wait for at the Inn, but had forgotten.
Is he come?

*Trueworth.* And in the house.—Some friends that met him,
As he alighted, laid strong hands upon him
And made him stop for dinner. We had else
Been earlier with you.

*Sir William.* Ha! I am glad he's come.

*Trueworth.* She may be smit with him.

*Sir William.* As cat with dog!

*Trueworth.* He heard her voice as we did mount the stairs,
And darted straight to join her.

*Sir William.* You shall see
What wondrous calm and harmony take place
When fire meets gunpowder!

*Constance.* [*Without*, R.] Who sent for you?
What made you come?

*Wildrake.* [*Without*, R.] To see the town, not you!—
A kiss!

*Constance.* I vow I'll not.

*Wildrake.* I swear you shall.

*Constance.* A saucy cub! I vow, I had as lieve
Your whipper-in had kissed me!

*Sir William.* Do you hear?

*Trueworth.* I do. Most pleasing discords!

*Enter* CONSTANCE *and* WILDRAKE, R.

*Constance.* Father, speak
To neighbour Wildrake.

*Sir William.* Very glad to see him.

*Wildrake.* I thank you, good Sir William! Give you joy
Of your good looks!

*Constance.* What, Phœbe!—Phœbe!—Phœbe!

*Sir William.* What want'st thou with thy lap-dog?

*Constance.* Only, Sir,
To welcome neighbour *Wildrake*! What a figure
To shew himself in town!

*Sir William.* Wilt hold thy peace?

*Constance.* Yes; if you'll lesson me to hold my laughter.
Wildrake!

*Wildrake.* Well?

*Constance.* Let me walk thee in the Park—
How they would stare at thee!

*Sir William.* Wilt ne'er give o'er?

*Wildrake.* Nay, let her have her way—I heed her not!
Though to more courteous welcome I have right;
Although I am neighbour Wildrake! Reason is reason.

*Constance.* And right is right! so welcome, neighbour Wildrake,
I am very, very, very glad to see you!

Come, for a quarter of an hour, we'll e'en
Agree together!—How do your horses, neighbour?

*Wildrake.* Pshaw!

*Constance.* And your dogs?

*Wildrake.* Pshaw!

*Constance.* Whipper-in and huntsman?

*Sir William.* Converse of things thou know'st to talk about.

*Constance.* And keep him silent, father, when I know
He cannot talk of any other things?
How does thy hunter? What a sorry trick
He played thee t'other day, to balk his leap,
And throw thee, neighbour! Did he balk the leap?
Confess! You sportsmen never are to blame!
Say you are fowlers, 'tis your dog's in fault;
Say you are anglers, 'tis your tackle's wrong;
Say you are hunters, why, the honest horse
That bears your weight, must bear your blunders, too!
Why, whither go you?

*Wildrake.* Any where from thee.

*Constance.* *With* me, you mean.

*Wildrake.* I mean it not.

*Constance.* You do!
I'll give you fifty reasons for't—and first,
Where you go, neighbour, I'll go!

[*They go out,* L.—WILDRAKE *pettishly.* CONSTANCE *laughing.*

*Sir William.* Do you mark?
Much love is there!

*Trueworth.* Indeed, a heap, or none.
I'd wager on the heap!

*Sir William.* Ay!—Do you think
These discords, as in the musician's art,
Are subtle servitors to harmony?
That all this war's for peace? This wrangling but
A masquerade, where love his roguish face
Conceals beneath an ugly visor!—Well?

*Trueworth.* Your guess and my conceit are not a mile
Apart. Unlike to other common flowers,
The flower of love shows various in the bud,
'Twill look a thistle, and 'twill blow a rose!

And with your leave, I'll put it to the test;
Affect myself, for thy fair daughter, love—
Make him my confidant—dilate to him
Upon the graces of her heart and mind,
Feature and form—that well may comment bear—
Till—like the practised connoisseur, who finds
A gem of art out in a household picture
The unskilled owner held so cheap, he grudged
Renewal of the chipped and tarnished frame,
But values now as priceless—I arouse him
Into a quick sense of the worth of that
Whose merit hitherto from lack of skill,
Or dulling habit of acquaintanceship,
He has not been awake to.

*Constance.* [*Without*, C. D.] Neighbour Wildrake!

*Sir William.* Hither they come. I fancy well thy game!
Oh, to be free to marry Widow Green!
I'll call her hence anon—then ply him well.

[*Goes out*, R

*Wildrake.* [*Without.*] Nay, neighbour Constance!

*Trueworth.* He's high in storm.

*Enter* WILDRAKE *and* CONSTANCE, L. D.

*Wildrake.* To Lincolnshire, I tell thee.

*Constance.* Lincolnshire!
What, prithee, takes thee off to Lincolnshire.

*Wildrake.* Too great delight in thy fair company.

*Trueworth.* Nay, Master Wildrake, why away so soon?
You're scarce a day in town!—Extremes like this,
And starts of purpose, are the signs 'tis love,
Though immatured as yet. [*Aside.*

*Constance.* He's long enough
In town! What should he in here! He's lost in town:
No man is he for concerts, balls or routs!
No game he knows at cards, save rare Pope Joan!
He ne'er could master dance beyond a jig;
And as for music, nothing to compare
To the melodious yelping of a hound,
Except the braying of his huntsman's horn!
Ask *him* to stay in town!

*Sir William.* [*Without*, R.] Hoa, Constance!

*Contance.* Sir!—
Neighbour, a pleasant ride to Lincolnshire!
Good-bye!

*Sir William.* [*Without*, R.] Why, Constance!

*Constance.* Coming, Sir! Shake hands!
Neighbour, good-bye! Don't look so wo-begone;
'Tis but a two-days' ride, and thou wilt see
Rover, and Spot, and Nettle, and the rest
Of thy dear country friends!

*Sir William.* [*Without*, R.] Constance! I say.

*Constance.* Anon!—Commend me to the gentle souls.
And pat them for me!—Will you, neighbour Wildrake!

*Sir William.* [*Without*, R.] Why, Constance! Constance!

*Constance.* In a moment, Sir!
Good-bye!—I'd cry, dear neighbour, if I could!
Good-bye!—a pleasant day, when next you hunt!
And, prithee, mind thy horse don't balk his leap!
Good-bye—and, after dinner, drink my health!
"A bumper, Sirs, to neighbour Constance!"—Do!—
And give it with a speech, wherein unfold
My many graces, more accomplishments,
And virtues topping either—in a word,
How I'm the fairest, kindest, best of neighbours!

[*They go out severally.*—TRUEWORTH *trying to pacify* WILDRAKE, L.—CONSTANCE *laughing*, R.

## ACT II

### SCENE I.—*A Room in Sir William's House.*

*Enter* TRUEWORTH *and* WILDRAKE, R.

*Wildrake.* Nay, Master Trueworth, I must needs be gone!
She treats me worse and worse! I am a stock,
That words have none to pay her. For her sake,
I quit the town to-day. I like a jest,

But hers are jests past bearing. I am her butt
She nothing does but practise on! A plague!—
Fly her shafts ever your way?

*Trueworth.* Would they did!

*Wildrake.* Art mad?—or wishest she should drive thee so!

*Trueworth.* Thou know'st her not.

*Wildrake.* I know not neighbour Constance?
Then know I not myself, or anything
Which as myself I know!

*Trueworth.* Heigh ho!

*Wildrake.* Heigh ho!
Why, what a burden that for a man's song!
'Twould fit a maiden that was sick for love.
Heigh ho! Come, ride with me to Lincolnshire,
And turn thy "heigh ho!" into "hilly ho!"

*Trueworth.* Nay, rather tarry thou in town with me.
Men sometimes find a friend's hand of avail,
When useless proves their own. Wilt lend me thine?

*Wildrake.* Or may my horse break down in a steeple-chase.

*Trueworth.* A steeplechase! What made thee think of that!
I'm for the steeple—not to ride a race
Only to get there!—not alone, in sooth;
But in fair company!

*Wildrake.* Thou'rt not in love!

*Trueworth.* Heigh ho!

*Wildrake.* Thou wouldst not marry!

*Trueworth.* With your help.

*Wildrake.* And whom, I prithee?

*Trueworth.* Gentle mistress Constance!

*Wildrake.* What!—neighbour Constance?—Never did I dream
That mortal man would fall in love with her. [*Aside.*
In love with neighbour Constance?—I feel strange
At thought that she should marry!—[*Aside.*] Go to church
With neighbour Constance! That's a steeplechase
I never thought of. I feel very strange;
What seest in neighbour Constance?

*Trueworth.* Lovers' eyes
See with a vision proper to themselves,

Yet thousand eyes will vouch what mine affirm.
First, then, I see in her the mould express
Of woman—stature, feature, body, limb—
Breathing the gentle sex we value most,
When most 'tis at antipodes with ours!

*Wildrake.* You mean that neighbour Constance is a woman
Why, yes; she is a woman, certainly.

*Trueworth.* So much for person. Now for her complexion.
What shall we liken to her dainty skin!
Her arm, for instance?—

*Wildrake.* Snow will match it.

*Trueworth.* Snow!—
It is her arm without the smoothness on't.
Then is not snow transparent. 'Twill not do.

*Wildrake.* A pearl's transparent!

*Trueworth.* So it is, but yet
Yields not elastic to the thrilled touch!
I know not what to liken to her arm,
Except its beauteous fellow! Oh, to be
The chosen friend of two such neighbours!

*Wildrake.* Would
His tongue would made a halt. He makes too free
With neighbour Constance! Can't he let her arms
Alone! I trust their chosen friend
Will ne'er be he! I'm vexed. [*Aside.*

*Trueworth.* But graceful things
Grow doubly graceful in the graceful use!
Hast marked her ever walk the drawing-room?

*Wildrake.* [*Snappishly.*] No.

*Trueworth.* No! Why, where have been your eyes?

*Wildrake.* In my head!
But I begin to doubt if open yet. [*Aside.*

*Trueworth.* Yet that's a trifle to the dance: down which
She floats as though she were a form of air;
The ground feels not her foot, or tells not on't;
Her movements are the painting of the strain,
Its swell, its fall, its mirth, its tenderness!
Then is she fifty Constances! each moment
Another one, and each, except its fellow,
Without a peer! You have danced with her?

*Wildrake.* I hate
To dance! I can't endure to dance! [*Crosses* L.] Of course
You have danced with her?
*Trueworth.* I have!
*Wildrake.* You have
*Trueworth.* I have.
*Wildrake.* I do abominate to dance!—Could carve
Fiddlers and company! A dancing man,
To me, was ever like a dancing dog!
Save less to be endured!—Ne'er saw I one,
But I bethought me of the master's whip.
*Trueworth.* A man might bear the whip to dance with her!
*Wildrake.* Not if I had the laying of it on!
*Trueworth.* Well; let that pass. The lady is the theme.
*Wildrake.* Yes; make an end of it!—I'm sick of it.
[*Aside.*
*Trueworth.* How well she plays the harpsichord and harp!
How well she sings to them! Whoe'er would prove
The power of song, should hear thy neighbour sing,
Especially a love song!
*Wildrake.* Does she sing
Such songs to thee?
*Trueworth.* Oh, yes, and constantly!
For such I ever ask her.
*Wildrake.* Forward minx! [*Aside.*
Maids should not sing love songs to gentlemen!
Think'st neighbour Constance is a girl to love?
*Trueworth.* A girl to love?—Ay, and with all her soul!
*Wildrake.* How know you that?
*Trueworth.* I have studied close the sex.
*Wildrake.* You town-rakes are the devil for the sex!
[*Aside.*
*Trueworth.* Not your most sensitive and serious maid
I'd always take for deep impressions. Mind
The adage of the brow. The pensive brow
I've oft seen bright in wedlock, and anon
O'ercast in widowhood; then bright again,
Ere half the season of the weeds was out.
While, in the airy one, I've known one cloud
Forerunner of a gloom that ne'er cleared up—
So it would prove with neighbour Constance. Not

On superficial ground she'll ever love;
But once she does, the odds are ten to one
Her first love is her last!
  *Wildrake.* I wish I ne'er
Had come to town! I was a happy man
Among my dogs and horses. [*Aside.*] Hast thou broke
Thy passion to her?
  *Trueworth.* Never.
  *Wildrake.* Never?
  *Trueworth.* No.
I hoped you'd act my proxy there.
  *Wildrake.* I thank you.
  *Trueworth.* I knew 'twould be a pleasure to you.
  *Wildrake.* Yes;
A pleasure!—an unutterable pleasure!
  *Trueworth.* Thank you! You make my happiness your own. [*Crosses*, L.
  *Wildrake.* I do.
  *Trueworth.* I see you do. Dear Master Wildrake!
Oh, what a blessing is a friend in need,
You'll go and court your neighbour for me?
  *Wildrake.* Yes.
  *Trueworth.* And says she "nay" at first, you'll press again?
  *Wildrake.* Ay, and again!
  *Trueworth.* There's one thing I mistrust—yea, most mistrust,
That of my poor deserts you'll make too much.
  *Wildrake.* Fear anything but that.
  *Trueworth.* 'Twere better far,
You slightly spoke of them.
  *Wildrake.* You think so?
  *Trueworth.* Yes,
Or rather did not speak of them at all.
  *Wildrake.* You think so?
  *Trueworth.* Yes.
  *Wildrake.* Then I'll not say a word
About them.
  *Trueworth.* Thank you! A judicious friend
Is better than a zealous.—You are both!
I see you'll plead my cause as 'twere your own;

Then stay in town and win your neighbour for me,
Make me the envy of a score of men
That die for her as I do.—Make her mine,
And when the last "Amen!" declares complete
The mystic tying of the holy knot,
And 'fore the priest a blushing wife she stands,
Be thine the right to claim the second kiss
She pays for change from maidenhood to wifehood.

[*Goes out*, L.

*Wildrake*. Take that thyself! The first be mine, or none
A man in love with neighbour Constance!—Never
Dreamed I that such a thing could come to pass!
Such person, such endowments, such a soul!
I never thought to ask myself before
If she were man or woman! Suitors too,
Dying for her! I'll e'en make one among 'em!
Woo her to go to church along with him,
And for my pains, the privilege to take
The second kiss? I'll take the second kiss,
And first one, too—and last! No man shall touch
Her lips but me. I'll massacre the man
That looks upon her! Yet what chance have I
With lovers of the town, whose study 'tis
To please your lady belles!—who dress, walk, talk,
To hit their tastes—what chance, a country squire
Like me? Yet your true fair, I've heard, prefers
The man before his coat at any time,
And such a one must neighbour Constance be.
I'll show a limb with any of them! Silks
I'll wear, nor keep my legs in cases more.
I'll learn to dance town-dances, and frequent
Their concerts! Die away at melting strains
Or seem to do so—far the easier thing,
And as effective, quite; leave naught undone
To conquer neighbour Constance.

*Enter* LASH, L.

*Lash*. Sir.
*Wildrake*. Well, sir.
*Lash*. So please you, sir, your horse is at the door.

*Wildrake.* Unsaddle him again, and put him up.
And, hark you, get a tailor for me, sir—
The rarest can be found.
*Lash.* The man's below, sir,
That owns the mare your worship thought to buy.
*Wildrake.* Tell him I do not want her, sir.
*Lash.* I vow,
You will not find her like in Lincolnshire.
*Wildrake.* Go to! She's spavined.
*Lash.* Sir!
*Wildrake.* Touched in the wind.
*Lash.* I trust my master be not touched in the head!
I vow, a faultless beast! [*Aside.*
*Wildrake.* I want her not,
And that's your answer—Go to the hosier's, sir,
And bid him send me samples of his gear,
Of twenty different kinds.
*Lash.* I will, sir.—Sir!
*Wildrake.* Well, sir.
*Lash.* Squire Brush's huntsman's here, and says
His master's kennel is for sale.
*Wildrake.* The dogs
Are only fit for hanging!
*Lash.* Finer bred—
*Wildrake.* Sirrah, if more to me thou talk'st of dogs,
Horses, or aught that to thy craft belongs,
Thou may'st go hang for me!—A cordwainer
Go fetch me straight—the choicest in the town.
Away, sir! Do thy errands smart and well,
As thou canst crack thy whip!—[*Exit* LASH, L.]—Dear neighbour Constance,
I'll give up horses, dogs, and all, for thee! [*Exit.*

## SCENE II.

*Enter* WIDOW GREEN *and* LYDIA, R.

*Widow Green.* Lydia, my gloves. If Master Waller calls,
I shall be in at three; and say the same
To old Sir William Fondlove. Tarry yet!—
What progress, think you, make I in the heart
Of fair young Master Waller? Gods, my girl,

It is a heart to win and man as well!
How speed I, think you? Didst, as I desired,
Detain him in my absence when he called,
And, without seeming, sound him touching me?

*Lydia.* Yes.

*Widow Green.* And affects he me, or not? How guess you?
What said he of me? Looked he balked, or not,
To find me not at home? Inquired he, when
I would be back, as much he longed to see me?
What did he—said he? Come!—Is he in love,
Or like to fall into it? Goes well my game,
Or shall I have my labour for my pains?

*Lydia.* I think he is in love.—Oh, poor evasion!
Oh, to love truth, and yet not dare to speak it! [*Aside.*

*Widow Green.* You think he is in love. I'm sure of it,
As well have asked you has he eyes and ears,
And brain and heart to use them? Maids do throw
Trick after trick away, but widows know
To play their cards! How am I looking, Lydia?

*Lydia.* E'en as you ever look.

*Widow Green.* Handsome, my girl?
Eh? Clear in my complexion? Eh?—brimful
Of spirits? not too much of me, nor yet
Too little?—Eh?—A woman worth a man?
Look at me, Lydia! Would you credit, girl,
I was a scare-crow before marriage?

*Lydia.* Nay!—

*Widow Green.* Girl, but I tell thee, "yea." That gown of thine—
And thou art slender—would have hung about me!
There's something of me now! good sooth, enough.
Lydia, I'm quite contented with myself;
I'm just the thing, methinks, a widow should be.
So Master Waller, you believe, affects me?
But, Lydia, not enough to hook the fish;
To prove the angler's skill, it must be caught;
And lovers, Lydia, like the angler's prey—
Which, when he draws it near the landing place
Takes warning, and runs out the slender line,
And with a spring perchance jerks off the hold—

When we do fish for them, and hook, and think
They are all but in the creel, will make the dart
That sets them free to roam the flood again!

*Lydia.* Is't so?

*Widow Green.* Thou'lt find it so, or better luck
Than many another maid! Now mark me, Lydia;
Sir William Fondlove fancies me. 'Tis well!
I do not fancy him! What should I do
With an old man?—Attend upon the gout,
Or the rheumatics! Wrap me in the cloud
Of a darkened chamber—'stead of shining out,
The sun of balls, and routs, and gala days!
But he affects me, Lydia; so he may!
Now take a lesson from me—Jealousy
Had better go with open, naked breast,
Than pin or button with a gem—Less plague,
The plague spot: that doth speedy make an end
One way or t'other, girl—Yet never love
Was warm without a spice of jealousy.
Thy lesson now—Sir William Fondlove's rich,
And riches, though they're paste, yet, being many,
The jewel love we often cast away for.
I use him but for Master Waller's sake.
Dost like my policy?

*Lydia.* You will not chide me?

*Widow Green.* Nay, Lydia, I do like to hear thy thoughts
They are such novel things—plants that do thrive
With country air! I marvel still they flower,
And thou so long in town! Speak freely, girl!

*Lydia.* I cannot think love thrives by artifice,
Or can disguise its mood, and show its face.
I would not hide one portion of my heart,
Where I did give it, and did feel 'twas right,
Nor feign a wish, to mask a wish that was,
Howe'er to keep it. For no cause except
Myself would I be loved. What wer't to me
My lover valued me the more, the more
He saw me comely in another's eyes,
When his alone the vision I would show
Becoming to? I have sought the reason oft,
They paint Love as a child, and still have thought,

It was because true love, like infancy,
Frank, trusting, unobservant of its mood,
Doth show its wish at once, and means no more!

*Widow Green.* Thou'lt find out better when thy time doth come.
Now would'st believe I love not Master Waller?
I never knew what love was, Lydia;
That is, as your romancers have it. First,
I married for a fortune. Having that,
And being freed from him that brought it me,
I marry now, to please my vanity,
A man that is the fashion. Oh, the delight
Of a sensation, and yourself the cause!
To note the stir of eyes, and ears, and tongues,
When they do usher Mistress Waller in,
Late Widow Green, her hand upon the arm
Of her young handsome husband! How my fan
Will be in requisition—I do feel
My heart begin to flutter now—my blood
To mount into my cheek! My honey-moon
Will be a month of triumphs!—"Mistress Waller!"
That name, for which a score of damsels sigh,
And but the widow had the wit to win!
Why, it will be the talk of East and West,
And North and South!—The children loved the man
And lost him so—I liked, but there I stopped;
For what is it to love, but mind, and heart,
And soul upon another to depend?
Depend upon another!—Nothing be
But what another wills! Give up the rights
Of mine own brain and heart!—I thank my stars
I never came to that extremity! [*Exit,* L.

*Lydia.* She never loved, indeed!—She knows not love
Except what's told of it!—She never felt it.
To stem a torrent, easy, looking at it;
But once you venture in, you nothing know
Except the speed with which you're borne away,
Howe'er you strive to check it. She suspects not
Her maid, not she, brings Master Waller hither.
Nor dare I undeceive her. Well might she say
Her young and handsome husband! Yet his face

And person are the least of him, and vanish
When shines his soul out through his open eye!
He all but says he loves me!—His respect
Has vanquished me! He looks the will to speak
His passion, and the fear that ties his tongue—
The fear?—He loves not honestly!—and yet
I'll swear he loves!—I'll swear he honours me!
It is but my condition is a bar,
Denies him give me all. But knew he me,
As I do know myself!—Whate'er his purpose,
When next we speak, he shall declare it to me.

[*Exit.* L

SCENE III.—*Sir William Fondlove's.*

*Enter* CONSTANCE, *dressed for riding, and* PHŒBE, R.

*Constance.* Well, Phœbe, would you know me? Are those locks
That cluster on my forehead and my cheek,
Sufficient mask? Show I what I would seem,
A lady for the chase? My darkened brows
And heightened colour, foreign to my face,
Do they my face pass off for stranger, too?
What think you?

*Phœbe.* That he'll ne'er discover you.

*Constance.* Then send him to me—say a lady wants
To speak with him—unless indeed it be
A man in lady's gear—I look so bold,
And speak so gruff!—Away! [*Exit* PHŒBE, R.] That I am glad
He stays in town, I own; but if I am,
'Tis only for the tricks I'll play upon him;
And now begin—persuading him his fame
Hath made me fancy him, and brought me hither
On visit to his worship. Soft! his foot!
*This* he?—Why, what has metamorphosed him,
And changed my sportsman to fine gentleman?
Well he becomes his clothes!—But I must check my wonder,
Lest I forget myself—Why, what an air
The fellow hath!—A man to set a cap at!

*Enter* WILDRAKE, R.

*Wildrake.* Kind lady, I attend your fair commands.

*Constance.* My veiléd face denies me justice, sir,
Else would you see a maiden's blushing cheek
Do penance for her forwardness, too late,
I own, repented of. Yet, if 'tis true,
By our own hearts of others we may judge,
Mine in no peril lies, that's shown to you,
Whose heart, I'm sure, is noble. Worthy sir,
Souls attract souls, when they're of kindred vein.
The life that you love, I love. Well I know,
'Mongst those who breast the feats of the bold chase
You stand without a peer; and for myself,
I dare avow, 'mong such none follows them
With heartier glee than I do.
*Wildrake.* Churl were he
That would gainsay you, madam!
*Constance.* [*Curtseying.*] What delight
To back the flying steed, that challenges
The wind for speed!—seems native more of air
Than earth!—whose burden only lends him fire!
Whose soul, in his task, turns labour into sport!
Who makes your pastime his! I sit him now!
He takes away my breath!—He makes me reel—
I touch not earth—I see not—hear not—All
Is ecstacy of motion!
*Wildrake.* You are used,
I see, to the chase.
*Constance.* I am, Sir! Then the leap!
To see the saucy barrier, and know
The mettle that can clear it. Then your time
To prove you master of the manage. Now
You keep him well together for a space,
Both horse and rider braced as you were one,
Scanning the distance—then you give him rein
And let him fly at it, and o'er he goes,
Light as a bird on wing.
*Wildrake.* 'Twere a bold leap,
I see, that turned you, madam.
*Constance.* [*Curtseying.*] Sir, you're good!
And then the hounds, sir! Nothing I admire
Beyond the running of the well-trained pack.
The training's everything! Keen on the scent!

At fault none losing heart!—but all at work!
None leaving his task to another!—answering
The watchful huntsman's caution, check, or cheer,
As steed his rider's rein! Away they go!
How close they keep together!—What a pack!
Nor turn, nor ditch, nor stream divides them—as
They moved with one intelligence, act, will!
And then the concert they keep up!—enough
To make one tenant of the merry wood,
To list their jocund music!

*Wildrake.* You describe
The huntsman's pastime to the life!

*Constance.* I love it!
To wood and glen, hamlet and town, it is
A laughing holiday!—Not a hill-top
But's then alive!—Footmen with horsemen vie,
All earth's astir, roused with the revelry
Of vigor, health, and joy! Cheer awakes cheer,
While Echo's mimic tongue, that never tires,
Keeps up the hearty din! Each face is then
Its neighbour's glass—where gladness sees itself
And, at the bright reflection, grows more glad!
Breaks into tenfold mirth!—laughs like a child!
Would make a gift of its heart, it is so free!
Would scarce accept a kingdom, 'tis so rich!
Shakes hands with all, and vows it never knew
That life was life before!

*Wildrake.* Nay, every way
You do fair justice, lady, to the chase;
But fancies change.

*Constance.* Such fancy is not mine.

*Wildrake.* I would it were not mine, for your fair sake.
I have quite given o'er the chase.

*Constance.* You say not so!

*Wildrake.* Forsworn, indeed, the sportsman's life, and grown.
As you may partly see, town gentleman.
I care not now to mount a steed, unless
To amble 'long the street; no paces mind,
Except my own, to walk the drawing-room,
Or in the ball-room to come off with grace:

No leap for me, to match the light coupé;
No music like the violin and harp,
To which the huntsman's dog and horn, I find,
Are somewhat coarse and homely minstrelsy:
Then fields of ill-dressed rustics, you'll confess,
Are well exchanged for rooms of beaux and belles,
In short, I've ta'en another thought of life—
Become another man!

*Constance.* The cause, I pray?

*Wildrake.* The cause of causes, lady.

*Constance.* He's in love. [*Aside.*

*Wildrake.* To you, of women, I would name it last;
Yet your frank bearing merits like return:
I that did hunt the game, am caught myself,
In chase I never dreamed of! [*Exit.*

*Constance.* He is in love!
Wildrake's in love! 'Tis that keeps him in town,
Turns him from sportsman to town-gentleman.
I never dreamed that he could be in love!
In love with whom?—I'll find the vixen out!
What right has she to set her cap at him?
I warrant me, a forward artful minx!
I hate him worse than ever.—I'll do all
I can to spoil the match. He'll never marry—
Sure he will never marry! He will have
More sense than that! My back doth ope and shut,
My temples throb and shoot—I'm cold and hot!
Were he to marry, there would be an end
To neighbour Constance—neighbour Wildrake—why
I should not know myself!

*Enter* TRUEWORTH, L.

Dear Master Trueworth,
What think you?—Neighbour Wildrake is in love!
In love!—would you believe it, Master Trueworth!
Ne'er heed my dress and looks, but answer me.
Know'st thou of any lady he has seen,
That's like to cozen him?

*Trueworth.* I am not sure—
We talked to-day about the Widow Green!

*Constance.* Her that my father fancies.—Let him wed her!
Marry her to-morrow—if he will, to-night.
I can't spare neighbour Wildrake—neighbour Wildrake!
Although I would not marry him myself,
I could not bear that other married him!
Go to my father—'tis a proper match!
He has my leave! He's welcome to bring home
The Widow Green. I'll give up house and all!
She would be mad to marry neighbour Wildrake:
He would wear out her patience—plague her to death,
As he does me.—She must not marry him!

[*Exeunt* TRUEWORTH C., CONSTANCE, R.

## ACT III

### SCENE I.—*A Room at Widow Green's.*

*Enter* LYDIA, R., MASTER WALLER *following.*

*Waller.* But thou shalt hear me, gentle Lydia.
Sweet maiden, thou art frightened at thyself!
Thy own perfections 'tis that talk to thee.
Thy beauty rich!—thy richer grace!—thy mind,
More rich again than that, though richest each!
Except for these, I had no tongue for thee,
Eyes for thee!—ears!—had never followed thee!—
Had never loved thee, Lydia!—Hear me!—
*Lydia.* Love
Should seek its match.—No match am I for thee.
*Waller.* Right! Love should seek its match; and that is love
Or nothing! Station—fortune—find their match
In things resembling them. They are not love!
Comes love (that subtle essence, without which
Life were but leaden dullness!—weariness!
A plodding trudger on a heavy road!)
Comes it of title-deeds, which fools may boast?

Or coffers vilest hands may hold the keys of?
Or that ethereal lamp that lights the eyes
To shed their sparkling lustre o'er the face,
Gives to the velvet skin its blushing glow,
And burns as bright beneath the peasant's roof,
As roof of palaced prince? Yes! Love should seek
Its match—then give my love its match in thine,
Its match, which in thy gentle breast doth lodge
So rich—so earthly, heavenly fair and rich,
As monarchs have no thought of on their thrones,
Which kingdoms do bear up.
*Lydia*. Wast thou a monarch,
Me wouldst thou make thy queen?
*Waller*. I would!
*Lydia*. What!—Pass
A princess by for me!
*Waller*. I would.
*Lydia*. Suppose
Thy subjects would prevent thee?
*Waller*. Then, in spite
Of them!
*Lydia*. Suppose they were too strong for thee?
*Waller*. Why, then I'd give them up my throne—content
With that thou'dst yield me in thy gentle breast.
*Lydia*. Can subjects do what monarchs do?
*Waller*. Far more!
Far less!
*Lydia*. Among those things, were more their power
Is marriage one?
*Waller*. Yes.
*Lydia*. And no part of love,
You say, is rank or wealth?
*Waller*. No part of love.
*Lydia*. Is marriage part of love?
*Waller*. At times it is,
At times is not. Men love and marry—love
And marry not.
*Lydia*. Then have they not the power;
So must they hapless part with those they love.
*Waller*. Oh, no! not part! How could they love and part?

*Lydia.* How could they love, not part, not free to wed?
*Waller.* Alone in marriage doth not union lie!
*Lydia.* Alone where hands are free!—Oh, yes—alone!
Love that is love, bestoweth all it can
It is protection, if 'tis anything;
Which nothing in its object leaves exposed
Its care can shelter.—Love that's free to wed,
Not wedding, doth profane the name of love,
Which is, on high authority to Earth's,
(For Heaven did sit approving at its feast,)
A holy thing!—Why make you love to me?
Women whose hearts are free, by nature tender
Their fancies hit by those they are besought by,
Do first impressions quickly—deeply take;
And, balked in their election, have been known
To droop a whole life through! Gain for a maid
A broken heart!—to barter her young love,
And find she changed it for a counterfeit!
*Waller.* If there is truth in man, I love thee!—Hear me
In wedlock, families claim property,—
Old notions, which we needs must humour often,
Ban us to wed where we are forced to love!
Thou hear'st?
*Lydia.* I do.
*Waller.* My family is proud;
Our ancestor whose arms we bear, did win
An earldom by his deeds. 'Tis not enough
I please myself!—I must please others, who
Desert in wealth and station only see.
Thou hear'st?
*Lydia.* I do.
*Waller.* I cannot marry thee,—
And must I lose thee?—Do not turn away!
Without the altar I can honour thee!
Can cherish thee, nor swear it to the priest
For more than life I love thee!
*Lydia.* Say thou hatest me,
And I'll believe thee.—Wherein differs love
From hate, to do the work of hate—destroy?
Thy ancestor won title by his deeds!
Was one of them to teach an honest maid

The deed of sin—first steal her love, and then
Her virtue? If thy family is proud,
Mine, Sir, is worthy! If we are poor, the lack
Of riches, Sir, is not the lack of shame!
That I should act a part, would raise a blush,
Nor fear to burn an honest brother's cheek!
Thou wouldst share a throne with me!—Thou wouldst rob
me of
A throne!—reduce me from dominion to
Base vassalage! Pull off my crown for me,
And give my forehead in its place a brand!
You have insulted me.—To show you, Sir,
The heart you make so light of—you are beloved—
But she that tells you so, tells you beside
She ne'er beholds you more! [*Exit*, R.

*Waller*. Stay, Lydia!—No!—
'Tis vain! She is in virtue resolute,
As she is bland and tender in affection.
She is a miracle, beholding which,
Wonder doth grow on wonder!—What a maid!
No mood but doth become her—yea, adorn her.
She turns unsightly anger into beauty!
Sour scorn grows sweetness, touching her sweet lips
And indignation, lighting on her brow,
Transforms to brightness, as the cloud to gold
That overhangs the sun! I love her!—Ay!
And all the throes of serious passion feel,
At thought of losing her!—So my light love,
Which but her person did at first affect,
Her soul has metamorphosed—made a thing
Of solid thoughts and wishes—I must have her!

*Enter* WIDOW GREEN, L., *unnoticed by* WALLER, *who continues abstracted*, R.

*Widow G*. What!—Master Waller, and contemplative!
Presumptive proof of love! Of me he thinks!
Revolves the point, "to be or not to be!"
"To be!" by all the triumphs of my sex!
There was a sigh! My life upon't, that sigh,
If construed, would translate "Dear Widow Green!"

*Waller.* Enchanting woman! [*Musing.*

*Widow Green.* That is I!—most deep
Abstraction, sure concomitant of love.
Now could I see his busy fancy's painting,
How should I blush to gaze upon myself!

*Waller.* The matchless form of woman! The choice culling
Of the aspiring artist, whose ambition
Robs Nature to out-do her—the perfections
Of her rare various workmanship combines
To aggrandize his art at Nature's cost,
And makes a paragon!

*Widow Green.* Gods! how he draws me!
Soon as he sees me, at my feet he falls!
Good Master Waller! (C.)

*Waller.* Ha! The Widow Green!

*Widow Green.* He is confounded!—So am I. Oh, dear!
How catching is emotion.—He can't speak!
Oh, beautiful confusion! Amiable
Excess of modesty, with passion struggling!
Now comes he to declare himself, but wants
The courage.—I will help him.—Master Waller!

*Enter* SIR WILLIAM FONDLOVE, L.

*Sir William.* Dear Widow Green!

*Widow Green.* Sir William Fondlove!

*Waller.* Thank
My lucky stars! [*Aside.*

*Widow Green.* I would he had the gout,
And kept his room! [*Aside.*]—you're welcome, dear Sir William!
'Tis very, very kind of you to call.
Sir William Fondlove—Master Waller. [*They advance a little.*] Pray
Be seated, gentlemen. He shall requite me
For his untimely visit. Though the nail
Be driven home, it may the clinching lack
To make the hold complete! For that I'll use him.

[*Aside—With ceremony they take chairs and sit.* WALLER *gets gradually away from the* WIDOW.

You are looking monstrous well, Sir William! and
No wonder. You're a mine of happy spirits!
Some women talk of such and such a style
Of features in a man.—Give me good humour;
That lights the homeliest visage up with beauty,
And makes the face where beauty is already,
Quite irresistible!

*Sir William.* That's hitting hard [*Aside.*
Dear Widow Green, don't say so! On my life,
You flatter me.—You almost make me blush.

*Widow Green.* I durst not turn to Master Waller now,
Nor need I.—I can fancy how he looks!
I warrant me he scowls on poor Sir William,
As he could eat him up.—I will improve
His discontent, and so make sure of him. [*Aside.*
I flatter you, Sir William? Oh, you men!
You men, that talk so meek, and all the while
Do know so well your power! Who would think
You had a marriageable daughter! You
Did marry very young.

*Sir William.* A boy!—A boy,
Who knew not his own mind.

*Widow Green.* Your daughter's twenty.
Come, you at least were twenty when you married;
That makes you forty.

*Sir William.* Oh, dear!—Widow Green.

*Widow Green.* Not forty?

*Sir William.* You do quite embarrass me!
I own I have the feelings of a boy,
The freshness and the glow of springtime yet,
The relish yet for my young school-day's sports;
Could whip a top—could shoot a taw—could play
At prison-bars and leap-frog, so I might—
Not with a limb, perhaps, as supple, but
With quite as supple will.—Yet I confess
To more than forty!

*Widow Green.* Do you say so? Well,
I'll never guess a man's age by his looks
Again.—Poor Master Waller! He must writhe
To hear I think Sir William is so young.
I'll turn his visit yet to more account. [*Aside.*

A handsome ring, Sir William, that you wear!

*Sir William.* Pray look at it.

*Widow Green.* The mention of a ring
Will take away his breath. [*Aside.*

*Waller.* She must be mine,
Whate'er her terms! [*Aside.*

*Widow Green.* I'll steal a look at him!

*Waller.* What! though it be the ring? the marriage ring?
If that she sticks at, she deserves to wear it!
Oh, the debate which love and prudence hold! [*Aside*

*Widow Green.* How highly he is wrought upon!—His hands
Are clenched!—I warrant me his frame doth shake!
Poor Master Waller! I have filled his heart
Brimful with passion for me.—The delight
Of proving thus my power!

*Sir William.* Dear Widow Green!
She hears not! How the ring hath set her thinking!
I'll try and make her jealous. [*Aside.*]—Widow Green!

*Widow Green.* Sir William Fondlove!

*Sir William.* Would you think that ring
Could tell a story?

*Widow Green.* Could it? Ah, Sir William!
I fear you are a rogue.

*Sir William.* Oh, no!

*Widow Green.* You are!

*Sir William.* No, on my honour! Would you like to hear
The story of the ring?

*Widow Green.* Much,—very much.

*Sir William.* Think'st we may venture draw our chairs apart
A little more from Master Waller?

*Widow Green.* Yes.
He'll bring it to a scene! Dear—dear Sir William,
How much I am obliged to him! A scene!
Gods, we shall have a scene!—Good Master Waller,
Your leave, I pray you, for a minute while
Sir William says a word or two to me.
He durst not trust his tongue for jealousy. [*Aside.*
Now, dear Sir William

*Sir William.* You must promise me
You will not think me vain.

*Widow Green.* No fear of that.

*Sir William.* Nor given to boast.

*Widow.* Oh! dear Sir William!

*Sir William.* Nor
A flirt!

*Widow Green.* Oh! who would take you for a flirt?

*Sir William.* How very kind you are!

*Widow Green.* Go on, Sir William.

*Sir William.* Upon my life, I fear you'll think me vain!
I'm covered with confusion at the thought
Of what I've done. 'Twas very, very wrong
To promise you the story of the ring;
Men should not talk of such things.

*Widow Green.* Such as what?
As ladies' favours?

*Sir William.* 'Pon my life, I feel
As I were like to sink into the earth.

*Widow Green.* A lady, then, it was gave you the ring?

*Sir William.* Don't ask me to say yes, but only scan
The inside of the ring. How much she's moved! [*Aside.*

*Waller.* [*Aside.*] They to each other company enough!
I, company for no one but myself.
I'll take my leave, nor trouble them to pay
The compliments of parting. Lydia! Lydia! [*Exit.*

*Widow Green.* What's here? "Eliza!"—So, it was a lady!
How wondrously does Master Waller bear it!
He surely will not hold much longer out. [*Aside.*
Sir William! Nay, look up! What cause to cast
Your eyes upon the ground? What an' it were
A lady?

*Sir William.* You're not angry?

*Widow Green.* No!

*Sir William.* She is.
I'll take the tone she speaks in 'gainst the word,
For fifty crowns. [*Aside.*]—I have not told you all
About the ring; though I would sooner die

Than play the braggart!—yet, as truth is truth,
And, told by halves, may from a simple thing,
By misconstruction, to a monster grow,
I'll tell the whole truth!

*Widow Green.* Dear Sir William, do!

*Sir William.* The lady was a maid, and very young,
Nor there in justice to her must I stop,
But say that she was beautiful as young,
And add to that that she was learned, too,
Almost enough to win for her that title,
Our sex, in poor conceit of their own merit,
And narrow spirit of monopoly,
And jealousy which gallantry eschews,
Do give to women who assert their right
To minds as well as we.

*Widow Green.* What! a blue stocking?

*Sir William.* I see.—She'll come to calling names at last. [*Aside.*
I should offend myself to quote the term.
But to return, for yet I have not done;
And further yet may go, then progress on
That she was young, that she was beautiful,
A wit and learned are naught to what's to come—
She had a heart!—

*Widow Green.* [*Who, during* SIR WILLIAM'S *speech has turned gradually.*] What, Master Waller gone! [*Aside.*

*Sir William.* I say she had a heart—

*Widow Green.* [*Starting up,*—SIR WILLIAM *also.*] A plague upon her!

*Sir William.* I knew she would break out! [*Aside.*

*Widow Green.* Here, take the ring.
It has ruined me!

*Sir William.* I vow thou hast no cause
For anger!

*Widow Green.* Have I not? I am undone,
And all about that bauble of a ring.

*Sir William.* You're right, it is a bauble.

*Widow Green.* And the minx
That gave it thee!

*Sir William.* You're right, she was a minx.
Knew she'd come to calling names at last. [*Aside.*

*Widow Green.* Sir William Fondlove, leave me.
*Sir William.* Widow Green!—
*Widow Green.* You have undone me, Sir!
*Sir William.* Don't say so!—Don't!
It was a girl—a child gave me the ring!
*Widow Green.* Do you hear me, Sir! I bade you leave me.
*Sir William.* If
I thought you were so jealous.
*Widow Green.* Jealous, Sir!
Sir William! quit my house.
*Sir William.* A little girl
To make you jealous!
*Widow Green.* Sir, you'll drive me mad!
*Sir William.* A child, a perfect child, not ten years old!
*Widow Green.* Sir, I would be alone, Sir!
*Sir William.* Young enough
To dandle still her doll!
*Widow Green.* Sir William Fondlove!—
*Sir William.* Dear Widow Green!
*Widow Green.* I hate you, Sir!—Detest you!—Never wish
To see you more! You have ruined me!—Undone me!
A blighted life I wear, and all through you!
The fairest hopes that ever woman nourished
You've cankered in the very blowing! bloom,
And sweet destroyed, and nothing left me, but
The melancholy stem.
*Sir William.* And all about
A little slut I gave a rattle to!—
Would pester me for gingerbread and comfits!
A little roguish feigning!—A love trick
I played to prove your love!
*Widow Green.* Sir William Fondlove!
If of my own house you'll not suffer me
To be the mistress, I will leave it to you!
*Sir William.* Dear Widow Green! The ring—
*Widow Green.* Confound the ring,
The donor of it, thee, and everything!

[*Exit, hurriedly.*

*Sir William.* She is over head and ears in love with me.
She's mad with love! There's love and all its signs.

She's jealous of me unto very death!
Poor Widow Green! I warrant she is now
In tears!—I think I hear her sob!—Poor thing!
Sir William! oh, Sir William! you have raised
A furious tempest! Set your wits to work
To turn it to a calm. No question that
She loves me!—None, then, that she'll take me;
I'll have the marriage settlements made out
To-morrow, and a special licence got,
And marry her the next day! I will make
Quick work of it, and take her by surprise!
Who but a widower a widow's match;
What could she see with else, but partial eyes
To guess me only forty! I'm a wonder!
What shall I pass for in my wedding suit!
I vow, I am a puzzle to myself,
As well as all the world besides.—Odds life!
To win the heart of buxom Widow Green! [*Exit.*

WIDOW GREEN *re-enters with* LYDIA.

*Widow Green.* At last the dotard's gone! Fly, Lydia, fly
This letter bear to Master Waller straight;
Quick, quick, or I'm undone!—He is abused,
And I must undeceive him—own my love,
And heart and hand at his disposal lay.
Answer me not, my girl—Obey me!—Fly. [*Exit,* R.

*Lydia.* Untowardly it falls!—I had resolved
This hour to tell her I must quit her service!
Go to his house!—I will not disobey
Her last commands!—I'll leave it at the door,
And as it closes on me, think I take
One more adieu of him!—Hard destiny! [*Exit,* L.

SCENE II.—*A Room in Sir William Fondlove's.*

*Enter* CONSTANCE, R.

*Constance.* The booby! He must fall in love, indeed!
And now he's naught but sentimental looks
And sentences pronounced 'twixt breath and voice!
And attitudes of tender languishment!
Nor can I get from him the name of her

Hath turned him from a stock into a fool.
He hems and haws, now titters, now looks grave!
Begins to speak and halts!—takes off his eyes
To fall in contemplation on a chair,
A table, or the ceiling, wall, or floor!
I'll plague him worse and worse! Oh, here he comes!

*Enter* WILDRAKE.

*Wildrake.* Despite her spiteful usage, I'm resolved
To tell her now. Dear neighbour Constance!
*Constance.* Fool!
Accost me like a lady, Sir! I hate
The name of neighbour!
*Wildrake.* Mistress Constance, then—
I'll call thee that.
*Constance.* Don't call me anything!
I hate to hear thee speak—to look at thee,
To dwell in the same house with thee!
*Wildrake.* In what
Have I offended?
*Constance.* What!—I hate an ape!
*Wildrake.* An ape!
*Constance.* Who bade thee ape the gentleman?
And put on dress that don't belong to thee?
Go! change thee with thy whipper-in or huntsman,
And none will doubt thou wearest thy own clothes.
*Wildrake.* A pretty pass! Mocked for the very dress
I bought to pleasure her! Untoward things
Are women! [*Aside—walks backwards and forwards.*
*Constance.* Do you call that walking? Pray,
What makes you twist your body so, and take
Such pains to turn your toes out? If you'd walk,
Walk thus! walk like a man, as I do now! [*Walking.*
Is yours the way a gentleman should walk?
You neither walk like man nor gentleman!
I'll show you how you walk. [*Mimicks him.*] Do you call
that walking?
*Wildrake.* My thanks for a drill-sergeant twice a day
For her sake! [*Aside.*
*Constance.* Now, of all things in the world,
What made you dance last night?

*Wildrake.* What made me dance?

*Constance.* Right! It was anything but dancing! Steps
That never came from dancing school—nor English,
Nor Scotch, nor Irish!—You must try to cut,
And how you did it!
[*Cuts*] That's the way to cut!
And then you chassè! Thus you went, and thus,
[*Mimicking him.*
As though you had been playing at hop, step,
And jump!—And yet you looked so monstrous pleased,
And played the simpleton with such a grace,
Taking the tittering for compliment!
I could have boxed you soundly for't. Ten times,
Denied I that I knew you.

*Wildrake.* Twenty guineas
Were better in the gutter thrown, than gone
To fee a dancing master! [*Aside.*

*Constance.* And you're grown
An amateur in music!—What fine air
Was that you praised last night?—"The Widow Jones!"
A country jig they've turned into a song.
You asked "if it had come from Italy?"
The lady blushed, and held her peace, and then
You blushed and said, "Perhaps it came from France!"
And then when blushed the lady more, nor spoke,
You said, "At least it came from Germany!"
The air was English!—a true English air;
A downright English air! A common air,
Old as "When Good King Arthur." Not a square,
Court, alley, street, or lane about the town,
In which it is not whistled, played, or sung!
But you must have it come from Italy,
Or Germany, or France.—Go home! Go home!
To Lincolnshire, and mind thy dog and horn!
You'll never do for town! "The Widow Jones"
To come from Italy! Stay not in town,
Or you'll be married to the Widow Jones,
Since you've forsworn, you say, the Widow Green!
And morn and night they'll din your ears with her!
"Well met, dear Master Wildrake.—A fine day!
Pray, can you tell whence came the Widow Jones?"

They love a jest in town!—To Lincolnshire!
You'll never do for town!—To Lincolnshire!
"The Widow Jones" to come from Italy! [*Exit*, L.

*Wildrake*. Confound the Widow Jones! 'Tis true! The air,
Well as the huntsman's triple 'most I know,
But knew not then, indeed, 'twas so disguised
With shakes and flourishes, outlandish things,
That mar, not grace, an honest English song!
Howe'er, the mischief's done! and as for her,
She is either into hate or madness fallen.
If madness, would she had her wits again,
Or I my heart—If hate—my love's undone;
I'll give her up. I'll e'en to Master Trueworth,
Confess my treason—own my punishment—
Take horse, and back again to Lincolnshire! [*Exit*.

*Constance*. [*Returning*.] Not here! I trust I have not gone too far!
If he should quit the house! Go out of town!
Poor neighbour Wildrake! Little does he owe me!
From childhood I've been used to plague him thus.
Why should he fall in love, and spoil it all!
I feel as I could cry! He has no right
To marry any one? What wants he with
A wife? Has he not plague enough in me?
Would he be plagued with anybody else?
Ever since I have lived in town I've felt
The want of neighbour Wildrake! Not a soul
Besides I care to quarrel with; and now
He goes and gives himself to another!—What!
Am I in love with neighbour Wildrake?—No.
I only would not have him marry—marry!
Sooner I'd have him dead than have him marry!

[*Exit*.

# ACT IV

## SCENE I.—*A Room in Master Waller's House.*

*Enter* ALICE *hastily,* L.

*Alice.* [*Speaking to the outside.*] Fly, Stephen, to the door! your rapier! quick!—
Our master is beset, because of one
Whose part he takes, a maid, whom lawless men
Would lawlessly entreat! In what a world
We live!—How do I shake!—With what address
[*Looking out of window.*
He lays about him, and his other arm
Engaged, in charge of her whom he defends!
A damsel worth a broil!—Now, Stephen, now!
Take off the odds, brave lad, and turn the scale!
I would I were a swordsman! How he makes
His rapier fly!—Well done!—Oh, Heaven there's blood,
But on the side that's wrong!—Well done, good Stephen!
Pray Heaven no life be ta'en!—Lay on, brave lad!
He has marked his man again! Good lad—Well done
I pray no mischief come! Press on him, Stephen!
Now gives he ground—Follow thy advantage up!
Allow no pause for breath!—Hit him again!
Forbid it end in death!—Lounge home, good Stephen!
How fast he now retreats! That spring, I'll swear,
Was answer to thy point!—Well fenced!—Well fenced!
Now Heaven forefend it end in death!—He flies!
And from his comrade, the same moment, hath
Our master jerked his sword.—The day is ours!
Quick may they get a surgeon for their wounds,
And I a cordial for my fluttered spirits.
I vow, I'm nigh to swoon!

*Waller.* (*Without,* L.] Hoa! Alice! Hoa!
Open the door! Quick, Alice! Quick!

*Alice.* Anon!
Young joints do take no thought of aged ones,
But ever think them supple as themselves.
*Waller.* Alice!
*Alice.* [*Opening the door.*] I'm here! A mercy!—Is she dead?

*Enter* WALLER, *bearing* LYDIA, *fainting.*

*Waller.* No!—She but faints—A chair!—Quick, Alice, quick!
Water to bathe her temples. [*Exit* ALICE, R.] Such a turn
Did fortune never do me! Shall I kiss
To life these frozen lips?—No!—Of her plight
'Twere base to take advantage. [ALICE *returns.*] All is well,
The blood returns.
*Alice.* How wondrous fair she is!
*Waller.* Thou think'st her so?—No wonder then should I [*Aside.*
How say you?—Wondrous fair?
*Alice.* Yes; wondrous fair!
Harm never come to her!—So sweet a thing
'Twere pity were abused!
*Waller.* You think her fair?
*Alice.* Ay, marry! Half so fair were more than match
For fairest she e'er saw mine eyes before!
And what a form! A foot and instep there!
Vouchers of symmetry! A little foot
And rising instep, from an ankle arching,
A palm, and that a little one, might span.
*Waller.* Who taught thee thus?
*Alice.* Why, who but her, taught thee?
Thy mother!—Heaven rest her!—Thy good mother!
She could read men and women by their hands
And feet!—And here's a hand!—A fairy palm!
Fingers that taper to the pinky tips,
With nails of rose, like shells of such a hue,
Berimmed with pearl, you pick up on the shore!
Save these the gloss and tint do wear without.
*Waller.* Why, how thou talk'st!
*Alice.* Did I not tell thee, thus
Thy mother used to talk? Such hand and foot,

She would say, in man or woman, vouched for nature
High tempered!—soil for sentiment refined;
Affection tender; apprehension quick—
Degrees beyond the generality!
There is a marriage finger! Curse the hand
Would balk it of a ring!

*Waller.* She's quite restored.
Leave us!—Why cast'st thou that uneasy look?
Why linger'st thou? I'm not alone with her—
My honour's with her, too! I would not wrong her.

*Alice.* And if thou would'st, thou'rt not thy mother's son.
[*Exit.*

*Waller.* You are better?

*Lydia.* Much!—Much!

*Waller.* Know you him who durst.
Attempt this violence in open day?
He seemed as he would force thee to his coach,
I saw attending.

*Lydia.* Take this letter, sir,
And send the answer—I must needs be go!

*Waller.* [*Throws the letter away.*] I read no letter! Tell me, what of him
I saw offend thee?

*Lydia.* He hath often met me,
And by design, I think, upon the street,
And tried to win mine ear, which ne'er he got,
Save only by enforcement. Presents—gifts
Of jewels and of gold to wild amount.
To win an audience, hath he proffered me;
Until, methought, my silence—for my lips
Disdained reply where question was a wrong—
Had wearied him. Oh, Sir! whate'er of life
Remains to me I had foregone, ere proved
The horror of this hour!—and you it is
That have protected me!

*Waller.* Oh, speak not on't!

*Lydia.* You that have saved me from mine enemy—

*Waller.* I pray you to forget it.

*Lydia.* From a foe
More dire than he that putteth life in peril—

*Waller.* Sweet Lydia, I beseech you, spare me.

*Lydia.* No!
I will not spare you.—You have brought me safety,
You whom I fear worse than that baleful foe. [*Rises to go.*
*Waller.* [*Kneeling and snatching her hand.*] Lydia!
*Lydia.* Now make thy bounty perfect. Drop
My hand. That posture, which dishonours thee,
Quit!—for 'tis shame on shame to show respect
Where we do feel disdain. Throw ope thy gate
And let me pass, and never seek with me,
By look, or speech, or aught, communion more!
*Waller.* Thou said'st thou lov'dst me!
*Lydia.* Yes! when I believed
My tongue did take of thee its last adieu,
And now that I do know it—for be sure,
It never bids adieu to thee again—
Again I tell it thee! Release me, sir!
Rise!—and no hindrance to my will oppose,
That would be free to go.
*Waller.* I cannot lose thee!
*Lydia.* Thou canst not have me!
*Waller.* No!
*Lydia.* Thou canst not. I
Repeat it.—Yet I'm thine—thine every way
Except where honour fences!—Honour, sir,
Not property of gentle blood alone;
Of gentle blood not always property.
Thou'lt not obey me! Still enforcest me!
Oh, what a contradiction is a man!
What in another he one moment spurns,
The next—he does himself complacently!
*Waller.* Would'st have me lose the hand that holds my life?
*Lydia.* Hear me and keep it, if thou art a man!
I love thee,—for thy benefit would give
The labour of that hand!—wear out my feet
Rack the invention of my mind! the powers
Of my heart in one volition gather up!
My life expend, and think no more I gave,
Than he who wins a priceless gem for thanks!
For such good will canst thou return me wrong?
*Waller.* Yet, for a while, I cannot let thee go.
Propound for me an oath that I'll not wrong thee;

An oath which, if I break it, doth entail
Forfeit of earth and heaven. I'll take it—so
Thou stay'st one hour with me.

*Lydia.* No!—Not one moment!
Unhand me, or I shriek!—I know the summons
Will pierce into the street, and set me free!
I stand in peril while I'm near thee! She
Who knows her danger, and delays escape,
Hath but herself to thank, whate'er befals!
Sir, I may have a woman's weakness, but
I have a woman's resolution, too,
And that's a woman's strength! One moment more!—

*Waller.* Lo! Thou art free to go!

[*Rises, and throws himself distractedly into a chair.* LYDIA *approaches the door—her pace slackens—she pauses with her hand upon the lock—turns and looks earnestly on* WALLER.

*Lydia.* I have a word
To say to thee; if by thy mother's honour
Thou swear'st to me thou wilt not quit thy seat.

*Waller.* I swear as thou propound'st to me

*Lydia.* [*After a pause, bursting into tears.*] Oh, why—
Why have you used me thus? See what you've done
Essayed to light a guilty passion up,
And kindled in its stead a holy one!
For I do love thee! Know'st thou not the wish
To find desert doth bring it oft to sight,
Where yet it is not? so for substance passes
What only is a phantasm of our minds!
I feared thy love was guilty—yet my wish
To find it honest, stronger than my fear,
My fear with fatal triumph overthrew!
Now hope and fear give up to certainty
And I must fly thee—yet must love thee still.

*Waller.* Lydia! By all—

*Lydia.* I pray you, hear me out!
Was't right? was't generous? was't pitiful?
One way or other I might be undone:
To love with sin—or love without a hope!

*Waller.* Yet hear me, Lydia!—

*Lydia.* Stop! I am undone!
A maid without a heart—robbed of the soil
Wherein life's hopes and wishes root and spring,
And thou the spoiler did me so much hate,
And vowed me so much love!—But I forgive thee!
Yea, I do bless thee!
[*Rushing up and sinking at his feet.*
Recollect thy oath!—
Or in thy heart lodged never germ of honour,
But 'tis a desert all!
[*Kisses his hand—presses it to her heart, and kisses it again.*
Farewell, then, to thee! [*Rises.*

May'st thou be happy! [*Going.*

*Waller.* Would'st ensure the thing

Thou wishest?
[*She moves towards the door with a gesture that prohibits further converse.*
Stop! [*She continues to move on.*

Oh, sternly resolute! [*She still moves.*

I mean thee honour! [*She stops and turns towards him.*]
Thou dost meditate—
I know it—flight.—Give me some pause for thought,
But to confirm a mind almost made up.
If in an hour thou hear'st not from me, then
Think me a friend far better lost than won!
Wilt thou do this?
*Lydia.* I will.
*Waller.* An hour decides! [*Exeunt severally.*

SCENE II.—*A Room in Sir William Fondlove's.*

*Enter* TRUEWORTH *and* WILDRAKE, R.

*Wildrake.* You are not angry?
*Trueworth.* No; I knew the service
I sent you on was one of danger.

*Wildrake.* Thank you.
Most kind you are—And you believe she loves me,
And your own hopes give up to favour mine?
Was ever known such kindness! Much, I fear,
Twill cost you.
*Trueworth.* Never mind! I'll try and bear it.
*Wildrake.* That's right. No use in yielding to a thing,
Resolve does wonders. Shun the sight of her—
See other women. Fifty to be found
As fair as she.
*Trueworth.* I doubt it.
*Wildrake.* Doubt it not.
Doubt nothing that gives promise of a cure,
Right handsome dames there are in Lancashire,
Whence called their women witches!—witching things!—
I know a dozen families in which
You'd meet a courtesy worthy of a bow
I'll give you letters to them
*Trueworth.* Will you?
*Wildrake.* Yes.
*Trueworth.* The worth of a disinterested friend!
*Wildrake.* Oh, Master Trueworth, deeply I'm your debtor!
I own I die for love of neighbour Constance!
And thou to give her up for me! Kind friend!
What won't I do for thee!—Don't pine to death;
I'll find thee fifty ways to cure thy passion,
And make thee heart-whole, if thou'rt so resolved.
Thou shalt be master of my sporting stud,
And go a hunting. If that likes thee not,
Take up thy quarters at my shooting lodge;
There is a cellar to't, make free with it:
I'll thank thee if thou emptiest it. The song
Gives out that wine feeds love—it drowns it, man!
If thou wilt neither hunt nor shoot, try games;
Play at loggats, bowls, fives, dominos, draughts, cribbage,
Backgammon—special recipes for love!
And you believe, for all the hate she shows,
That neighbour Constance loves me?
*Trueworth.* 'Tis my thought.
*Wildrake.* How shall I find it out?

*Trueworth.* Affect to love
Another. Say your passion thrives; the day
Is fixed; and pray her undertake the part
Of bridemaid to your bride. 'Twill bring her out.

*Wildrake.* You think she'll own her passion?

*Trueworth.* If she loves.

*Wildrake.* I thank thee! I will try it! Master Trueworth
What shall I say to thee, to give her up,
And love her so?

*Trueworth.* Say nothing.

*Wildrake.* Noble friend!
Kind friend! Instruct another man the way
To win thy mistress! Thou'lt not break thy heart?
Take my advice, thou shalt not be in love
A month! Frequent the play-house!—walk the Parks!
I'll think of fifty ladies that I know,
Yet can't remember now—enchanting ones!
And then there's Lancashire!—and I have friends
In Berkshire and in Wiltshire, that have swarms
Of daughters! Then my shooting lodge and stud!
I'll cure thee in a fortnight of thy love!
And now to neighbour Constance—yet almost
I fear accosting her—a hundred times
Have I essayed to break my mind to her,
But still she stops my mouth with restless scorn!
Howe'er, thy scheme I'll try, and may it thrive!
For I am sick for love of neighbour Constance.
Farewell, dear Master Trueworth! Take my counsel—
Conquer thy passion! Do so! Be a man!
[*Exit.*

*Trueworth.* Feat easy done that does not tax ourselves!

*Enter* PHŒBE, R.

*Phœbe.* A letter, sir. [*Exit.*

*Trueworth.* Good sooth, a roaming one!
And yet slow traveller. This should have reached me
In Lombardy.—The hand! Give way, weak seal.
Thy feeble let too strong for my impatience!
Ha! Wronged!—Let me contain myself!—Compelled
To fly the roof that gave her birth!—My sister!
No partner in her flight but her pure honour!

I am again a brother.—Pillow, board,
I know not till I find her.

*Enter* WALLER.

*Waller*. Master Trueworth!

*Trueworth*. Ha! Master Waller! Welcome, Master Waller!

*Waller*. Good Master Trueworth, thank you. Finding you
From home, I e'en made bold to follow you,
For I esteem you as a man, and fain
Would benefit by your kind offices.
But let me tell you first, to your reproof
I am indebted more than e'er I was
To praise of any other. I am come, sir,
To give you evidence I am not one
Who owns advice is right, and acts not on't.

*Trueworth*. Pray you, explain.

*Waller*. Will you the bearer be
Of this to one has cause to thank you, too,
Though I the larger debtor?—Read it, sir.

*Trueworth*. [*Reading the letter.*] "At morn to-morrow I will make you mine.
Will you accept from me the name of wife—
The name of husband give me in exchange?"

*Waller*. How say you, sir?

*Trueworth*. 'Tis boldly—nobly done!

*Waller*. If she consents—which affectation 'twere
To say I don't—bid her prepare for church,
And you shall act the father, sir, to her
You did the brother by.

*Trueworth*. Right willingly,
Though matter of high moment I defer
Mind, heart, and soul, are all enlisted in't.

*Waller*. May I implore you, haste! A time is set!—
How light an act of duty makes the heart!

[*Exeunt together.*

SCENE III.—*Another Chamber in Sir William's House.*

CONSTANCE, *discovered*, C.

*Constance*. I'll pine to death for no man! Wise it were.
Indeed, to die for neighbour Wildrake—No!—

I know the duty of a woman better—
What fits a maid of spirit! I am out
Of patience with myself, to cast a thought
Away upon him. Hang him! Lovers cost
Naught but the pains of living. I'll get fifty,
And break the heart of every one of them!
I will! I'll be the champion of my sex,
And take revenge on shallow fickle man,
Who gives his heart to fools, and slights the worth
Of proper women! I suppose she's handsome!
My face 'gainst hers at hazard of mine eyes!
A maid of mind! I'll talk her to a stand,
Or tie my tongue for life! A maid of soul!
An artful, managing, dissembling one!
Or she had never caught him—he's no man
To fall in love himself, or long ago,
I warrant, he had fallen in love with me!
I hate the fool—I do. Ha, here he comes!
What brings him hither? Let me dry my eyes;
He must not see I have been crying. Hang him,
I've much to do, indeed, to cry for him!

*Enter* WILDRAKE.

*Wildrake.* Your servant, neighbour Constance.
*Constance.* Servant, sir!
Now what, I wonder, comes the fool to say,
Makes him look so important!
*Wildrake.* Neighbour Constance,
I am a happy man.
*Constance.* What makes you so?
*Wildrake.* A thriving suit.
*Constance.* In Chancery?
*Wildrake.* Oh, no!
In love.
*Constance.* Oh, true! You are in love! Go on!
*Wildrake.* Well, as I said, my suit's a thriving one.
*Constance.* You mean you are beloved again?—I don't
Believe it.
*Wildrake.* I can give you proof.
*Constance.* What proof?
Love-letters? She's a shameless maid

To write them! Can she spell? Ay, I suppose
With prompting of a dictionary!

*Wildrake.* Nay,
Without one.

*Constance.* I will lay you ten to one
She cannot spell. How know you she can spell!
You cannot spell yourself! You write command
With a single M——C—O—M—A—N—D:
Yours to Co-mand.

*Wildrake.* I did not say she wrote
Love-letters to me.

*Constance.* Then she suffers you to press
Her hand, perhaps?

*Wildrake.* She does.

*Constance.* Does she press yours!

*Wildrake.* She does.—It goes on swimmingly! [*Aside.*

*Constance.* She does!
She is no modest woman! I'll be bound,
Your arm the madam suffers round her waist?

*Wildrake.* She does!

*Constance.* She does! Outrageous forwardness!
Does she let you kiss her?

*Wildrake.* Yes.

*Constance.* She should be—

*Wildrake.* What?

*Constance.* What you got thrice your share of when at school
And yet not half your due! A brazen face!
More could not grant a maid about to wed.

*Wildrake.* She is so.

*Constance.* What?

*Wildrake.* How swimmingly it goes! [*Aside.*

*Constance.* [*With suppressed impatience.*] Are you about to marry, neighbour Wildrake?
Are you about to marry?

*Wildrake.* Excellent.

*Constance.* [*Breaking out.*] Why don't you answer me?

*Wildrake.* I am.

*Constance.* You are—
I tell you what, sir—You're a fool!

*Wildrake.* For what?

*Constance.* You are not fit to marry! Do not know
Enough of the world, sir! Have no more experience,
Thought, judgment, than a school-boy! Have no mind
Of your own—your wife will make a fool of you,
Will jilt you, break your heart. I wish she may,
I do! You have no more business with a wife
Than I have. Do you mean to say indeed,
You are about to marry?

*Wildrake.* Yes, indeed.

*Constance.* And when?

*Wildrake.* I'll say to-morrow! [*Aside.*

*Constance.* When, I say?

*Wildrake.* To-morrow.

*Constance.* Thank you: much beholden to you!
You've told me on't in time! I'm very much
Beholden to you, neighbour Wildrake! And,
I pray you, at what hour?

*Wildrake.* That we have left
For you to name.

*Constance.* For me!

*Wildrake.* For you.

*Constance.* Indeed,
You're very bountiful. I should not wonder,
Meant you I should be bridesmaid to the lady?

*Wildrake.* 'Tis just the thing I mean.

*Constance.* [*Furiously.*] The thing you mean!
Now pray you, neighbour, tell me that again,
And think before you speak; for much I doubt
You know what you are saying. Do you mean
To ask me to be bridesmaid?

*Wildrake.* Even so.

*Constance.* Bridesmaid?

*Wildrake.* Ay, bridesmaid!—It is coming fast
Unto a head. [*Aside.*

*Constance.* And 'tis for me you wait
To fix the day? It shall be doomsday, then!

*Wildrake.* Be doomsday?

*Constance.* Doomsday!

*Wildrake.* Wherefore doomsday?

*Constance.* [*Boxes him.*] Wherefore!—
Go ask your bride, and give her that from me.

Look, neighbour Wildrake! you may think this strange,
But don't misconstrue it! For you are vain, Sir!
And may put down for love what comes from hate.
I should not wonder, thought you I was jealous;
But I'm not jealous, sir!—would not be so,
Where it was worth my while—I pray henceforth
We may be strangers, sir—you will oblige me
By going out of town—I should not like
To meet you on the street, sir. Marry, sir!
Marry to-day! The sooner, sir, the better.
And may you find you have made a bargain, sir.
As for the lady!—much I wish her joy.
I pray you, send to me no bride-cake, sir!
Nor gloves—If you do, I'll give them to my maid
Or throw them into the kennel—or the fire.
I am your most obedient servant, sir! [*Exit* R.

*Wildrake.* She is a riddle, solve her he who can! [*Exit* L.

## ACT V

### SCENE I.—*A Room in Sir William's.*

SIR WILLIAM *seated with two* LAWYERS, *discovered.*

*Sir William.* How many words you take to tell few things
Again,—again say over that, said once,
Methinks, were told enough.

*1st Lawyer.* It is the law,
Which labours at precision.

*Sir William.* Yes; and thrives
Upon uncertainty—and makes it, too,
With all its pains to shun it. I could bind
Myself, methinks, with but the twentieth part
Of all this cordage, sirs.—But every man,
As they say, to his own business. You think
The settlement is handsome?

*1st Lawyer.* Very, sir.

*Sir William.* Then now, sirs, we have done, and take my thanks,
Which, with your charges, I will render you
Again to-morrow.

*1st Lawyer.* Happy nuptials, sir! [*Exeunt Lawyers.*

*Sir William.* Who passes there? Hoa! send my daughter to me.
And Master Wildrake, too! I wait for them.
Bold work!—without her leave to wait upon her,
And ask her go to church!—'Tis taking her
By storm. What else could move her yesterday,
But jealousy? What causeth jealousy
But love? She's mine the moment she receives
Conclusive proof like this, that heart and soul,
And mind and person, I am all her own!
Heigh ho! These soft alarms are very sweet,
And yet tormenting, too! Ha! Master Wildrake,

*Enter* WILDRAKE, L.

I am glad you're ready, for I'm all in arms
To bear the widow off. Come! Don't be sad;
All must go merrily, you know, to-day!—
She still doth bear him hard, I see! The girl
Affects him not, and Trueworth is at fault,
Though clear it is that he doth die for her. [*Aside.*
Well, daughter—So I see you're ready, too.

*Enter* CONSTANCE, R.

Why, what's amiss with thee?

*Enter* PHŒBE, L.

*Phœbe.* The coach is here. [*Exit,* L.

*Sir William.* Come, Wildrake, offer her your arm.

*Constance.* [*To* WILDRAKE] Thank you!
I'm not an invalid!—can use my limbs!
He knows not how to make an arm befits
A lady lean upon.

*Sir William.* Why, teach him, then.

*Constance.* Teach him! Teach Master Wildrake! Teach, indeed!

I taught my dog to beg, because I knew
That he could learn it.
  *Sir William.* Peace, thou little shrew!
I'll have no wrangling on my wedding-day!
Here, take my arm.
  *Constance.* I'll not!—I'll walk alone!
Live, die alone! I do abominate
The fool and all his sex!
  *Sir William.* Again!
  *Constance.* I have done.
When do you marry, Master Wildrake? She
Will want a husband goes to church with thee!

[*Exeunt*, L.

SCENE II.—*Widow Green's Dressing Room.*

WIDOW GREEN *discovered at her Toilet, attended by* AMELIA —*Waller's letter to Lydia in her hand.*

*Widow Green.* Oh, bond of destiny!—Fair bond, that seal'st
My fate in happiness!—I'll read thee yet
Again—although thou'rt written on my heart.
But here his hand, inditing thee, did lie!
And this the tracing of his fingers! So
I read thee that could rhyme thee, as my prayers!
"*At noon to-morrow will I make thee mine,*
*Wilt thou receive from me the name of wife—*
*The name of husband give me in exchange?*"
The traitress! to break ope my billet-doux,
And take the envelope!—But I forgive her,
Since she did leave the rich contents behind
Amelia, give this feather more a slope,
That it sit droopingly. I would look all
Dissolvement, naught about me to bespeak
Boldness! I would appear a timid bride,
Trembling upon the verge of wifehood, as
I ne'er before had stood there! That will do.
Oh, dear!—how I am agitated—don't
I look so? I have found a secret out.
Nothing in women strikes a man so much
As to look interesting! Hang this cheek

Of mine! It is too saucy; what a pity
To have a colour of one's own!—Amelia!
Could you contrive, dear girl, to bleach my cheek,
How I would thank you! I could give it then
What tint I chose, and that should be the hectic
Bespeaks a heart in delicate-commotion.
I am much too florid: stick a rose in my hair,
The brightest you can find; 'twill help, my girl,
Subdue my rebel colour—Nay, the rose
Doth lose complexion, not my cheek! Exchange it
For a carnation. That's the flower, Amelia!
You see how it doth triumph o'er my cheek.
Are you content with me?

*Amelia.* I am, my lady.

*Widow Green.* And whither, think you, has the hussy gone
Whose place you fill so well?—Into the country?
Or fancy you she stops in town?

*Amelia.* I can't
Conjecture.

*Widow Green.* Shame upon her! Leave her place
Without a moment's warning—with a man, too;
Seemed he a gentleman that took her hence?

*Amelia.* He did.

*Widow Green.* You never saw him here before?

*Amelia.* Never.

*Widow Green.* Not lounging on the other side
Of the street, and reconnoitering the windows?

*Amelia.* Never.

*Widow Green.* 'Twas planned by letter. Notes, you know
Have often come to her—But I forgive her,
Since this advice she chanced to leave behind
Of gentle Master Waller's wishes, which
I bless myself in blessing!—[*A knock.*] Gods, a knock!
'Tis he! Show in those ladies are so kind
To act my bridesmaids for me, on this brief
And agitating notice. [*Amelia goes out,* R.] Yes, I look
A bride sufficiently! And this the hand
That gives away my liberty again?
Upon my life it is a pretty hand,
A delicate and sentimental hand!

No lotion equals gloves; no woman knows
The use of them that does not sleep in them!
My neck hath kept its colour wondrously
Well; after all, it is no miracle
That I should win the heart of a young man.
My bridesmaids come, Oh, dear!

*Enter two* LADIES, R.

1*st Lady*. How do you? A good morning to you—Poor dear,
How much you are affected! Why, we thought
You ne'er would summon us.
*Widow Green*. One takes, you know
When one is flurried, twice the time to dress.
My dears, has either of you salts! I thank you!
They are excellent; the virtue's gone from mine,
Nor thought I of renewing them.—Indeed,
I'm unprovided quite for this affair
1*st Lady*. I think the bridegroom's come!
*Widow Green*. Don't say so! How
You've made my heart jump!
1*st Lady*. As you sent for us,
A new-launched carriage drove up to the door;
The servants all in favours.
*Widow Green*. 'Pon my life,
I never shall get through it; lend me your hand.
[*Half rises and throws herself back on her chair again.*
I must sit down again! There came just now
A feeling like to swooning over me.
I'm sure, before 'tis over, I shall make
A fool of myself! I vow, I thought not half
So much of my first wedding-day! I'll make
An effort. Let me lean upon your arm,
And give me yours, my dear. Amelia, mind
Keep near me with the smelling bottle.

*Enter* SERVANT, R.

*Servant*. Madam,
The bridegroom's come. [*Exit*, R.

*Widow Green.* The brute has knocked me down!
To bolt it out so! I had started less
If he had fired a cannon at my ear
How shall I ever manage to hold up
Till all is done! I'm tremor head to foot.
You can excuse me, can't you? Pity me.
One may feel queer upon one's wedding-day. [*Exeunt*, R.

## SCENE III.—*A Drawing-Room.*

*Enter* Servants, R., *showing in* SIR WILLIAM FONDLOVE, CONSTANCE, *and* WILDRAKE.—Servants *exeunt*, C.

*Sir William.* [*Aside to Wildrake.*] Good Master Wildrake look more cheerfully!—Come,
You do not honour to my wedding-day.
How brisk am I? My body moves on springs!
My stature gives no inch I throw away;
My supple joints play free and sportfully;
I'm every atom what a man should be.
*Wildrake.* I pray you, pardon me, Sir William
*Sir William.* Smile then,
And talk, and rally me! I did expect
Ere half an hour had passed, you would have put me
A dozen times to the blush. Without such things,
A bridegroom knows not his own wedding-day.
I see! Her looks are glossary to thine:
She flouts thee still,—I marvel not at thee;
There's thunder in that cloud! I would to-day
It would disperse, and gather in the morning.
I fear me much, thou know'st not how to woo.
I'll give thee a lesson. Ever there's a way,
But knows one how to take it! Twenty men
Have courted Widow Green. Who has her now?
I sent to advertise her, that to-day
I meant to marry her. She would not open
My note. And gave I up? I took the way
To make her love me! I did send again,
To pray her leave my daughter should be bridesmaid
That letter, too, came back. Did I give up?
I took the way to make her love me! Yet
Again I sent to ask what church she chose

To marry at; my note came back again;
And did I yet give up? I took the way
To make her love me. All the while, I found
She was preparing for the wedding. Take
A hint from me! She comes! My fluttering heart
Gives note the empress of its realms is near.
Now, Master Wildrake, mark and learn from me
How it behoves a bridegroom play his part.

*Enter* Widow Green, L., *supported by her* Bridesmaids *and followed by* Amelia.

*Widow Green.* I cannot raise my eyes—they cannot bear
The beams of his, which, like the sun's, I feel
Are on me, though I see them not, enlightening
The heaven of his young face; nor dare I scan
The brightness of his form, which symmetry,
And youth and beauty, in enriching vie.
He kneels to me! Now grows my breathing thick,
As though I did await a seraph's voice,
Too rich for mortal ear.

*Sir William.* My gentle bride!

*Widow Green.* Who's that? who speaks to me?

*Sir William.* These transports check.
Lo, an example to mankind I set,
Of amorous emprise; and who should thrive
In love, if not Love's soldier, who doth press
The doubtful siege, and will not own repulse.
Lo! here I tender thee my fealty,
To live thy duteous slave. My queen thou art,
In frowns or smiles, to give me life or death.
Oh, deign look down upon me! In thy face
Alone I look on day; it is my sun
Most bright; the which denied, no sun doth rise.
Shine out upon me, my divinity!
My gentle Widow Green! my wife to be!
My love, my life, my drooping, blushing bride!

*Widow Green.* Sir William Fondlove, you're a fool!

*Sir William.* A fool?

*Widow Green.* Why come you hither, sir, in trim like this
Or rather, why at all?

*Sir William.* Why come I hither?
To marry thee!
*Widow Green.* The man will drive me mad!
Sir William Fondlove, I'm but forty, sir,
And you are sixty, seventy, if a day;
At least you look it, sir. I marry you!
When did a woman wed her grandfather?
*Sir William.* Her brain is turned!
*Widow Green.* You're in your dotage, sir,
And yet a boy in vanity! But know
Yourself from me; you're old and ugly, sir.
*Sir William.* Do you deny you are in love with me?
*Widow Green.* In love with thee!
*Sir William.* That you are jealous of me?
*Widow Green.* Jealous!
*Sir William.* To very lunacy?
*Widow Green.* To hear him!
*Sir William.* Do you forget what happened yesterday?
*Widow Green.* Sir William Fondlove!—
*Sir William.* (R.) Widow Green, fair play!—
Are you not laughing? Is it not a jest?
Do you believe me seventy to a day?
Do I look it? Am I old and ugly? Why,
Why do I see those favours in the hall.
These ladies dressed as bridesmaids, thee as bride,
Unless to marry me? [*Knock.*
*Widow Green.* He is coming, sir,
Shall answer you for me!

*Enter* WALLER, L., *with* Gentlemen *as* Bridesmen.

*Waller.* Where is she? What!
All that bespeaks the day, except the fair
That's queen of it? Most kind of you to grace
My nuptials so! But that I render you
My thanks in full, make full my happiness,
And tell me where's my bride?
*Widow Green.* She's here.
*Waller.* Where?
*Widow Green.* Here.
Fair Master Waller!
*Waller.* Lady, do not mock me.

*Widow Green.* Mock thee! My heart is stranger to such mood;
'Tis serious tenderness and duty all.
I pray you, mock not me, for I do strive
With fears and soft emotions, that require
Support. Take not away my little strength,
And leave me at the mercy of a feather.
I am thy bride! If 'tis thy happiness
To think me so, believe it, and be rich
To thy most boundless wishes. Master Waller.
I am thy waiting bride, the Widow Green!

*Waller.* Lady, no widow is the bride I seek,
But one the church has never given yet
The nuptial blessing to!

*Widow Green.* What mean you, sir?
Why come a bridegroom here, if not to me
You sued to be your bride? Is this your hand, sir?
[*Showing letter*

*Waller.* It is! addressed to your fair waiting-maid.

*Widow Green.* My waiting-maid! The laugh is passing round,
And now the turn is yours, sir. She is gone
Eloped! run off! and with the gentleman
That brought your billet-doux.

*Waller.* Is Trueworth false?
He must be false. What madness tempted me
To trust him with such audience as I knew
Must sense, and mind, and soul of man entrance,
And leave him but the power to feel its spell!
Of his own lesson he would profit take,
And plead at once an honourable love,
Supplanting mine, less pure, reformed too late!
And if he did, what merit I, except
To lose the maid I would have wrongly won,
And, had I rightly prized her, now had worn?
I get but my deservings!

*Enter* TRUEWORTH, *leading in* LYDIA *richly dressed and veiled from head to foot.*

Master Trueworth,
Though for thy treachery thou hast excuse,

Thou must account for it, so much I lose!
Sir, you have wronged me to amount beyond
Acres, and gold, and life, which makes them rich.
And compensation I demand of you,
Such as a man expects, and none but one
That's less than man refuses. Where's the maid
You falsely did abstract?

*Trueworth.* I took her hence.
But not by guile, nor yet enforcement, sir,
But of her free will, knowing what she did.
That, as I found I cannot give her back,
I own her state is changed, but in her place
This maid I offer you, her image, far
As feature, form, complexion, nature go.
Resemblance halting only there, where thou
Thyself didst pause—condition; for this maid
Is gently born and generously bred.
Lo! for your fair loss, fair equivalent!

*Waller.* Show me another sun, another earth,
I can inhabit, as this Sun and Earth;
As thou did'st take the maid, the maid herself
Give back herself, her sole equivalent!

*Trueworth.* Her sole equivalent I offer you!
My sister, sir, long counted lost, now found,
Who fled her home unwelcome bands to 'scape
Which a half-father would have forced upon her.
Taking advantage of her brother's absence
Away on travel in a distant land!
Returned, I missed her; of the cause received
Invention, coward, false and criminating!
And gave her up for lost, but happily
Did find her yesterday—Behold her, sir!

[*Removes veil.*

*Waller.* Lydia!

*Widow Green.* My waiting-maid!

*Waller.* Thy sister, Trueworth!
Art thou fit brother to this virtuous maid?

*Trueworth.* [*Giving* LYDIA *to* WALLER.] Let this assure thee.

*Lydia.* [*To* WIDOW GREEN.] Madam, pardon me.
My double character, for honesty—

No other end—assumed, and my concealment
Of Master Waller's love. In all things else,
I trust I may believe you hold me blameless;
At least, I'll say for you I should be so,
For it was pastime, madam, not a task,
To wait upon you! Little you exacted,
And ever made the most of what I did
In mere obedience to you.

*Widow Green.* Give me your hand;
No love without a little roguery.
If you do play the mistress well as maid,
You will bear off the bell! There never was
A better girl! [WALLER *and* LYDIA *go up.*] I have made myself a fool;
I am undone, if goes the news abroad,
My wedding-dress I donned for no effect,
Except to put it off! I must be married.
I'm a lost woman, if another day
I go without a husband!—What a sight
He looks by Master Waller!—Yet he is physic
I die without, so needs must gulp it down.
I'll swallow him with what good grace I can.
Sir William Fondlove!

*Sir William.* Widow Green!

*Widow Green.* I own
I have been rude to you. Thou dost not look
So old by thirty, forty years, as I
Did say. Thou'rt far from ugly—very far!
And as I said, Sir William, once before,
Thou art a kind and right good-humoured man:
I was but angry with you! Why, I'll tell you
At more convenient season—and you know
An angry woman heeds not what she says,
And will say anything!

*Sir William.* I were unworthy
The name of man, if an apology
So gracious came off profitless, and from
A lady! Will you take me, Widow Green?

*Widow Green.* Hem! [*Curtsies.*

*Trueworth.* [*To* WILDRAKE.] Master Wildrake dressed to go to church!

She has acknowledged, then, she loves thee?—No?
Give me thy hand, I'll lead thee up to her.

*Wildrake.* 'Sdeath! what are you about? You know her not.
She'll brain thee!

*Trueworth.* Fear not: come along with me.
Fair Mistress Constance!

*Constance.* Well, sir!

*Wildrake.* [*To* TRUEWORTH.] Mind!

*Trueworth.* Don't fear.
Love you not neighbour Wildrake?

*Constance.* Love, sir!

*Trueworth.* Yes,
You do.

*Constance.* He loves another, sir, he does!
I hate him. We were children, sir, together.
For fifteen years and more; there never came
The day we did not quarrel, make it up,
Quarrel again, and make it up again:
Were never neighbours more like neighbours, sir,
Since he became a man, and I a woman,
It still has been the same; nor cared I ever
To give a frown to any other, sir.
And now to come and tell me he's in love,
And ask me to be bridesmaid to his bride!
How durst he do it, sir!—to fall in love!
Methinks at least he might have asked my leave
Nor had I wondered had he asked myself, sir!

*Wildrake.* Then give thyself to me!

*Constance.* How! what!

*Wildrake.* Be mine!
Thou art the only maid thy neighbour loves.

*Constance.* Art serious, neighbour Wildrake?

*Wildrake.* In the church
I'll answer thee, if thou wilt take me; though
I neither dress, nor walk, nor dance, nor know
"The Widow Jones" from an Italian, French,
Or German air.

*Constance.* No more of that.—My hand.

*Wildrake.* Giv'st it as free as thou didst yesterday?

*Constance.* [*Affecting to strike him.*] Nay!

*Wildrake.* I will thank it, give it how thou wilt.

*Widow Green.* A triple wedding! May the Widow Green
Obtain brief hearing e'er she quits the scene,
The Love-Chase to your kindness to commend
In favour of an old, now absent friend!

# FRIDAY

## THE DANCING GIRL
## (1891)

*A Drama in Four Acts*

By

HENRY ARTHUR JONES

## PERSONS REPRESENTED.

THE DUKE OF GUISEBURY............................................

THE HON. REGINALD SLINGSBY....................................

DAVID IVES.............................................................

JOHN CHRISTISON....................................................

MR. CRAKE, the Duke's land agent...............................

GOLDSPINK, the Duke's valet.......................................

CAPTAIN STEPHEN LEDDRA........................................

STEPHEN LEDDRA, his son, a child..............................

MR. AUGUSTUS CHEEVERS.........................................

LORD MAITLAND.......................................................

LORD BRISLINGTON..................................................

SIR HENRY DRYSDALE...............................................

SIR LIONEL BALDWIN...............................................

MR. AUGUSTUS ANSTRUTHER....................................

MR. VANSTONE........................................................

SIGNOR PONIATOWSKI..............................................

CHARLES, a footman..................................................

JAMES, a footman.....................................................

DRUSILLA IVES........................................................................

FAITH IVES. ........................................................................

SIBYL CRAKE........................................................................

LADY BAWTRY, the Duke's aunt..................................................

MRS. CHRISTISON..................................................................

MRS. LEDDRA........................................................................

SISTER BEATRICE..................................................................

LADY POPEROACH..................................................................

ISABEL POPEROACH................................................................

LADY BRISLINGTON................................................................

LADY MAITLAND....................................................................

LADY BALDWIN......................................................................

MISS BALDWIN.......................................................................

MISS ANSTRUTHER.................................................................

FISHERMEN, TENANTS, VILLAGERS, GUESTS, CHILDREN, ETC.

# ACT I

Scene. *The Island of Saint Endellion, off the Cornish Coast.*

*Time, an Autumn evening.*

## ACT I

### THE BEAUTIFUL PAGAN

SCENE.—*The Isle of Endellion*

John Christison *discovered looking in at the window of* David's *house.*

*John.* Thou miracle of grace and beauty! Thou one desire of my heart! No! Grant me this, that loving her so much I may ever love Thee more! Grant me that she may never come betwixt my soul and Thee!

*Enter* Faith *from house. She is in Quaker dress, about twenty, very modest, pleased, timid.*

*Faith.* You have left work early to-day John?

*John.* I can't work. These last few weeks my thoughts go astray, my hands rebel against me. My body's down there at the breakwater, but my heart and spirit and soul are here—here in your house, Faith.

*Faith.* [*Pleased, trembling, turns her head aside.*] John!

*John.* Is there any hope for me? Does she ever— speak of me?

*Faith.* She?

*John.* Drusilla.

[FAITH, *after an effort, speaks in a quiet, unmoved tone.*

*Faith.* How long have you loved her?

*John.* Ever since she came back from London.

*Faith.* Three weeks.

*John.* It's seven years if you measure it by the love I've loved her with.

[DRUSILLA *passes the window inside cottage.* FAITH *takes off a white silk scarf she has been wearing round neck, and after a struggle, kisses it; then hiding her feeling so far as she can, gives it to him.*

*Faith.* John, I've been forgetting all this while—this handkerchief has been a sore temptation to me since you gave it to me——

*John.* Nay, it's harmless.

*Faith.* Nay, I'm inclined to gauds and finery. Indeed my heart is full of vain thoughts. Take it back, John. You would not have it lead me away from heavenly things.

*John.* What can I do with it? It's a woman's belongings.

*Faith.* Give it to Drusilla. She is more staid and thoughtful than I am. [*Very fervently.*] I hope she will love thee. Indeed she shall! It will be pleasant to have thee for a brother. Stay here! I'll bring her to thee.

[FAITH *runs into the house.* DAVID IVES, *a Quaker, about fifty, comes on.* JOHN *is looking into cottage, he puts handkerchief into his pocket.*

*David.* You've come early to week-night meeting, John.

*John.* The spirit moved me, David.

*David.* Don't be ashamed, John. It is the spirit that moves young men towards maidens. Love doesn't come from the Devil. The spirit moved me to wed the best mother of the best two maidens.—I mustn't boast. Which is it, John? Faith or Drusilla?

*John.* [*After a shame-faced pause.*] Drusilla.

*David.* [*A little surprised.*] Drusilla?! I thought it was likely to be Faith. Drusilla?! You've not seen her for seven years. She's never been home here in Endellion except for a week or two at a time.

*John.* But she's grown so beautiful!

*David.* [*Quickly.*] Hold thy peace! Choose a wife for her beauty!

*John.* Thy wife, her mother, was beautiful!

*David.* [*After a pause, very impressively.*] Ay—and her goodness was of a piece with her beauty! I made an idol of her, and sometimes I think I was punished. She only lived three months after Faith's birth. [*A long deep sigh; then, having dismissed the subject, changes his tone.*] Drusilla! But she must go back to her situation in London——

*John.* Let me persuade her to stay in Endellion.

*David.* And keep her near me? You know how my heart has ached for her all the seven years she has been away from me! But I've denied myself lest I should make an idol of her too, and she should be taken from me as her mother was. Besides, she's happy in London, and she's with godly people, though they're not of our persuasion. John, why do you tempt me?

*John.* You said just now "Love doesn't come from the Devil."

*David.* Speak to her, John. Ask her to be your wife. Not one word, good or bad, will I say. [JOHN *grasps* DAVID'S *hand very warmly.*] But hold—times are bad, and Endellion is little better than a barren rock. There's your dear mother to keep, and you've set yourself a giant's task to build that breakwater. There's years of work before you, and you mustn't give it up, John.

*John.* Give it up!? Do you think I could ever forget that night, and my promise to my father?

*David.* That's right. A promise always binds—but a promise to a dying father binds seven times.

*John.* I'll never rest till the last stone is laid. But I could work with double the strength if Drusilla would wed me. I could keep her in comfort, David, and perhaps I could prevail with the Duke to give me some help.

*Enter from house,* FAITH *and* DRUSILLA. DRUSILLA *is very beautiful, demure, dressed in Quaker fashion, but handsomely. They enter behind* DAVID and JOHN, *and come down unobserved.*

*David.* [*Very scornfully.*] The Duke! Trust no Duke, lad! Trust to thine own right hand, and thy work shall stand sure and drive back the Atlantic. [*Scornfully.*] The Duke! Let him waste his substance in riotous living with his sinful companions! You'll get no help from him! leave him to dance to destruction with his dancing baggages—this what d'ye call her? Some heathen name—Diana Valrose!——

[*Suddenly sees* DRUSILLA, *stops short, drops his voice.*

I was speaking of matters, my dear, that you know nothing of. John wants to speak with you. Weigh well what he says.

*Faith.* [*Aside to* JOHN.] I've said a good word for thee. She says she has no thought of marriage, but she will hear thee.

[*Exit* FAITH.

*David.* [*Calling into house.*] Faith, get me a cup of tea—and—[*glancing at himself.*] And I'll give myself a wash for the week-night meeting.

[*Goes to door of house, glances round with great pride at* DRUSILLA.

My firstling!

[*Exit into house.* JOHN *goes to* DRUSILLA, *who stands very demurely, with eyes cast down on the ground; pause.*

*Drusilla.* Why dost thou not speak?

[JOHN, *very much embarrassed, awkward, trembling, jerky in his utterance, does not look at her.*

*John.* Thou art quite happy in London, Drusilla?

*Drusilla.* Alas, friend John, I am quite happy! And that is what makes me so sad.

*John.* Sad because you are happy?

*Drusilla.* Yes, John, for to tell you the honest truth, I am not quite good and therefore I ought not to be quite happy—but alas! *I am.*

*John.* I do not understand you.

*Drusilla.* That's not strange, for I do not understand myself.

*John.* [*Very earnestly.*] Drusilla—could you live all your life in Endellion?

*Drusilla.* I could, John, but I do not think I should live very long.

*John.* Why not?

*Drusilla.* I could not live in an island where they play harmoniums on Sunday afternoon.

*John.* [*Embarrassed.*] Then I may not ask you to——

*Drusilla.* [*With cordial encouragement.*] Ask me anything you please, friend John.

*John.* [*Very hopeful.*] Then, Drusilla—will you——?

*Drusilla.* [*Unconcerned, demure.*] Will I live in Endellion? [*Considering.*] It is very healthy—Sarah Bazeley has lived to a hundred and two——

*John.* [*Dubiously.*] Yes——

*Drusilla.* But I should like to die while I am well-favoured, and have all my wits, and teeth, and hair, because I should be very sorrowful hereafter without them.

*John.* But wilt thou live in Endellion?

*Drusilla.* The air is soft and pleasant, and moreover all who live here must needs be very good.

*John.* Why?

*Drusilla.* Because they have no means of falling into evil.

*John.* It is indeed a favoured spot.

*Drusilla.* Ah, friend John, but what merit is there in goodness when it is forced? Now as I told thee, there is little goodness in me——

*John.* Thou are all goodness! Oh, Drusilla, have pity on me! [*Approaching her.*

*Drusilla.* [*Starts away from him.*] Nay, but John, have pity on me! [*Lifting up her foot.*

*John.* What ails thee?

*Drusilla.* There is a stone in my slipper. It hurts me.

[JOHN *takes off her slipper.*

The shoemaker who made my slippers told me I had the prettiest foot in London. Is it not wicked of him to fill my heart with vanity?

*John.* [*Kneeling still.*] Have you found it?

*Drusilla.* [*Putting on slipper.*] There is nothing in it.

*John.* [*Suddenly.*] I love thee! Love me, or I shall die!

*Drusilla.* You are foolish!

[*Going away from him ; looking at him.*

*John.* [*Rises, comes up to her with fierce passion.*] I love thee! Wilt thou wed me?

*Drusilla.* I have not thought of it.

*John.* [*Same tone as before.*] I love thee! Wilt thou wed me? [*Seizing her arm.*

*Drusilla.* You should not woo me so—you are too rough! [*Withdrawing her arm.*

*John.* I know not how to woo—I love thee! Wilt thou wed me? Say me yea or nay.

*Drusilla.* I am sorry, friend John, but I must say thee "nay." [*He looks at her.*]

Indeed I mean it.

[*His hands drop with a despairing gesture ; he stands quiet, hopeless, stricken for a few seconds.*

*John.* [*Very hopelessly.*] If you ever want a man's love, you know where to find it.

[*Goes off very slowly, downcast, despairing.*

*Drusilla.* [*Sighs.*] Poor fellow. [*Looking after him.*] He looked rather handsome! Should I——

FAITH *enters from house.*

*Faith.* What answer have you given him? You will marry him?

*Drusilla.* No, indeed. I do not love him—and yet he looked very comely with his red and tanned face. Tell me, Faith—don't you love him yourself?

*Faith.* No—at least six weeks ago——

*Drusilla.* Tell me.

*Faith.* I had never thought about any man—but when he returned from Penzance, he brought me a handkerchief and he took my hand that night, and looked at me a long while——

*Drusilla.* Go on.

*Faith.* My heart beat very fast, and the next day when I saw him coming, I hid away from him—I was ashamed! Drusilla, have you never had thoughts of love?

*Drusilla.* Thoughts are like birds! They will come and roost!

*Faith.* But in London—has no man tried to persuade you to love him?

*Drusilla.* One or two men have tried.

*Faith.* You know *I* would tell *you everything.* Tell me everything about yourself. Do you love any man?

*Drusilla.* We are commended to love *all* men.

*Faith.* Yes, but with that *surpassing* love.

*Drusilla.* I do not think I could love any man with a *surpassing* love. And yet—[*Yawns, stretches out her arms above her head, sighs.*] I don't know—if I could have a man after my own heart——

*Faith.* A very good man——

*Drusilla.* A *perfect* man! I could love him—all a summer afternoon. [*Jumps up.*

Ah! We are talking foolishly. I wonder where John has gone.

[*Looking after* JOHN; *meets* REGY SLINGSBY *who enters.* REGY *is a modern, old-young man, about thirty-three, nearly bald. He shows great surprise at seeing* DRUSILLA, *stops dead—takes off his hat and bows.* DRUSILLA *looks at him unmoved.*

Friend! Why dost thou look at me? I do not know thee.

[REGY *disconcerted, stands, hat in hand, looking at her.*

Put on thy hat. Sunstrokes are frequent in Endellion, and when one has a weak place, it is foolish to expose it to injury.

*Regy.* [*Puts on his hat.*] I beg pardon—I mistook you—I—— [*Laughs foolishly.*

*Drusilla.* Do not make that mistake again, friend. Come, Faith!

[*Takes* FAITH'S *arm, goes with her towards house;* REGY *is still staring.*

*Faith.* A tourist! Why does he stare at you?

*Drusilla.* He thinks he knows me. It's strange! So many folks make that mistake.

[*Exeunt* DRUSILLA *and* FAITH *into house.*

*Regy.* Well, I—if it isn't her——

[*Goes up path; meets* DUKE OF GUISEBURY *who enters; both exclaim "Hillo!"*

Guise! Well, I am—What the devil——

*Guisebury.* Hush, Regy! You're in the Island of Endellion where bad language, scarlet fever, hydrophobia and immorality have never entered.

*Regy.* But you're here—and——

*Guisebury.* My yacht's off that point. I've only called in for a few hours, strictly incog.

*Regy.* Incog.? I say, do you know who's down here?

[DRUSILLA *passes the window.*

There—it is Diana Valrose!

*Guisebury.* Nonsense, Regy!

*Regy.* I'll swear it is! And you down here too! It must be——

*Guisebury.* That young lady is Drusilla Ives—the eminently respectable Quaker daughter of one of my eminently respectable Quaker tenants. Now come—I'll show you my new yacht.

*Regy.* No. If that *isn't* Diana Valrose, I shall try and get an introduction to her.

*Guisebury.* You'll oblige me, Regy, by not noticing that lady.

*Regy.* Look here, Guise—own up. It is Diana—Miss Valrose—Why I met her at your table.

*Guisebury.* Hush! The fact is she's a native of this place.

*Regy.* How did you get to know her, then?

*Guisebury.* I'll tell you. Her father sent her up to a situation in London, and five years ago she called on me as her father's landlord for a subscription to some charity affair—I saw she was two-thirds delightful Quaker innocence, and one-third the devil's own wit and mischief, so—I gave her the subscription!

*Regy*. And now?

*Guisebury*. Well, don't ask me any more, Regy. I've been a confounded fool all through, but somehow—I can't help it. It's a damned silly thing to say—I really love that woman!

*Regy*. But where did she get her style and tone from? Anyone would think she was a lady.

*Guisebury*. [*With meaning.*] I've never met, Regy, with anyone who has presumed to think otherwise in my presence. She had the best masters. She astonished me with the amount of things she learnt, and the way she dropped the Quaker, and became—well, she's a Pagan! Three years ago she took a fancy to dancing. Last season she began dancing for some charities, and her long skirts took the town by storm. She got asked to lots of places, and—that's the whole history of it, Regy.

*Regy*. And her people?

*Guisebury*. Oh, they think she's in a situation in London. Most people believe what pleases them. It's good for them. I never disturb a good, comfortable fiction—it's against my conservative principles.

*Regy*. She's made you dance to a pretty tune, Guise. House in Mayfair, race-horses, carriages, diamonds—what would it all tot up to, Guise? A hundred thousand pounds!

*Guisebury*. Perhaps. But she's never bored me.

*Regy*. Can't you pull up?

*Guisebury*. What for? She's never bored me.

*Regy*. Do you mean to let her ruin you?

*Guisebury*. Why not? She's never bored me.

*Regy*. Not down in this hole?

*Guisebury*. Don't you go depreciating my property. I've only just got here. She, like a dutiful daughter, took a fancy to visit her people, and I, like a dutiful landlord, took a fancy to visit my tenants. I haven't been to Endellion for eighteen years.

*Regy*. You're a model landlord.

*Guisebury.* I am. I take two thousand a year from Endellion in rents, and I spend three in repairs, and keeping the sea out. What brings you to—this hole?

*Regy.* I wanted to get out of town, away from everybody—so I came here. The fact is, Guise—[*confidentially*]—I've made a fool of myself!

*Guisebury.* What, again! The third time! After Bowler's cross-examination, and after those damages—as exemplary as your behaviour.

[*Shaking his head.*

Regy, Regy, you're a bad lot—bad lot, Regy!

*Regy.* No, no, old fellow. Not that—I've been really going straight lately.

*Guisebury.* Ah, twice bit, once shy, I see! What silly mess have you got yourself into now?

*Regy.* [*Calmly.*] I'm engaged to be married.

[*The two men look at each other calmly for some seconds.*

*Guisebury. What, again!* [*Calmly.*] Who's landed you?

*Regy.* One of the Poperoach girls—Isabel.

*Guisebury.* Isabel? Oh, yes. Tall girl, with large features, high cheek-bones, and a lot of wispy, straw-coloured hair—eh?

*Regy.* [*Dubiously.*] Yes. It *may* turn out all right, you know?

*Guisebury.* Think so?

*Regy.* Lady Poperoach has been trying to catch me all the season. I could see their game. Will you walk into my parlour? And in I walked. And the old woman slammed the door. And there it was staring at me in the *Morning Post* the next morning.

[*Looks very depressed;* GUISE *laughs.*

*Regy.* [*Piteously.*] Don't be hard on a fellow. Isabel's got some good points—eh? [*Anxiously.*] What do you think of her? Really now—not bad, take her altogether?

*Guisebury.* I'd rather take her in instalments!

*Regy.* It isn't Isabel so much as the old woman. Lady Poperoach does come the old soldier over everybody. It's awful!

*Guisebury.* How is it you're not on duty?

*Regy.* Well, as soon as it was all—you know—settled, I thought I should like to have a few days to myself and think it over. So I got away—just—well, just to get used to the idea.

*Guisebury.* [*Benevolently.*] Get used to it, Regy—don't hurry, but get used to it.

*Regy.* [*Valiantly*]. Oh, I'm in for it, and I mean to go through it like a man.

DAVID *enters.*

*Guisebury.* [*To* REGY.] One of my Quaker tenants. They don't know me—don't know I'm in the island. Regy, here's a chance of hearing an honest opinion of myself.

*Regy.* I say——[GUISEBURY *puts him away.*] Well I'm—— [*Exit.*

*Guisebury.* Very charming spot, this Isle of Endellion!

*David.* We're highly favoured in many respects, friend.

*Guisebury.* Who's the owner of this property?

[DRUSILLA *comes to door and listens.*

*David.* Valentine Danecourt——His Grace the Duke of Guisebury and the Earl of St. Endellion, they call him.

*Guisebury.* Of course. You are highly favoured. A philanthropist, isn't he?

*David.* I've heard him called many names, but I've never heard that title given to him.

*Guisebury.* Perhaps you don't know him.

*David.* No, friend, but I have received a very evil report of him.

*Guisebury.* Ah! From the Radical papers!

*David.* No, from his own actions. He wants no other accusers.

*Guisebury.* What particular shape does his infamy take?

*David.* All shapes. A spendthrift, a libertine, a gambler with cards and horses.

*Guisebury.* The rascal! The damned rascal!

*David.* Yes, friend. That's a strong word to use, but it's the right one!

*Guisebury.* [*Amused.*] He hasn't killed anybody, I suppose?

*David.* Yes, he has.

*Guisebury.* [*Highly amused.*] A murderer as well! [*Aside.*] I'm getting on!

*David.* The law wouldn't call it murder, but his conscience would, if he had one.

*Guisebury.* What do you mean?

*David.* Two years ago, my friend Mark Christison was struck in the high tide, as he was trying to save his home from destruction. He died and his wife went out of her mind. What Valentine Danecourt wastes on his dancing creatures would have built a breakwater, and saved Mark Christison's life.

*Guisebury.* [*Aside.*] He's right. I am a blackguard. [*Stands thoughtful.*]

*Drusilla.* [*To her father.*] Your tea's ready, father!

*Guisebury.* [*Aside.*] Di's father!

*Drusilla.* What have you been saying to the stranger?

*David.* I've been telling him my opinion of Valentine Danecourt.

*Drusilla* [*Mischievously.*] I hope you have been pleasantly entertained, friend.

*Guisebury.* [*Ironically.*] Oh, most pleasantly.

*Drusilla.* In London, where I live, there is grievous talk of the Duke's misdeeds.

*Guisebury.* So there is in Endellion, it seems.

*David.* [*To* GUISEBURY.] Do you know this Duke?

*Guisebury.* I have met him, but if he's as bad as you say, I shall keep out of his way for the future.

*David.* Aye, do, friend. Come, Drusilla.

REGINALD *runs on.*

*Regy.* I say, Guisebury, old fellow——

*David.* [*Turns sharply round.*] Guisebury! Guisebury! Go indoors, Drusilla!

[DRUSILLA *exits into house.* DAVID *turns to* GUISEBURY.]

Then you are Valentine Danecourt, yourself?

*Guisebury.* At your service.

*David.* [*After a pause.*] I suppose I may take a year's notice to quit my house and land.

*Guisebury.* Not at all. I'm a very bad landlord,

Mr. Ives, but you're a very good tenant. I'm glad to have heard your candid opinion of me.

*David.* You're quite welcome.

*Guisebury.* I regret to say that all you have said of me is quite true. I am a thoroughly bad lot, and the worst of it is there's not the least chance of my reformation. However, if you want any repairs doing, my agent, Crake, is down here with me—let him know and they shall be done.

*David.* Thank you.

*Guisebury.* And in the meantime, friend Ives, as I never knew Mr. Christison, have no precise knowledge of high tides, and was at Monte Carlo at the time of his death, I think you may stretch a point in my favour and call it manslaughter for the future—eh, friend?

*David.* [*Seriously.*] Harkee, friend—Remember your promise—Keep out of the Duke of Guisebury's way for the future. You'll be wise.

[*Exit into house.*

*Regy.* I'm afraid I've put my foot in it again!

*Guisebury.* What made you blurt out my name when I told you I was here incog.?

*Regy.* I'm awfully sorry, old fellow. Hallo! Here's what's-his-name.

[*Enter* CRAKE, *the* DUKE'S *steward and land agent, about* 50.

*Guisebury.* Here's Crake—you know Crake?

*Crake.* [*A little surprised on seeing Regy.*] Mr. Slingsby, how d'ye do?

*Regy.* I'm not very well.

*Crake.* I saw the joyful news in the *Morning Post.*

*Regy.* [*Sheepishly.*] Yes. It's the right sort of thing to do, eh, Crake?

[CRAKE *does not reply.*

No, but candidly, Crake—after a fellow's knocked about for a great many years as I have, there comes a time when he thinks "I'm having a jolly good time of it now, but who's going to nurse me and take care of me when I get into the sere and yellow leaf?" A man must look at it a little in that light.

[CRAKE *goes up a little.* SYBIL CRAKE *enters; an odd, elfin girl, about* 20, *lame, with crutches, very bright, sprightly, alert, she hops on, comes up to* GUISEBURY. GUISEBURY'S *manner towards her is protecting, something like a master to a favourite dog.*

*Guisebury.* Well, Midge, what have you been doing?

*Sybil.* Wishing I was a millionaire, or a bricklayer, or a horsewhip.

*Guisebury.* Why?

*Sybil.* If I were a millionaire, I could build that breakwater; if I were a bricklayer, I could help poor young Christison build it; if I were a horsewhip, I might whip all the people who brought you up, and between them spoiled a good man in the making.

*Crake.* [*Very reprovingly.*] Sybil! Sybil!

*Guisebury.* I've spoiled myself, Midge.

*Sybil.* [*Hops across to* REGY.] Mr. Slingsby, how are you?

*Regy.* I'm not very well.

*Sybil.* I've heard some good news about you.

*Regy.* Yes? She's rather a jolly girl, you know. Very good at repartee.

*Guisebury.* That's an awkward talent in a wife, Regy.

*Regy.* Look here, Guise, you needn't choke me off; I'm in for it now, and I'm going to try it! It may not suit me, but I'm going to try it!

*Guisebury.* Very well, Regy—try it! Come and dine with me on my yacht. We'll make it half-past eight to give you plenty of time.

*Regy.* All right. See you at dinner, Guise. [*Piteously.*] I knew I was putting my foot in it. [*Exit very despondent.*

*Guisebury.* Well, Crake, what's to be done with this confounded island?

*Crake.* Take your rents while you can, and then let the island pitch headforemost into the sea.

*Sybil.* And then let the people pitch headforemost into the sea after it.

*Crake.* The people must move off.

*Sybil.* But they love their homes—isn't it senseless of them?

*Crake.* My dear Sybil, this is a practical question.

*Sybil.* Yes, I've been talking with the fishermen's wives—they're horribly practical. What do you think? They want to keep a roof over their children.

*Guisebury.* Can't something be done, Crake?

*Crake.* Your Grace! I would prefer not to speak of your affairs. [*Glancing at* SYBIL.

*Guisebury.* Oh, Midge knows I'm a pauper. Go on.

*Crake.* This breakwater would cost fifty thousand pounds at least. Indeed you can't possibly raise the money.

*Sybil.* Oh, that needn't stand in your way—it never has.

*Enter* CAPTAIN *and* MRS. LEDDRA, Villagers, Tenants, *and* Children.

Here are some of your tenants coming to meeting. That's Captain Leddra and his wife. I wish you knew your tenants.

*Guisebury.* Introduce me.

*Sybil.* May I? Captain Leddra, Mrs. Leddra—here is the Duke of Guisebury come to pay you a visit. [*General surprise.*

*Leddra.* [*A bronzed seafarer.*] The Duke! [*Comes to* GUISEBURY.] You're welcome, your Grace! We've been looking out for you for the last dozen years or so. We thought you'd forgotten there was such a place as Endellion.

*Guisebury.* No. Captain Leddra—I've not forgotten Endellion, and if I can do anything for the island——

*Leddra.* If you've a mind to do anything for us, your Grace, you must be quick about it. We're at our wits' ends! The sea's washing us away!

[DAVID IVES *comes to door of house.*

*Crake.* But can't you find employment elsewhere?

*Leddra.* Oh, yes, Mr. Crake, there's plenty of employment at the North Pole.

*Crake.* The North Pole?

*Leddra.* We've been offered berths with this new Arctic Expedition that Captain Curvengen is fitting out at Plymouth. He sails next spring. It's a desperate venture, but we shall have to go.

*Sybil.* Yes, you'll leave all your bones at the North Pole, but there'll be two hundred pounds apiece for your widows. And you'll have snow for a shroud, and an iceberg for a hearse and white bears for undertakers—so there'll be no funeral expenses.

*Mrs. Leddra.* [*With a cry, clings to her husband.*] You shan't go, Steve—you shan't go!

*Leddra.* Let be, Hester. What's the use of staying here? I will go, I tell you, woman, unless—unless I happen to get killed first as Mark Christison was!

*Mrs. Leddra.* Hush!

MRS. CHRISTISON, *a white-haired old peasant woman comes on, very gentle, dreamy, absorbed.*

*Guisebury.* Who's this?

*Sybil.* Mark Christison's widow. She's mad! You needn't take any notice of her.

*Mrs. Christison.* [*To* DAVID.] Is there any news from Mark yet, David?

*David.* No, Rachel, there's no news yet.

*Mrs. Christison.* It's unkind of him not to write to me. [*Seeing* GUISEBURY.] A stranger gentleman! I beg your pardon, friend. Do you come from London? [GUISEBURY *nods.*] My husband Mark Christison has gone up there to ask the Duke to help him. Mark's left me for two years, and he never writes to me. I know he hasn't forgotten me, because when man and wife love as we loved, there's never any forgetting on either side of the grave.

*Sybil.* [*watching* GUISEBURY.] She's mad. You needn't take any notice of her.

*Guisebury.* I haven't met your husband, Mrs. Christison, but I believe he's well—quite well.

[*Takes her hand kindly with a soothing gesture.*

*Mrs. Christison.* Thank you, friend. The Duke may be keeping him in London. It's week-night meeting. I'm going to pray for him to come back.

[GUISEBURY *gives her his hand with great courtesy and leads her towards the meeting-house.*

I pray, and I pray, and I pray, but he never comes.

*Sybil.* You might say a good word for the Duke while

you're about it, Mrs. Christison. They tell me he needs it more than your husband.

*Mrs. Christison.* Yes, I'll say a good word for the Duke.

[*Exit into meeting-house.*

*Guisebury.* [*Sharply.*] Crake! [JOHN CHRISTISON *re-enters;* FAITH *and* DRUSILLA *come to cottage door.*] Send for an engineer from London, get him to prepare plans, and give me an estimate for a breakwater that will protect all the south-west coast of the island.

*Crake.* [*Deprecatingly.*] Your Grace—it's madness—it's impossible!

*Guisebury.* Yes, Crake, I know it's impossible, but it's going to be done. Captain Leddra, you and your friends may remain in the bosom of your families instead of trying to climb the legendary North Pole. I'm glad you have such excellent lungs. But you'd better save your shouts till the breakwater is built.

*John.* [*Comes eagerly forward.*] Your Grace, I want to thank you. My name's John Christison. I promised my father when he was dying that if you did nothing, I would build the breakwater with my own hands. Oh it's weary work! For as fast as we lay one stone upon the other, the tide and storm dash them to pieces. My courage is well-nigh spent, but if you will lend me some men and money, I'll begin again with a new heart, and please God, the work shall prosper in our hands. You'll help me, Duke—you'll help me?

*Guisebury.* Certainly, Mr. Christison. I shall be very glad of your advice and assistance. We will consider the building of this breakwater as our joint enterprise, and you shall be my overlooker at a salary of two hundred pounds a year.

*John.* Thank you, Duke. You do mean it! You'll go through with it?

*Guisebury.* I keep my word, Mr. Christison. It's a habit of mine, and I give you my word of honour I'll build that breakwater.

*John.* Forgive me, your Grace! I don't doubt you. I can't thank you. Ah! But I'll ask a blessing for you from the place that used to be my father's.

[*Goes quickly up to the meeting-house door.*

*Drusilla.* Shall I come with you, friend John?

*John.* [*Eagerly.*] Will you? If you would help me, I could work like a giant!

*Drusilla.* Perhaps I will. Come!

[*They go into meeting-house,* FAITH *watching them.*

*Faith.* [*Aside.*] She does not love him, yet she makes him love her.

[*Looks after them in the meeting-house, and goes in.*

*Mrs. Leddra.* My blessings on you too, your Grace. [*To her child.*] There, Stephen, look at him, and remember him all your life! He saved your father from going to his grave up there in the ice and snow! Yes, that you have! [*Hysterically.*] You've saved my husband's life.

*Guisebury.* [*Very much amused.*] Midge, I've *saved* a man's life!

*Sybil.* Why don't you save your own?

*Guisebury.* [*Turns to* MRS. LEDDRA, *who is sobbing.*] Come, my dear lady, bear up! If your husband's life is saved, you needn't indulge in this violent sorrow about it.

*Mrs. Leddra.* [*Unsuspectingly.*] Sorrow! Your Grace, I'm beside myself with joy! Oh, your Grace, I've had no peace since Steve threatened to go! I've had such dreams —oh, your Grace! May you never have such dreams as I've had!

*Guisebury.* I trust not! I trust not!

*Leddra.* [*She is sobbing on his shoulder.*] There! There! Hold your peace, Hester! Don't take any notice of her, your Grace. She can't help it! She's only a woman, and she's fond of me and the children—that's what makes her so foolish—she's fond of me—that's what it is. Your Grace—our best hearty thanks.

[*The people have gradually gone into the meeting-house.*

*Leddra.* [*Going into the meeting-house with* DAVID.] Well, David, what do you think of his Grace's promise?

*David.* His promise! [*Looks at* GUISEBURY.] Wait and see whether he keeps it!

[*All the people have gone into the meeting-house, leaving* GUISEBURY, CRAKE *and* SYBIL.

*Guisebury.* [*Watching the people going into the meeting-house.*] Poor devils! They take life very seriously!

*Sybil.* Three-fourths of the world do, that the other fourth may see what a splendid jest it is!

*Crake.* Duke, will you follow me into figures?

*Guisebury.* I'd rather not—anywhere but there, Crake. Arithmetic is so relentless.

*Crake.* Your Grace, excuse my putting it plainly—if you build this breakwater, you'll beggar yourself.

*Guisebury.* My good Crake, what is a landlord for, except to beggar himself for his tenants? I know my duty, Crake. I very rarely *do* it but I yield to no man in *knowing* it!

*Crake.* Will you tell me how the money is to be raised?

*Guisebury.* That's what I want you to do. You shall have a bottle of my grandfather's port at dinner to-night, and then *you* shall tell *me* how it is to be raised. Go and take another look at the place, and see what this young Christison has been doing.

[SYBIL, *who has been up stage, hops down to* GUISEBURY.

*Crake.* [*Going off.*] If I'd been wise I should have left him ten years ago, but I suppose I shall be fool enough to stay till the smash comes. [*Exit.*

*Sybil.* I want to ask you a question.

*Guisebury.* Well?

*Sybil* Why are you such a hypocrite?

*Guisebury.* Am I a hypocrite?

*Sybil.* Yes. You pretend to be a great deal worse than you are.

*Guisebury.* Most people pretend to be a great deal better than they are, so somebody must restore the moral balance. But you don't know what a bad fellow I am, Midge.

*Sybil.* Yes, I do. You *are* bad—but you aren't half so bad as you think you are. I've found you out in lots of good deeds, and you always do them and seem ashamed of them. You're kind; you're truthful; you don't slander anybody—except yourself—and you are brave.

*Guisebury*. Brave—am I?

*Sybil*. If you hadn't been brave you wouldn't have rushed in and picked me from under the horses' feet ten years ago—You would have let them trample me to death instead of only laming me for life, and curdling my wits.

*Guisebury*. They were my horses, and it was my infernal groom that put you behind them. I couldn't stop myself—it was mere impulse—and sometimes I've asked myself whether it was a kindness to save you.

[*Looking at her crutches.*

*Sybil*. What does it matter? I don't mind it. At least, so long as people don't pity me. At first I used to lie all night and beat my fists against the wall in agony—But now——

*Guisebury*. Now?

*Sybil*. Now I've found out that the world was not constructed for the sole purpose of making me happy. And besides, perhaps some day I shall pull *you* out from under the horses' feet.

*Guisebury*. What horses?

*Sybil*. Don't you know? Can't you see where you are driving?

*Guisebury*. No.

*Sybil*. Why not pull up?

*Guisebury*. I can't Midge. I've got my life into a horrible mess, and it's too much bother to get it straight now.

*Sybil*. Doesn't your conscience plague you sometimes?

*Guisebury*. No. I suppose I've got a conscience, but it's rusty—the works have stopped. What does it matter? The world wasn't constructed for the sole purpose of making me good.

*Sybil*. Suppose life should be serious after all!

*Guisebury*. My dear Midge, don't preach at me!

*Sybil*. I won't; preaching won't tame wild horses. [*Hops up the cliff.*] I'll wait till they're trampling you under their feet. [*Exit.*

*Guisebury*. [*Looks after her, turns round, fills pipe.*] Suppose life should be serious after all! What a jest it would be!

[Drusilla *creeps out of meeting-house.*

*Drusilla.* Guisebury!

*Guisebury.* What mischief now?

*Drusilla.* Catch me!

*Guisebury.* Come then!

[*She jumps into his arms.*

*Drusilla.* Oh, I'm so glad you've come! I've had three awful weeks! These people are so good, and so stupid! They'll kill me! I'm simply dying of goodness. Two more ounces of goodness, and I'm dead!

*Guisebury.* Don't be alarmed!

*Drusilla.* You'll catch it! It's in the air. The long faces they pull, the dresses they wear, the way they talk, the books they read—oh, so good, oh, so stupid! And the things they think sinful! Living is sinful! Loving is sinful! Breathing is sinful! Eating and drinking are sinful! Flowers are sinful! Everything is sinful! Oh, so good! Oh, so stupid! And the time they give to their prayers, and their harmoniums! There's an epidemic of harmoniums! And the way they spend their Sundays! Oh, so good! Oh, so stupid! How's everything and everybody in London? What have you been doing with yourself? Have you missed me? Have you brought my dear old Bully Boy?

*Guisebury.* Yes, I've brought the dog. He's fond of me.

*Drusilla.* Guisebury—what's the matter with you?

*Guisebury.* Nothing. Tell me what *you've* been doing with *yourself*.

*Drusilla.* Going to meeting; pulling a long face; chaffing my father and sister up my sleeve; wondering how on earth they came to be my father and sister; boring myself; sighing a little for you—not much, and making that boy John Christison fall madly in love with me.

*Guisebury.* You shouldn't do that.

*Drusilla.* Shouldn't make people fall in love with me? Oh, I must.

*Guisebury.* You should remember——

*Drusilla.* What?

*Guisebury.* [*with much quiet tenderness.*] How deeply I'm attached to you.

*Drusilla.* So's John Christison! And he can make love—in his way. You can't make love as he does.

*Guisebury.* The devil take John Christison!

*Drusilla.* Ah, you're jealous! You needn't be! But are you attached to me, Guisbury?

*Guisebury.* Am I attached to you? I met you, Di, when I was thirty. If you'd been another sort of woman, Di, I should have been another sort of man. I wonder what my life would have been without you?

*Drusilla.* Very dull. You've bought me that yacht?

*Guisebury.* Yes. Have you ever had a wish, a caprice that I haven't gratified? Haven't I done every mad thing that you asked me?

*Drusilla.* [*She is putting flower in his coat.*] Suppose for once I asked you to do something sensible?

*Guisebury.* Well?

*Drusilla.* [*After a pause, drops her eyes, then glances up at him furtively*] I read in one of the weekly papers that I am to be the Duchess of Guisebury.

*Guisebury.* [*Startled.*] My dear Di, don't be absurd!

*Drusilla.* I read it in the paper, Guisebury. Why is it absurd? I've been thoroughly educated. I've been asked to several very good houses. And then my family—sound Quaker stock on both sides for two hundred years—you couldn't have better breeding than that! And no cosmetics but the sea and wind! Guisebury, I could play the part to perfection!

*Guisebury.* My dear child, don't ask for the one thing I cannot give you.

*Drusilla.* You won't? Very well. [*Bites her lip.*] Heigho!

[GUISEBURY *stands, looking glum and thoughtful.*

What's the matter with you? What makes you so serious?

*Guisebury.* Suppose life should be serious after all!

*Drusilla.* Don't suppose anything so dreadful. They'll be coming out of meeting soon. [*Creeps up to meeting-house door, looks in.*] Oh the Captain is preaching! That means forty minutes at least! And on such a lovely moonlight night too!

[JOHN *creeps stealthily out of the meeting-house door and hides behind a shrub.*

I've been practising a new dance, a shadow dance. Shall I show you?

[DRUSILLA *carefully looks all round, takes up her skirts, gives one or two turns, and catches sight of* JOHN'S *face watching her through the shrubs, stops suddenly.*

*John.* [*Advancing.*] Woman! What art thou?!

CURTAIN.

[*Two years between Act* 1 *and* 2.]

## ACT II

### THE BROKEN BOWL.

[DIANA VALROSE'S *boudoir at Richmond. A very elegantly furnished room, with light, pretty furniture. Discover* DRUSILLA *in handsome morning dress arranging flowers in large china bowl. Enter* Footman, *announcing* MR. CHRISTISON. *Enter* JOHN. *Exit* Footman

*Drusilla.* Well, friend John!

*John.* Your father and Faith are in London.

*Drusilla.* I know—they've written to me.

*John.* They're searching everywhere for you. I've been with them the last three days pretending to help them find you, throwing them off your track—deceiving them, lying at every step.

*Drusilla.* How kind and thoughtful of you!

*John.* Kind and thoughtful!

*Drusilla.* To me and to them It would pain them to know the truth about me. My father and sister do not understand me.

*John.* Who does understand you? I don't. What made you bring me up to London? Why have you kept me here for nearly two years—feeding me with false hopes and promises—making me eat the bread of idleness and deceit, till there isn't a sound place in me? Why have you done it? Why?—You do not love me!

*Drusilla.* [*Very seductive.*] How do you know that I do not love you, friend John?

*John.* Love me! Oh, it would be horrible! It would be past grace and mercy for you and me to love each other after—this. [*Looking round the room.*] After all—after what I know of you. And yet——

[*Coming up to her, fiercely seizing her hands.*

Do you love me?

*Drusilla.* You've never gone the right way to make me love you. I like you—when you're not in one of these moral fits. When you're moral, you're dull and tiresome, friend John! You are really. Why don't you take things more quietly? What harm has been done?

*John.* What harm? How have I passed my time since I left Endellion?

*Drusilla.* You came to London to superintend the plans for the breakwater, and the Duke appointed you overlooker at two hundred a year.

*John.* I've taken the money, and I've not done one hour's work for it. I've lied to my dead father! I've broken my promise to him!

*Drusilla.* You mean you haven't kept it at present. There's plenty of time.

*John.* Yes—there's plenty of time to repent—hereafter!

*Drusilla.* Friend John, you are very foolish—why should you trouble yourself? Tell me about my father and Faith.

*John.* They are terribly distressed because they cannot find you. Your father seems broken-hearted.

*Drusilla.* Why couldn't they stay at Endellion! The climate and the meeting-house suited them so well!

[*Comes up to him, puts her hand on his shoulder, caressingly.*

Friend John, I want you to do me a little favour.

*John.* What?

*Drusilla.* Persuade them there has been some mistake, and get them quietly back to Endellion. When they are at home I'll write and explain everything to my father. I'll find some good excuse.—He'll believe me! For the sake of old times, John. It will be kind to spare them anxiety about me. I'm really not so bad as you think me—I'm really not indeed—will you, John?

*John.* You know I shall do whatever you ask me!

*Drusilla.* Thank you, friend John.

[GUISEBURY *passes the window.*

Here's the Duke!

*John.* I want to see him.

*Drusilla.* Very well, I'll leave you to him. And, John, you'll tell them some pretty little fairy tale, and get them comfortably off home, eh?

*John.* Yes. I'll keep up the lies now I've begun them. Oh, I'm lost anyhow.

*Drusilla.* Yes, friend John, we are lost! But never mind—we shall be in very good company! [*Exit.*

*John.* If I could break off your chains! If I could!

*Enter* GUISEBURY.

*Guisebury.* Ah, Mr. Christison!

*John.* Your Grace, I wish to speak about the salary you've allowed me.

*Guisebury.* The last quarter hasn't been paid.

*John.* I don't want your money. I'm sorry I took it.

*Guisebury.* Why?

*John.* I've not earned it.

*Guisebury.* That's a very absurd reason for not taking it, Mr. Christison. However, I'll respect your scruples. You needn't be under any further apprehension about being paid. Is there anything else?

*John.* Yes! Two years ago you spoke of beginning the breakwater at Endellion, and I was to work under you and for you. There's not a stone been laid since. I don't understand your feelings—but I know what my own are every night as I lay my head upon my pillow and think, "Another day gone, and I've done nothing to redeem my promise." I thought perhaps your feelings might be something like mine.

*Guisebury.* [*Touched*] You're right, Mr. Christison! I've allowed two years to go by, and I've done nothing to keep my word! You're right! And I've sacrificed those men's lives!

*John.* Are you sure they've perished?

*Guisebury.* They've given up all hope at the Admiralty. You've nothing more to say, Mr. Christison?

*John*. No, Duke. As soon as I am able, I shall go back to Endellion and get on with the work as well as I can. I shan't trouble your Grace any further about it.

*Guisebury*. Very well, Mr. Christison. [*Rings bell.*

*John*. Your Grace, David Ives is in London.

*Guisebury*. Indeed! [*Exit* JOHN.

[GUISEBURY *alone, takes several turns about the room, his walk, mien and gesture indicate supreme self-contempt, his eyes on floor, bites his thumb, kicks the footstool savagely, sits on sofa; finds the cushion uncomfortable, pitches it about, reclines again, finds it still more uncomfortable, pitches it the other end of the room and breaks an old China bowl which drops in pieces and falls on floor.*

I suppose there is some poor devil somewhere that's in a worse all-round mess than I am! But if there is, I should like to shake hands with him, and ask him how he feels.

[*Gets up savagely, walks across the room, walks into back room, looks out of window.*

Hillo, Bully Boy—what is it, old chap?

[*Opens the French window; admits a ferocious looking, ugly bulldog.*

Come in, old boy! Sit up there! I like you, Bully Boy! There's a splendid absence of all moral squeamishness about that ugly old mug of yours! Birds of a feather, eh, old boy? I'm a bad lot, but you don't mind that, do you? [*Caressing the dog.*] You love me, don't you, as much as if I were a paragon pattern of all the virtues. I'm in a devilish scrape, Bully Boy! I've come nearly to the end of my tether! I broke my word to those poor beggars! I let them join that cursed Arctic Expedition, and there they are, up there, making a cold supper for the Polar bears! How would you feel, Bully Boy, if you had sent a dozen poor beggars to Kingdom Come? You wouldn't mind, would you? And why should I? I've ruined myself for her, Bully Boy, and now she's growing tired of me!

Strange, isn't it! A few shillings will buy a faithful dog, but all the money in the world won't buy a faithful woman!

[*Enter* Servant *announcing* MR. SLINGSBY. REGY. *enters.* Servant *then goes up and takes the dog.*

*Guisebury.* Well Regy, this is a surprise!

*Regy.* Yes. They told me you called the other day, but I wasn't at home, so as I was driving by to-day I thought I'd give you a look up.

*Guisebury.* Thanks. [*To* Servant, *who is going off with dog.*] Where are you taking that dog?

*Servant.* I beg pardon, your Grace, Miss Valrose said he was to be sent up to town.

*Guisebury.* Oh, very well, I'll take him back to town with me to-night. Poor Bully Boy! She's getting tired of you too, is she?

[*Exit* Servant *with Dog.*

*Regy.* Well, Guisebury, what have you been doing with yourself all the while?

*Guisebury.* Playing the fool, and scandalizing society.

*Regy.* Did you see that article in yesterday's *Trafalgar Square Gazette* on "The decline of our Aristocracy?" They did give it you hot.

*Guisebury.* Ah! I met the editor a few months ago, and he assured me that when he writes about the blackguard Duke our differences are—like Satan and Michael's—merely political! What did the article say of me?

*Regy.* That the spectacle of your career has hastened the downfall of the House of Lords by twenty years.

*Guisebury.* Well. What more do the Radicals want? And yet they've never given me a testimonial! What have you been doing with yourself, Regy?

*Regy.* [*Very solemnly.*] Guisebury—I tell you this—things are coming to a crisis.

*Guisebury.* Yes, Regy. I've lived in one chronic crisis ever since I left Eton! Why don't you ask her to name the day, and get it all over?

*Regy.* Not if I know it. While there's life there's hope—and Lady Poperoach—

[*With a mysterious, threatening manner.*

had better not drive me to bay! That's my candid advice to Lady Poperoach—"Don't drive me to bay!"

*Guisebury.* What should you do, Regy?

*Regy.* Well, don't let Lady Poperoach drive me to bay, that's all!—Guisebury, if I ask you a plain, straightforward question, will you give me a plain, straightforward answer?

*Guisebury.* Rely on me, Regy.

*Regy.* Will you tell me what the devil I wanted to go and tie myself up to Isabel Poperoach for? That's what I want to know. I'd everything I wanted—nicest little bachelor's quarters in London, nobody to bully-rag me, or order me about—What did I do it for?

*Guisebury.* Well, why did you?

*Regy.* Because I was a silly fool—that's why! There's no other reason.

*Guisebury.* Well—that seems sufficient.

*Regy.* [*Continuing, taking no notice of* GUISEBURY.] Some people want to get married—very well, let them! Let them go in and get married forty times over! I don't interfere with them! Why should I be dragged like a victim to the slaughter?

*Guisebury.* Just so, Regy—why should you?

*Regy.* It's hard lines on a fellow, isn't it, Guisebury? It's devilish hard lines! What would you advise me to do?

*Guisebury.* I should get married.

*Regy.* [*Disgusted.*] Get married! Oh, hang it all, Guisebury—I didn't expect this from you! No, candidly, what would you advise me to do? Eh?

*Guisebury.* [*Yawns.*] I should not get married.

*Regy.* [*Shakes hands with him.*] Thank you old fellow, thank you. I knew I might rely on you. But. I say—how am I to get out of it, eh?

*Guisebury.* That's it, Regy! How are we to get out of it?

*Regy.* You! You haven't been and landed yourself!

*Guisebury.* Yes, in no end of a mess! Debts, difficulties, duns, unfulfilled engagements everywhere—all the Danecourt property under water with these floods—no rents—no money——no self-respect—no nothing!

*Regy*. [*Cheerfully*.] Poor old Guisebury! I'm awfully sorry for you, I am indeed. But—I say, Guisebury, what am I to do?

*Guisebury*. Why not marry her? It couldn't be worse than the life we've lived for the last fifteen years! The other Saturday night I sat in that big house of mine alone till I felt that if I stayed five minutes longer I should get out my pistols and blow my brains out. Well, I went out, and I got amongst some people marketing—I watched some little cad and his wife buying their Sunday's dinner with four squalling snub-nosed brats hanging round them! He was happy—that little cad! I wonder what grudge Providence had against me to give me a title and thirty thousand a year, instead of making me a greasy little cad like that!

*Regy*. [*Supremely occupied with his own concerns*. What I ask myself is this—what's the object of my getting married? That's what I want to know! Where does the joke come in? What shall I have to show for it?

*Guisebury*. What have we both got to show for it as it is? That little cad had his wife and children's love, and his shoulder of mutton and his onions. And he *was happy!*

*Regy*. Happy be hanged! All women are alike!

*Guisebury*. That's the last cursed word of cynicism. All women are alike. And the devil of it is—it's true! That is it's true for such men as you and I. [*With a chuckle*.] My God, Regy, what a farce of a world it is!

*Regy*. It is, old boy. But I stick to my Goschens—oh dear, yes! I've got a nice little fifteen thousand a year, dear old fellow—just keeps me going. But I say, old fellow, what's the matter with you?

*Guisebury*. Everything. Crake has left me. She's tired of me. And those poor beggars who went with that fool Curgenven to find the North Pole—they're lost, Regy!

*Regy*. Well, what the devil could they expect? Suppose they do find the North Pole—what the deuce is the good of it? It's no business of yours.

*Guisebury*. I never missed a night's sleep in my life till lately. Now, every night, just as I'm falling off, my heart gives a kind of a start. Perhaps I doze off again for a few minutes. Another start—and then I'm wide awake and going through every detail of the Arctic Expedition. Up to 83 North, going all through the plans of the Endellion breakwater—and there I lie, hour after hour, night after night, just the same! And when at last I drop off, they're at me again—thousands and thousands of poor lank, starved wretches with their faces grey and pinched like corpses; and their limbs dropping off with grangrene and frostbite, hanging over me in my sleep.

*Regy.* Put on your hat, dear old boy, and go to a doctor.

*Guisebury.* I've been. Gave me sleeping draughts. Chloral, opium—I took them—tumbler fulls of them. No good. Ordered me abroad. I went. No good. I've tried drink. I've tried everything. It's no good, Regy my boy. My heart, or my liver, or my conscience, or some damned thing inside of me is all wrong, and I don't know how the devil to get it right!

*Regy.* [*Looks at him half critically, half compassionately.*] Let me tell you this, my dear old Guisebury—you'd better take care of yourself. You're in a bad way.

*Guisebury.* I know I am. I never bothered myself about duty and conscience and all that grandmother's stuff, but I'm damned, Regy, if I don't begin to think there's something in it after all!

*Regy.* [*Cheerfully.*] Wish I could help you, dear old fellow—upon my word I do. If there's anything I can do for you——

*Guisebury.* You know, Regy, there are really a great many natural resources in Endellion, and if any thorough, good-hearted fellow would advance the money, and would take a small risk, I believe the thing would pay itself back in a few years. I want to keep my word, Regy! It would make a new man of me. I wouldn't take a shilling for myself. It's for those poor beggars. You don't happen to know any thorough good fellow who would put his hand in his pocket, eh?

*Regy.* Oh, I'd do it myself for you with pleasure, dear old fellow, but when I said just now fifteen thousand a year I didn't mean fifteen thousand clear. The fact is, when the charges on the estate are paid, it's not much over six, and I've got so many calls. In fact my life's nothing but one eternal monotonous fork out, fork out, fork out!

*Enter* Servant, *announcing* Mr. *and* Miss Crake; *enter* Crake *and* Sybil. Regy *takes out his watch suddenly.*

*Regy.* By Jove! I had to be back in Piccadilly at five! Ta, ta, old fellow, ta, ta! If I can be of any use to you, you let me know. [*To* Crake *and* Sybil *as he passes them.*] How d'ye do? How d'ye do? [*Exit very hurriedly.*

*Crake.* You received my note, your Grace?

*Guisebury.* Yes, Crake. [*Shakes hands.*] Ah, Midge, you haven't forsaken me, then?

*Sybil.* No, I always come to your funerals. I followed your character when it went to its early grave; and when you broke your word and buried your self-respect—[Guisebury *winces.*]—I was the chief mourner. To-day we are going to bid farewell to the remains of your fortune, and when the little that is left of you goes to its last home, I'm sure I shall be following.

*Guisebury.* But don't shed one tear over me, Midge—I'm not worth it. [*Taking her hand.*

*Sybil.* No. [*Looking at bowl.*] You've had a smash here!

[*Goes up to the broken china bowl, picks up the pieces and is all through the interview trying to put them together.*

*Guisebury.* [*In a sharp quick tone.*] Now, Crake, let's get this over.

*Crake.* Your Grace, I don't want to prolong it. It's a bitter day for me. [*Takes out bunch of keys.*] There's the strong room, that's the jewels, those are the deed boxes at the Bank. I've been through everything with the new steward. I hope your Grace doesn't blame me?

*Guisebury.* No, Crake.

*Crake.* I advised your Grace for the best.

*Guisebury.* You did, Crake.

*Crake.* There's nothing else, your Grace?

*Guisebury.* Nothing. I've already thanked you for your faithful service. I wish I had deserved it better. [*Giving hand.*]

*Crake.* [*Moved.*] Don't say any more, your Grace.

[*The two men stand with hands clasped for some moments.* CRAKE *speaks with great feeling, very low tone of voice.*

Good day, your Grace.

*Guisebury.* Good-bye, Crake.

[*Shakes hands very cordially.*

*Crake.* Come, Sybil.

[*Leaves the room hurriedly, much affected.* GUISEBURY *stands despondent.*

*Sybil.* [*Occupied with the vase.*] Yes—it's smashed all to pieces; but you can put it together again.

*Guisebury.* What?

*Sybil.* This bowl.

[*Leaves it, hops down to him.*] And your life. [GUISEBURY *shrugs his shoulders, shakes his head sadly.*

Yes! Look! Of course it will never be the same again, but it will hold together. Oh, why don't you pick up the pieces?

*Guisebury.* Too late!

*Sybil.* No! Try—try—Pick up the pieces!

*Guisebury.* You'll come and see me again, Midge?

*Sybil.* Yes, when you are right under the horses' hoofs.

[*Exit after* CRAKE. GUISEBURY *goes up to the table where she had been playing with the pieces, puts the bowl together.*

*Guisebury.* Yes, the pieces will join, but the bowl is broken.

*Enter* SERVANT

*Servant.* Your Grace, there are two people in the hall asking to see you. The man says his name is David Ives.

*Guisebury.* [*Showing slight surprise.*] Show them in here and—[*with meaning to the* SERVANT]—When they are here, find Miss Valrose and tell her that Mr. David Ives is with me here. [*Exit* SERVANT] David Ives! What brings him here? Can he know?

*Re-enter* SERVANT *announcing* MR. IVES, DAVID *enters followed by* FAITH. *They look round the room with great curiosity.*

*David.* You remember me?

*Guisebury.* Perfectly, Mr. Ives. The last time I saw you, you reminded me that my neglect had lost a man's life.

*David.* Now it has lost another. More than two years ago you brought John Christison up to London. You've kept him idling here ever since. When shall you have done with him?

[DRUSILLA *very cautiously appears at back and stands behind the curtains,* JOHN *follows her, peeping over her shoulders.*

*Guisebury.* I've done with him now.

*David.* Then pay him his wages and let him go. I don't understand the lad. He seems lost and dazed. I can't get him back to Endellion with me. What's the reason?

*Guisebury.* Am I his keeper? I believe Mr. Christison intends leaving London. He is free to do so. He is his own master.

*David.* No. There's somebody up here in London who's got the mastery over John Christison, and an evil mastery it is! Who is it?

*Guisebury.* It's not I, Mr. Ives.

*David.* Who is it?

*Guisebury.* It must be one of the other five million Londoners. You had better ask him yourself.

*David.* I will! You've changed the lad's nature. You've made him like yourself.

*Guisebury.* You flatter me! How?

*David.* He's a promise-breaker.

[GUISEBURY *winces;* JOHN'S *face shows through the curtain, full of pain and shame.*

But when the sea rakes his dead father out of his resting place, as it will before long, perhaps John Christison will remember the promise he gave, and come back to Endellion and fulfill it. [JOHN'S *face withdraws.*
That's all I have to say to you. [*Curtly, going.*] Good morning. Come, Faith.

*Faith.* Good morning, your Grace. My father is not quite himself to-day. We've been beside ourselves with grief the last few days. We cannot get any news of my sister

Drusilla. She is not at the place where her letters are sent. We fear some mischief has happened to her.

*Guisebury.* I'm sorry—I hope your fears are groundless.

*David.* [*To* GUISEBURY.] What business is it of yours what has become of my child?

*Guisebury.* Wait here a few minutes. I may have some news that will surprise you——

[*Exit* GUISEBURY, *the moment he has left* JOHN *comes forward from behind the curtains.*

*John.* David, I've heard all you said. There was someone in London who had a mastery over me, and an evil mastery it was. But I'll break it—I'll go back to Endellion this very night.

*David.* You will? Ah, that's the John Christison I knew! That's the lad his father and I brought up after our own hearts. The lad I would have given my Drusilla to for wife!

*John.* Don't say any more. Wait till I've proved myself. We'll get away from this place. You've nothing more to do here?

*Faith.* He asked us to wait till he returned.

*John.* You'll see him to-morrow. Don't stay here. Go! You and Faith—wait a little while along the road for me—I'll come to you soon. I entreat you, don't stay.

*Faith.* You won't fail us? You'll come to us?

*John.* Yes. I have one thing to do here first—when that is done I shall be my own master. Don't ask me any more—go!

*David.* Come, Faith. [*Exit* DAVID.

*Faith.* Oh, you have made our hearts rejoice. Now if we could but find Drusilla, and take her home with us—then all would be well.

[JOHN *almost pushes* FAITH *off at door, shuts it, turns round;* DRUSILLA *enters from between the curtains from other room.*

*Drusilla.* That was splendidly done, friend John. Now you will get them home to-night, and I'll write a letter and explain. I think I have imagination enough for that!

[*She goes up to window; looks out.*

They've gone! [*Shows relief.*] It's really a shame to fib to them, but what can one do?

[JOHN *has stood stern and fixed, nerving himself.*

*John.* [*Calm, stern, strong.*] Listen to me! I depart from London to-night for Endellion, and as I live, I will never return to you. Perhaps I shall never see you again!

*Drusilla.* Friend John! [*Approaching him.*]

*John.* [*Repulsing her.*] Whether your father and sister will come with me I cannot tell. But they will surely come back to Endellion before many days. You know what I have done, how I have lied to them and deceived them to keep them from knowing the truth about you. From this time forth I have done with lies! I will not betray you. If they ask me of you, I will keep silent. Not one word good or bad will I speak of you. From this day it shall be to me as though you were dead!

[*Going.* DRUSILLA *throws her arms around him.*

*Drusilla.* And you said you loved me! Who spoke a lie then?

*John.* I *did* love you.

*Drusilla.* And you love me still! You do! You do! You love me now!

*John.* I—no—I—I do not love you! I will not love you!

[*Trying to take her arms from him.*

*Drusilla.* You do! You shall! Come, you will do as I wish, friend John. I cannot tell you what a strange sweet feeling has been growing in my heart. [*Drawing him away from door.*] I think I am beginning to love you at last, a little. I must have you near me—because I know you are true as steel—John, you won't go to Endellion—you'll get rid of them to-night and come back to me to-morrow? Yes, friend John——

*John.* [*After a struggle.*] I cannot! I dare not! Let me go!

[*Tearing himself away from her.*

*Drusilla.* You shall not go! You shall not! If you should leave me—I—don't know what will become of me! Perhaps I shall kill myself! I don't care what becomes of me! It will be your work! I love you, John, and you can do as you please with me! Who knows? You might make me a good woman! Won't you try? I could do anything for you! Ask me anything in the world—I'll do it!

*John.* Do you mean that? Then leave this house now forever. Come back to your home with your father and sister and me. Live the rest of your life so that I may forget what you have been. I will help you and be as your own brother. Will you do that?

*Drusilla.* No—it's impossible! I hate Endellion—I must live in London! Oh, you are tiresome—you want to go—very well! Go! Go! Go! There is the door. I hate you! I hate you! And I had begun to love you—Go!

*John.* [*Tortured*]. Drusilla!

*Drusilla.* Leave me! You do not love me!

*John.* I do not love you? Do I not? Ask me anything—see if I will not do it!

*Drusilla.* Stay in London. I like you to be near me—and perhaps some day I will reward you as you never hoped for. Who knows? Perhaps some day I will give you myself!

*John.* [*Fiercely*] Ah, do you think I would take you? Do you think it means nothing what we were taught! That you can give yourself first to him and then to me! Oh, when I knew of it, I thought I would kill him—and many times I've been near doing it! Very well—give yourself to me! I'll take you! But let me kill him first—and then come to me and let us kill ourselves together. Will you do that? Will you do that? Do you love me enough for that?

*Drusilla.* You're mad! Come, be sensible,—you won't go, John—I must have you for my friend. You'll stay with me?

*John.* [*Has recovered his calmness.*] No—I leave here to-night. I have said it and I'll keep my word.

*Drusilla.* You do not love me! You do not love me!

*John.* I do not love you! Tear out this heart of mine and see! What do you want of the man that loves you? His life? You can have mine. I'd suffer anything—I'd dare anything—I'd be your bondslave and pay your penalty—I'd give myself for years beyond number to make you fit to be loved at the last! Take all my strength, my hopes, my worldly comfort, every drop of joy that my tongue shall ever taste—That's nothing—all is nothing! All is less than dust! Set any price upon yourself! I'll pay it! I'll give you all—all—save only my word, my faith, my duty, my soul! I will not pay them for you! Not them! Not them! No! No! No!

[*Rushes off wildly. Drusilla sits crying, looks up from her tears, flings her handkerchief on the ground, goes to door, calls* "JOHN!" *rushes up to back, meets* GUISEBURY *who enters.*]

*Guisebury.* [*Very calmly*]. What is it?

*Drusilla.* [*Controls herself.*] Nothing.

*Guisebury.* Where are you going in such a hurry?

*Drusilla.* Nowhere.

*Guisebury.* Di! Di! I have something to say to you. I've been looking for you all over the grounds. Where are your father and sister?

*Drusilla.* Gone.

*Guisebury.* Perhaps it's better. I shall see your father to-morrow, and can speak to him then. Di, will you give me a few moments? You'll be pleased to hear what I have to say.

*Drusilla.* If it's short and sweet I shall.

*Guisebury.* I think it will be sweet. I'll make it short.

[*Goes to her with great tenderness.*

I wish you to do me the honour of becoming my wife.

*Drusilla.* What? What? Say it again!

*Guisebury.* I offer you my hand. Will you be my wife?

*Drusilla.* You don't mean it?

*Guisebury.* Indeed I do. I don't profess to be a pattern, but I don't want to sink any lower than I am! I know my love isn't worth much, but such as it is you have it all. I'm fond of you, Di! You've always been able to twist me round your finger. You can't say that I haven't valued very highly the privilege of being ruined by you.

*Drusilla.* It's been very pleasant, hasn't it?

*Guisebury.* Delightful while it lasted. Only——

*Drusilla.* Only——

*Guisebury.* I'm ruined!

*Drusilla.* Yes, and when a man's ruined, it's time for him to turn over a new leaf.

*Guisebury.* Yes. My only reason for turning over a new leaf is that I feel wretched and contemptible as I am. Di—I'm in your hands. We've wasted our lives——

*Drusilla.* Excuse me, Val—I'm not twenty-five. I've only wasted part of mine at present.

*Guisebury.* Don't waste the other part, and don't let me waste what is left of mine. I daresay everybody will cut us—most respectable people have cut me for the last five years—but we'll hold on to each other. We'll be married quietly, and go into some quiet little continental place—[*Approaching her very tenderly.*]

*Drusilla.* No—Val—we will not.

*Guisebury.* Well, we'll live where you please. I can't provide for you in the style you are used to. We must cut down everything. But you're welcome to all I have. Di, you'll stick to me now? Mine's a broken life, but I want to pick up the pieces. You'll help me? You'll be my wife?

*Drusilla.* My dear Val, don't ask me for the one thing I cannot give you.

*Guisebury.* You don't mean it, Di! I know I've knocked about the old title and tarnished it, but I'll polish it up as well as I can now you are going to wear it.

*Drusilla.* No, Val. I'm really sensible of the honour you have done me, but I must decline. I must indeed.

*Guisebury.* Don't throw me over, Di. If you do, I don't know what will become of me. I've been thoroughly shaken the last few months—I'm as weak as a child, and I want somebody to cling to. You're the only woman who has ever had what I've got in the way of a heart—you have it still—Di, we've thrown away our best chances of happiness—let's save what we can from the wreck.

*Drusilla.* No, my dear Val—no, no, no!

*Guisebury.* You refuse me?

*Drusilla.* I refuse you. To live cheaply in a little continental town, my dear Val, it would be purgatory! I must have my London, my Paris, my theatre, my dancing, my public to worship me.

*Guisebury.* [*Greatly hurt and piqued.*] You refuse me?

*Drusilla.* Yes. We've had our cake and eaten it—Now

the feast is over, and there's nothing to do but to say good-bye and part friends. Good-bye.

*Guisebury.* No, Di. The feast is not over. We won't say good-bye.

*Drusilla.* You won't say good-bye?

*Guisebury.* Not now—we will say good-bye—but not now!

[DRUSILLA *shrugs shoulders and exit.* GUISEBURY *bursts into a very bitter laugh; stands silent for some moments, then bursts into a little mocking laugh.*

This world has given me a few good kicks—I've had just enough of it. I'll give this world one good kick back, and then I'll get out of it!

CURTAIN.

*Six months pass between Acts 2 and 3.*

## ACT III

SCENE.—*Hall and Staircase at the Duke of Guisebury's, Guisebury House, Saint-James's Square. The wide handsome staircase takes up the centre of stage and leads to a gallery which runs along the top, and ends in doors on the right and left.*

## ACT III

### *The Last Feast*

*Discover* Footman, *Enter* GOLDSPINK.

*Goldspink.* Dinner over, Charles?

*Footman.* I've left them at dessert. They're going to have coffee here.

*Goldspink.* This is a rummy go, Charles! He's had a few rummy goes in his time—in fact I should say his whole life has been a series of rummy goes—but this is the rummiest of all!

*Footman.* Where's he going?

*Goldspink.* He hasn't taken any passage for anywhere, he hasn't made any enquiries about any vessels, or shown any interest in foreign countries. And yet he's on the hop somewhere—and shortly.

*Footman.* He's been in tremendous spirits all through dinner. Such raillery, Mr. Goldspink! Such delicate persiflage! It's been quite a feast of wit!

*Goldspink.* I don't understand Guisebury lately. He's never had any scerets from me! Never troubled to lock up his letters, or any meannesses of that sort. But this last week he's puzzled me, Charles!

*Footman.* There's something curious about this little tête-à-tête dinner with her, and the big reception afterwards.

*Goldspink.* Just so! There's more in it, Charles, than meets the eye! I don't know what the dénōuement will be—but you mark my words, Charles, there will be a dénōuement of some kind or the other.

*Footman.* He's give Martin orders to have out all the 68 Château Lafitte and the 74 P—J—for the reception to-night. Fancy turning all them blessed old dowagers on to 68 Lafitte. It's disgusting!

*Goldspink.* Guisebury always was a damned fool with his wine and his money! But I ain't the one to shy stones at him for that! He's chucked enough about for me to be the owner of six houses in Gladstone Terrace, Freetrade Road, Peckham.

*Enter* GUISEBURY.

*Guisebury.* I'm glad to hear it, Goldspink! You might perhaps have invested my money in something less extremely radical.

*Goldspink.* Your Grace—if you'll pardon my saying so—my political convictions are exactly the same as your Grace's. And I'll try to get the name of the terrace altered.

*Guisebury.* I wouldn't, Goldspink. I've no doubt it's admirably descriptive. And I don't propose to take the least interest in English politics for the future. Lady Bawtry has not come yet?

*Footman.* No, your Grace. Her Ladyship said she should be here at five minutes to twelve. [*Exit.*

*Guisebury.* Did you get my sleeping draught made up?

*Goldspink.* Yes your Grace. It's in your bedroom. [*Exit.*

*Enter* DRUSILLA.

*Drusilla.* Well?

*Guisebury.* Well?

*Drusilla.* This is really the end of it then?

*Guisebury.* The very end.

*Drusilla.* I should like to cry.

*Guisebury.* Why?

*Drusilla.* I don't want to give you up. That's the worst of life. Its taste is never half as sweet as its perfume! It is only the flowers that we don't gather that are worth gathering at all.

*Guisebury.* What! You're never going to take life seriously, Di? Just as I've discovered what a superb jest it is!

*Drusilla.* No, it isn't. It's something between jest and earnest—something between a laugh and a cry. Only to-night, now we are parting, it seems a little nearer a cry! I shall miss you, Val! Shall you miss me?

*Guisebury.* Not in the least. Two lumps.

*Drusilla.* Oh, but you must. It will be unkind. It will be ungallant to forget me!

*Guisebury.* When you and I have parted after the reception to-night, I shan't give you twenty thoughts for the rest of my life.

*Drusilla.* But that's monstrous! That's a challenge to me to win you again!

*Guisebury.* You can't wring a wren's neck twice!

*Drusilla.* Do you know, Val, you've been charming the last few days and to-night at dinner I felt if I had a heart I could lose it to you.

*Guisebury.* If you had a heart I should have won it years ago.

*Drusilla.* And broken it!

*Guisebury.* Most likely! You liked our dinner to-night?

*Drusilla.* It was exquisite. And you were the most delightful companion. What is the matter with you?

You seem so light-hearted to-night—so unlike yourself.

*Guisebury.* [*Gaily.*] I've paid all my debts—except one, and that will give me no trouble. That's quite unlike myself.

*Drusilla.* And you've sold Danecourt?

*Guisebury.* Yes, my cousin and I put it in the pot. Samuelson the stockbroker made us a splendid bid—I found it would just clear me and leave me a few thousands to the good, and I thought I couldn't do better than give you the most recherché dinner possible and a big reception afterwards.

*Drusilla.* In my honour?

*Guisebury.* In your honour and for your honour. You know, my dear Di, there have been rumours about you and me, rumours which might affect your future—so just to show there is absolutely no foundation—I have asked my aunt, Lady Bawtry, to do the honours for me, and I've invited all my set.

*Drusilla.* Oh, but that's perfectly delightful of you!

*Guisebury.* Half of them were scandalized and declined. The other half were scandalized and accepted. You shall dance yourself out of my life, and I'll take leave of you all. To-night when I bid my last guest farewell, I shan't have a single care or anxiety in the world. Tell me, Di, when I've left England, what are you going to do with yourself?

*Drusilla.* I have some dancing engagements at private houses. They pay me very well. I shall go on with that while I'm the fashion. That will be this season—and perhaps next——

*Guisebury.* Apres?

*Drusilla.* Then I shall go to America—or into a convent.

*Guisebury.* A convent?

*Drusilla.* Yes. The Catholic is such an artistic religion. No harmoniums. I think I should like to try it for three months.

*Guisebury.* And then?

*Drusilla.* And then? And then? Who knows? I don't! Lately I seem to be pursuing something that always escapes me. At first I thought it was love for that boy John Christison. Guise, do you know where I went the other week when the Richmond Place was broken up?

*Guisebury.* Where?

*Drusilla.* To Endellion.

*Guisebury.* Endellion? You saw your father?

*Drusilla.* No. He is still in London.

*Guisebury.* In London? What's he doing up here?

*Drusilla.* Looking for me. Poor father! I wish I could let him know I am quite safe—without telling him in what way.

*Guisebury.* What did you do in Endellion?

*Drusilla.* I only stayed there a few hours—and I saw no one but John Christison. He has begun the breakwater, and he looked grubby and good and happy in his dismal way. I was rather disgusted with him.

*Guisebury.* Why?

*Drusilla.* Because he is forgetting me. I have lost my power over him. As I have lost my power over you. I want you to worship me as you did, and I can't make you. I feel that everything is slipping away from me; I feel that I'm going to be cheated out of my youth and beauty and the homage that men owe me! Just when I long for more life, more pleasure, more empire! Oh! I hope I shall never live to grow old!

*Guisebury.* It would be a pity!

*Drusilla.* What makes you such a stone towards me? Am I losing my power over everybody, as I have lost it over you!

*Guisebury.* Try! There will be a crowd here to-night. Practise on them. You'll give us a dance?

*Drusilla.* Yes Isn't my dress maddening? If you knew what trouble I've taken over it for you——

*Guisebury.* For me? You are kind. I wished to make your dance a great success. My aunt, Lady Bawtry, will be here soon.

*Drusilla.* And I've got to put the finishing touch to my dress. But I must have another word with you before we part forever.

*Guisebury.* Yes, one word more—but only one—Adieu!

*Drusilla.* Oh, don't say it yet. [*Exit.*

*Guisebury.* One word more, old love—Adieu—One word more, old world—Adieu. Ten minutes to twelve. About another two hours' consciousness, and perhaps another hour more—without consciousness! Strange! I shan't drop off to sleep to-night—I shall drop off to death. But really one drops off to death every night for eight hours. Except when one has insomnia. Life's nothing more than insomnia after all—and I've had it badly. It would be rather interesting to leave behind me an account of my feelings for this last hour or so. 'Pon my word, I don't know that I have been such a fool after all. I've had a great deal of pleasure in life—and I've got two or three more hours. Let me see how I really feel. I did sleep last night. I can understand now why a condemned man always sleeps so pleasantly the last night. Yes—life is insomnia—nothing more. [*Feeling his pulse*] It's steady and regular—about seventy, I should think. I never remember such a feeling of absolute serenity and superiority! To think that all these poor devils who are coming to my reception to-night will be full of cares and anxiety, worrying themselves about all sorts of silly social conventions, dressing themselves up the most expensive ridiculous way, loving, hating, fighting, eating, drinking and scrambling for happiness, or what they think happiness—with not a bit of chance of reaching it—and I shall be the only really happy one among them. Yes, decidedly I'm master of the situation. Is it seventy-five? Perhaps—but then it's the thought of to-night's frolic. How they will chatter to morrow—what faces they will pull! How they will moralize at my expense! I wonder if there is one single soul in this world that will be sorry that I have left it? Yes, one—Midge. I wish I could take her across the ferry with me! I'll scribble her a line of adieu. The letters to Crake and Dyson, I'd forgotten them! Have I made Crake thoroughly understand? About Di's settlement? It will be at least sufficient to ensure her from want in the event of her dancing engagements failing. Yes—that will do—now for a line to Midge. "My dear Midge, by the time you get this I shall be well on my way to the new world. I sail early to-morrow. The weather is very fair and the outlook favourable——"

Goldspink, you paid all those little bills?

GOLDSPINK *enters.*

*Goldspink*. Yes, your Grace.

*Guisebury*. I've left fifty pounds in your name at the Bank in case any claims arise after I've left England.

*Goldspink*. I'm sorry your Grace won't allow me to accompany you on your travels.

*Guisebury*. Well, the fact is, Goldspink, I don't think I shall require a valet.

*Goldspink*. Your Grace will be rather at a loss without one.

*Guisebury*. Perhaps, Goldspink, perhaps. But in these new countries one must expect to rough it a little at first.

*Goldspink*. Your Grace is taking a very small wardrobe.

*Guisebury*. Quite sufficient, Goldspink, quite sufficient. I wish these three letters to be posted early to-morrow morning.

*Goldspink*. I'll post them myself, your Grace.

*Guisebury*. Early to-morrow morning—not to-night. You understand. You'll see the last of poor Bully-boy?

*Goldspink*. Yes, your Grace. I've got the poison.

*Guisebury*. I tried to do it myself, but he licked my hand, and I hadn't the heart. You're sure he won't suffer?

*Goldspink*. Not a bit, your Grace. I had to put my old terrier out of the way last year, and he went off as quiet as a baby going to sleep. I hope you and me, your Grace, will go as comfortably, when our time comes.

*Guisebury*. I hope so, Goldspink. [*Exit* GOLDSPINK

*Enter* CHARLES, *announcing* LADY BAWTRY. *Enter* LADY BAWTRY.

*Guisebury*. My dear aunt! I knew you would come and do the honours for me, and shed a halo of respectability over my last reception!

[*Exit* CHARLES.]

*Lady Bawtry*. You wretched sinner! I've shed so many haloes of respectability over you and your antics that I've scarcely a halo left to cover my own little peccadilloes.

*Guisebury*. Your peccadilloes always become you so well, Auntie, that they form a halo in themselves.

*Lady Bawtry*. If my faults are charming, it is because I have the good taste to keep them decently dressed. Nobody ever saw more than the ankle of any of my indiscretions!

*Guisebury.* It was cruel of your faults to preserve their modesty.

*Lady Bawtry.* I wish your faults had any modesty to preserve. Your vices are so terribly décolletée. Really, Guise, you are too outrageous for words. And what have you gained by shocking society?

*Guisebury.* Nothing. But see what society has gained by being shocked.

*Lady Bawtry.* Well, what? You've scandalized everybody, offended everybody, made things uncomfortable, for all your connections. It isn't that you are worse than anybody else—I know dozens of men far worse than you. Look at Bawtry for instance—he's going on dreadfully. But you've not played the game fairly. Society's the best tempered creature that ever lived—society allows you to do as you please, believe as you please, be as wicked as you please—only society says, "Don't do it openly—I want to wink at your little follies, because I want you to wink at mine."

*Guisebury.* In short, "Be as immoral as you like, but don't make a fuss about it."

*Lady Bawtry.* Exactly, and keep it out of the newspapers. We all must have our little follies and indiscretions. Human nature is just what it always was and always will be. The world is just what it always was and always will be. Society is just what it always was and always will be. What is the use of making yourself a nuisance by trying to reform it on the one hand, or shocking it and defying it on the other? No, no, you good-for-nothing fellow. Turn over a new leaf this very night, and if you're ever so much better than your neighbours, or ever so much worse, don't make them uncomfortable by letting them know it.

*Guisebury.* I'm going to turn over a new leaf—this very night.

*Lady Bawtry.* That lady is not coming to-night?

*Guisebury.* A lady is coming who has promised to dance.

*Lady Bawtry.* It's too bad of you, Guise—I will not meet her?

*Guisebury.* You applauded her dancing last year.

*Lady Bawtry.* That was for charity. And everybody runs after her—it's disgraceful. I'm not squeamish, Guise, but really, society is getting too mixed.

*Guisebury*. It is mixed—but so it will be by and by—in both the other places—whatever principle of selection is adopted.

*Lady Bawtry*. I heard you had broken off with her.

*Guisebury*. I've not seen her for some time till to-night.

*Lady Bawtry*. Why did you bring her here to-night?

*Guisebury*. Because having done some injury to her reputation, I thought, my dear auntie, that for the sake of your scapegrace nephew——

*Lady Bawtry*. I won't, Guise, positively, I won't——

*Guisebury*. Yes, you will, Auntie. You'll be generous enough to take her under your wing, if at any time she should stand in need of a friend when I've left England.

*Lady Bawtry*. I won't! I'll never forgive you, never!

*Guisebury*. You'll forgive me to-morrow at this time, Auntie.

*Lady Bawtry*. I won't! You're too shocking for anything!

*Guisebury*. Come, Auntie—we shan't see each other for a long while. Don't let us part bad friends!

*Lady Bawtry*. [*Kissing him.*] There! You wretch! I don't know where you're going, but wherever it is, you'll shock them.

*Enter* CHARLES, *announcing* "MR. REGINALD SLINGSBY."

*Enter* Regy.

*Regy*. How d'ye do, Guise? How d'ye do, Lady Bawtry?

*Lady Bawtry*. Well, Mr. Slingsby, when shall we have the pleasure of congratulating you?

CHARLES *enters, announcing* SIR LIONEL *and* LADY BALDWIN *and* MISS BALDWIN, *who enter.*

*Regy*. If I were to ask your advice on a little delicate matter, Lady Bawtry, would you give it fearlessly and frankly?

[*Exit* CHARLES

*Lady Bawtry*. Certainly, Mr. Slingsby. I'm not a very charitable woman, but I never refuse advice.

*Regy*. You've been to my little place—you know my man Crapper? Well, my prospective mother-in-law, Lady Poperoach, has made herself so very objectionable to poor Crapper that things have come to a crisis and it's a question of my forbidding her the house or losing Crapper altogether.

*Lady Bawtry.* What a pity! You'll have to let him go, then?

*Regy.* Let him go? Life would not be worth living without Crapper!

*Lady Bawtry.* Can't you persuade him to stay?

*Regy.* No, Crapper's as firm as a rock. He said to me an hour ago as he was dressing me, "Heaven forbid, sir," he said, "that I should prognosticate you against matrimony, but in the name of humanity," he said, "if it's like this before marriage, what's it going to be like after?" And I said, "By Jove, you're right, Crapper," and I sat down there and then and I wrote my ultimatum to Lady Poperoach and Crapper's taken it and she's reading it this moment. Now, Lady Bawtry, don't you think I've done right?

*Lady Bawtry.* But—it will lead to breaking off the engagement!

*Regy.* Well, of course, it will be very unfortunate for me—but if things come to the worst I may get another mother-in-law like Lady Poperoach, but I shall never get another valet like Crapper.

*Enter* CHARLES *announcing* MR. AUGUSTUS CHEEVERS; LORD *and* LADY BRISLINGTON.

*They enter and* CHARLES *exit.*

*Regy.* Guise, old fellow, this is a devilish momentous night for me.

*Guise.* Is it?

*Regy.* Yes, my fate is trembling in the balance. The next three or four hours will decide what becomes of me!

*Guise.* And does it matter what becomes of you—Regy?

[CHARLES *enters announcing* LADY POPEROACH, MISS ISABEL POPEROACH. REGY *immediately rushes up stairs and off. Enter* LADY POPEROACH *and* MISS POPEROACH. *Exit* CHARLES

*Lady Brislington.* I was rather doubtful about coming because—well, because of the scandal—but when I found everybody else was coming——

*Cheevers.* And bringing their daughters——

*Lady Brislington.* I thought there could be no harm

in it. Besides I wasn't sure that the—the—a—a—would be present.

*Cheevers.* Oh, yes, the—a—a—will be present.

*Lady Brislington.* Is she going to dance?

*Cheevers.* Yes. Didn't you see the platform?

*Lady Brislington.* I'm glad she's going to dance. Because it really puts her on the level of an entertainer—and, of course, entertainers and artists, and those people—they have morals of their own, haven't they?

*Cheevers.* Oh, yes! Plenty! Of their own!

*Lady Bawtry.* I think great allowance ought to be made for——

*Cheevers.* For everybody who goes wrong. So do I. I believe with Socrates that all wrongdoing is quite involuntary. I've only one rule in dealing with it—to extend to all man and womankind that plenary indulgence which I lavish upon myself.

*Lady Brislington.* Oh, there's that dear Poniatowski!

*Enter* PONIATOWSKI *left and off upstairs.*

*Cheevers.* The fiddler who eloped with Mrs. Brocklehurst?

*Lady Brislington.* They say he has played divinely ever since. We mustn't miss his solo.

*Exeunt crowd following* PONIATOWSKI.

*Cheevers.* Curious hangings, Guise! Where did you pick them up?

*Guisebury.* They are the funeral draperies of His Majesty, the late Emperor of China.

*Cheevers.* A funeral must be rather a festive affair in China.

*Guisebury.* Why not? Why shouldn't it be here? If a man must die why should he make all his friends miserable? The Romans used to feast at their funerals. Some more music. Tell Poniatowski to play again—keep it up. [SYBIL *enters walking with aid of cane.*] I hope when I die that not one eye will be the wetter, or one heart the heavier because a good-for-nothing fellow has gone——

*Sybil.* Where?

*Guisebury.* I don't know. [*Exit* CHEEVERS *up stairs*]. The Chinaman thinks he's going into nothingness and this is his mourning. We think we are going to Paradise and our friends wear black kid gloves, crape hat-bands and hire a dozen men in black. We can't be going to a more comic world than this.

*Sybil.* No, nor to a sadder.

*Guisebury.* I didn't expect you, Midge, I thought you wouldn't face the crowd!

*Sybil.* Oh, your rooms are so large. And I so much wanted to see Nero fiddling while Rome was blazing.

*Guisebury.* I haven't provided that attraction. But there's the Hungarian Band—and Poniatowski—if he'll do?

*Sybil.* Yes, he'll do for Nero—he can fiddle while your soul's—not freezing. I want to talk to you. My foot's really better—what's the matter with you?

*Guisebury.* Nothing.

*Sybil.* What are you going to do after to-night?

*Guisebury.* I leave the country early to-morrow morning.

*Sybil.* Where are you going?

*Guisebury.* On a voyage of discovery.

*Sybil.* Where?

*Guisebury.* That's a secret.

*Sybil.* Is it anywhere—anywhere that a friend could ever come to you?

*Guisebury.* What friend?

*Sybil.* Myself!

*Guisebury.* You! I think not!

*Sybil.* You're not going after those Arctic voyagers?

*Guisebury.* Yes, I'm going after those Arctic voyagers!

*Sybil.* Then you are going to try and do something for them at last. Oh, I'm glad you're setting yourself to something! But won't it be very dangerous?

*Guisebury.* Not very, I think. Midge, what's the matter? Tears.

*Sybil.* What shall I do when you're gone?

*Guisebury.* You have your poor people.

*Sybil.* Oh, but they're only my chicks.

*Guisebury.* Your chicks?

*Sybil.* I had a black hen at Danecourt with a lot of chicks and one duckling in her brood—it was the duckling that was always getting into harm and giving her trouble, but it was the duckling that she loved—poor silly creature!

My poor people are my chicks—it's a pleasure to look after them! But I don't want that—I want the trouble and hopelessness of looking after you!

*Guisebury.* [*Aside.*] I wish she hadn't come!

*Sybil.* Besides, if you go away, I shall never pull you from under the horses' hoofs. *Must* you go?

*Guisebury.* I must! I've made every arrangement for going—and none for staying.

*Cheevers.* Now, Lady Brislington, Miss Valrose is going to dance, if you want to get a good place.

*Sybil.* [*to* GUISEBURY.] Must you go?

*Guisebury.* I must! Where are you going, Midge?

*Sybil.* Home. I don't care much to look at dancing. Where are you going?

*Guisebury.* To the dance!

[*Exit.*

*Sybil.* Is he really going after those Arctic voyagers? A letter for me! In his handwriting! Strange; I don't understand it! I'll wait and see Nero fiddling.

[*Exit* SYBIL *upstairs.*

[*Enter* DAVID IVES, *forcing his way,* CHARLES *opposing him.*

*David.* This is the Duke of Guisebury's?

*Charles.* Yes. What is your business?

*David.* Tell thy master that David Ives would speak to him.

*Charles.* You cannot speak to him now.

*David.* I can and I will. Take him my message or—what's that noise? What's that shouting?

*Charles.* Miss Valrose is dancing.

*David.* Miss Valrose dancing! Where?

[*The crowd of guests enter, applauding* DRUSILLA *who is in dancing costume led by* GUISEBURY. *They come downstairs followed by guests.*

*Guisebury.* David Ives.

*Drusilla.* You!

*David.* Thy name, woman! Dost thou hear? Who art thou? I want to know thy name?

*Drusilla.* Drusilla Ives!

*David.* Drusilla Ives! I thought it was Delilah or Jezebel

or Valrose! Drusilla Ives! Then it seems that thou art my daughter! Get a cloak or shawl to cover thy infamy and come with me! There lies thy way!

*Drusilla.* No! That is your way! This is mine!

*David.* [*To guests.*] I don't know your ways, but I suppose you're made of flesh and blood the same as I am—and you have fathers and children—that's my child—my firstborn—I want to speak to my child alone! Perhaps you'll give me leave.

*Guisebury.* Your father wishes to speak to you—your father!

*David.* I'll deal with thee to-morrow!

*Guisebury.* [*To David.*] To-morrow! If you please! Some music there—please! Tell them to give us some music! Some music! Get them away! I beg you! Will you go—if you please!

[*Exeunt* GUISEBURY *and guests leaving* DAVID *and* DRUSILLA.

*David.* Now, thou shameless one!

*Drusilla.* Spare yourself, father! Words will not move me—nor threats.

*David.* What will then? Thou—thou wanton! Thou betrayer of men! What hast thou to say?

*Drusilla.* Strike me then, if you will! You'll be reasonable?—very well! Listen to reason then! You gave me life—you gave me health and strength and beauty! You brought me up as you thought best—But your mean, narrow life stifled me, crushed me! I couldn't breathe in it! I wanted a larger, freer, wider life—I was perishing for want of it! I've kept up a life of deception for five years to spare you pain—for your sake—not for mine! Now it's over! You know me! You see me as I am—I am the topmost rose on the topmost branch and I love the sunshine—I want admiration—applause! I want to live and live in every pulse of me! For every moment of my life—and I will! I will be myself! You cannot change me! Leave me! Let me go!

*David.* Let thee go! Let thee go to destruction! Stay—art thou indeed my child? No—surely thou art some changeling—thou art not the little golden-haired maiden that would climb on my knees, and throw her arms around my neck on Sunday evenings and whisper her prayers in my ear, while my prayers and thanks went up to Him who had given her to me! Oh, if there is any of my blood left in thee, if there was any faith and virtue in me when I wedded thy mother—if there was faith and virtue and truth in her—if her love for me was not a lie—own thyself my child again! My heart is breaking to gather thee to me! I will forgive thee! It is I, thy father! I will not be angry with thee any longer—I will plead with thee—I will win thee back again to repentance and righteousness! Come back with me, my daughter!

*Drusilla.* Hear me, father—you and I live in a different world—all the old things have gone—the very words you use—righteousness, repentance, and the rest seem strange to me! I have forgotten them—they are no longer in use—they are old-fashioned and out-worn! Do you hear? You are mad to think you will change me. I tell you the old life is gone! Waste no more words on me! It's vain! I am your daughter no longer! Leave me! Leave me and forget me!

*David.* Forget thee! I would I could forget thee! Forget thee! No—come with me, my child—I, thy father, command thee. Get some cloak to cover thee! Dost thou hear? Get rid of these! I'll strip thy shame from thee! I'll leave thee none of it!

*Drusilla.* Are you mad? Stay there! If you come a step nearer—stop there, I say! Now, have you any more to say to me?

*David.* Yes—thou hast scorned and defied me—shut the gate on my love and forgiveness. If that word "father" means anything—if there is any reverence and authority left in it—may thy stubborn, rebellious heart be broken as thou hast broken mine—may thy beauty wither and canker thee—may thy frame be racked—I, thy father, pray it—that thy soul may be gnawn with sorrow and despair—that thy spirit may be humbled and thy proud neck bowed with agony to the dust—till thou turn to thy God and thy father's God at the last! I have said it! It is my last word to thee! [*Exit.*

[DRUSILLA *falls on stairs; and the guests enter, and group round her. She beats her way through the people and exit. A burst of music, very loud.* GUISEBURY *enters, looks round. Music suddenly stops; a loud hubbub at left on gallery.* LADY BAWTRY *enters, very distressed.*

*Lady Bawtry.* Guise! the people are asking what has happened. They are all talking about the scene here! There will be a dreadful scandal to-morrow! Half of them have gone off terribly offended.

[*Hubbub of departing guests. Carriages called.* GUISEBURY *leans against staircase taking no notice of anything, staring in front of him.*

What's the matter with you? Can't you say anything to them? Speak to them. Say something! [*He does not heed her.*]

[LADY BAWTRY *makes a gesture of despair and comes downstairs. Exit.*

[*Hubbub and chatter of departing guests.*

CHEEVERS *and* LADY BRISLINGTON *have entered.*

*Lady Brislington.* [*to* CHEEVERS *who is helping with her cloak.*] I'm sorry I came here! [*With marked emphasis.*] It was a mistake.

*Cheevers.* Guise, old fellow, this is very unfortunate.

*Lady Brislington.* Mr. Cheevers, will you see if my carriage is ready?

[CHEEVERS *gives arm,* LADY BRISLINGTON *passes* GUISEBURY *with marked discourtesy. Hubbub continues, shouting for carriages, etc. Guests all exeunt, leaving* GUISEBURY *standing alone motionless. Enter* GOLDSPINK.

*Goldspink.* What time shall I call your Grace? [GUISEBURY *takes no notice.*] What time shall I call your Grace? Good night, your Grace. [*Exit.*

[*Clock strikes two*]

*Guisebury.* There goes my knell! Bankrupt! Suicide! Who'll find me! Where will they bury me? The cathedral or the cross-roads? For this part of me I don't mind—and for the other—Nirvana—nothingness! Heaven—hell—who knows—who cares! Bankrupt! Suicide! Beggar in honour—in estate—in friends—in love. I won't do it like a coward, I'll die game! I've lived like a careless fool and I'll die like a careless fool. A little less light—

[*Switches off electric light. Enter* SYBIL *on stairs.*]

Come, Nirvana—[*Takes out bottle.*] My very good friends, who have liked me—my very good enemies who have hated me—my dear, good women who haven't loved me, my dear weak women who have—emperors, charlatans, pickpockets, brother fools, good fellows all—here's forgetfulness and forgiveness in this world and a merry meeting in the next! Good night! Good night! Good night!

[*Raises phial;* SYBIL *has come down stairs behind him, she draws down his hand, away from the poison.*

CURTAIN.

[*Two years pass between Acts III and IV.*]

## ACT IV

### THE DESIRED HAVEN.

*Same scene as in Act I.*

GUISEBURY *discovered, changed, aged.*

*Guisebury.* My work done! My promise kept! Only that one last stone to lay. Yes, Endellion's safe. I've done something at last. It's about the only thing I have done. I don't remember what else there is to go on my tombstone.

SYBIL *enters.*

*Sybil.* Thoughts? Sad or pleasant?

*Guisebury.* Sadly pleasant. I was composing my epitaph.

*Sybil.* [*Quickly, a little alarmed.*] But you don't intend to need one—at present?

*Guisebury.* No, Midge. But I was thinking what a poor epitaph mine will be—when it has to be written. "Here lies Valentine Danecourt, Duke of Guisebury. He lived at issue with the Ten Commandments and died at peace with all men."

*Sybil.* "P.S. He built Endellion breakwater." And then will follow the rest of your good deeds—which you haven't done yet.

*Guisebury.* I haven't done this—it isn't I who have built it.

*Sybil.* Yes, it is—not with your hands, but with your head and heart. Where would it have been in the gale last November if you hadn't stood by the men day and night and kept up their courage? Don't you remember how they were running away from it, and you stood there and made them all ashamed of themselves? Oh, it has changed you!

*Guisebury.* I shall never be the same man that I was before my illness. That dreadful two months. You pulled me through, Midge, but—I'm maimed for life. Oh, Midge, those thirty-five wasted years.

*Sybil.* They don't count. It's your two well-spent years that count. That's life. To save a little out of the wreck—to show a balance on the right side. That's life.

*Guisebury.* Midge, sometimes you make me feel almost good.

*Sybil.* But you are good—didn't you know that?

*Guisebury.* Am I? I don't go to church very often.

*Sybil.* Yes, you do—in your way.

*Guisebury.* And I don't believe in much.

*Sybil.* Yes, you do. You believe in work, and you believe in all the great things that people call by different names.

*Guisebury.* What things?

*Sybil.* The things that all our wise people pretend to be quarrelling about. But they're only quarrelling about words—they all believe in the things.

*Guisebury.* What things do you mean?

*Sybil.* Why, all the watchwords and passwords—Faith, Duty, Love, Conscience, God. Nobody can help believing them. Turn them out at the door, they only fly in at the window—trample them into the ground, they spring up again stronger than ever. Prove them falsehoods in Greek and Latin, and you only find that they are the first truths that the mother tells to her baby.

[GUISEBURY *nods.*

*Guisebury.* Midge, what would you have done if you had been too late that night—if I had done it?

*Sybil.* Oh, I don't know. I think I should have come after you, and snatched you back somehow.

*Guisebury.* [*Startled, takes her hands.*] Midge, is it too late to pick up the pieces?

*Sybil.* Hush! [DAVID IVES, *much older, in deep mourning, enters from house. As he passes* GUISEBURY *the two men look at each other for a moment, but make no sign.* DAVID *turns and goes on sternly.*

*Guisebury.* You've not spoken to me since I've been in the island. Can't you forget the past?

*David.* [*Calmly, without resentment.*] I'm in mourning for my daughter Drusilla.

[GUISEBURY *exits with great despair.*

[SYBIL *hops up to* DAVID.

*Sybil.* There's a certain little passage, Mr. Ives, you know the passage I mean—something about forgiveness—you've said it every night and morning for fifty years—if I were you, Mr. Ives, when you say that little passage to-night, I should ask myself what it means. [*Hops off.*

*David.* [*Looking after her.*] Perhaps you're right—who knows? It is in Thy hands! [*Exit.*

*Enter up from path by beach a Sister of Mercy, Sister Beatrice.*

*Sister Beatrice.* Can you tell me which is Mr. David Ives' house?

*David.* I am David Ives.

*Sister Beatrice.* I am Sister Beatrice who wrote you eight months ago from New Orleans.

*David.* Concerning the death of my daughter Drusilla. It was thou who nursed her. [*Shakes hands, a pause.*] Did she repent?

*Sister Beatrice.* She died in peace, and received pardon from the Church.

*David.* Tell me—what was her manner of life before—before she died? I saw in a newspaper that she was dancing in public in New Orleans. Was it so?

*Sister Beatrice.* You have forgiven her. She is dead. Don't ask any more.

*David.* Nay, but I will know. Tell me the truth. Hide nothing—the truth—the whole truth. She was dancing —how long before she died?

*Sister Beatrice.* She was dancing on the——

*David.* Go on.

*Sister Beatrice.* On the Sunday night.

*David.* And died—when?

*Sister Beatrice.* The Wednesday morning.

[DAVID *utters a great cry of pain and sinks onto rock overcome.*

Be comforted. Heaven is full of forgiveness.

[DAVID *after a pause, rises as if half-dazed, speaks in a quiet, hoarse, indifferent tone.*

*David.* You have some things of hers. Where are they?

*Sister Beatrice.* In the sailing boat that brought me over.

*David.* If you'll show me where they are, I'll bring them up. [*Exit* SISTER BEATRICE *down cliff.* Dancing before all the city one Sunday night—in her grave the next. [*Exit down cliff after* SISTER BEATRICE.

*Enter* FAITH *and* JOHN

*John.* Take care, dear one, thou must not tax they strength.

*Faith.* But I am well-nigh recovered. I do not need to lean on you.

*John.* Yet do it—if not from need, lean on me from love.

*Faith.* It is sweet to breathe the air again. Why dost thou look at me with such a strange, new tenderness?

*John.* Because thou art so strangely dear to me.

*Faith.* Dost thou love me more than when I wedded thee?

*John.* Indeed I do. When I told thee of all that had happened to me in London and thou didst forgive me all my shameful past, I thought I could not love thee more. Oh, Faith, I do not deserve such happiness as thou hast given me!

*Faith.* [*Suddenly.*] Hush! *Listening towards the cottage door.*] Dost thou not hear?

*John.* No, there's nothing.

*Faith.* [*Nodding.*] Yes. My ears are quicker than thine. [*Exit into cottage.*

*John.* [*Looking after her.*] How could I ever stray from thee? Thou hast brought me home.

[*Enter from cliff above,* REGY *and* CRAKE.

*Crake.* Ah, Mr. Christison, so we shall get this last stone laid to-morrow?

*John.* Yes, the Duke has been kind enough to put off laying the last stone till my wife could be there. And it's to be to-morrow.

*Regy.* That's a comfort. I promised poor old Guisebury I'd wait till it was over. Now I can toddle back to town on Tuesday. London's good enough for me.

*Crake.* [*Looking down over cliff below.*] Look, that boat has come round the corner now—she's making for the breakwater.

*John.* A boat to-day! Where does she come from?

*Crake.* There's a large sailing vessel standing off the point, and the boat got off from her about half an hour ago.

*John.* Put in for water, I suppose. They're calling to the men on shore. There's quite a crowd gathering. All the folks are coming out of their houses. Look, they're all running to the breakwater. What can it be?. [*Exit hurriedly down cliff.*

*Regy.* Come back with me to town on Tuesday, Crake?

*Crake.* No, I must stay on with the Duke.

*Regy.* He's very glad he's got you back again.

*Crake.* Ah, I ought never to have left him. It was a shabby thing to do—And though I was making a good thing out of the Chichester property, I was very glad to throw it up and come back to Guisebury.

*Regy*. Poor old Guisebury. Fancy his sticking down here for two years. Look at the place. It's bad enough on a week day. Look at it on a Sunday afternoon. What was it made for?

*Crake*. Well, why did you come here?

*Regy*. I'm a little bit goey on the chest, and I've done Monte Carlo till I'm sick of it. My doctor happened to mention Penzance, and so, as old Guise was down here, I thought, like a fool, I'd come and give him a look up. Well, I came and when I'd been here ten minutes, I sat down on the top of a rock, and I solemnly asked myself this question, "What am I here for? Why did I give up my club, and my decent cooking, and my snug little rooms in the Albany to come down to this benighted spot and play Robinson Crusoe for the benefit of the sea-gulls?" What am I doing it for, Crake, eh?

*Crake*. Just so. What are you?

*Regy*. [*Confidentially*.] I say, Crake, sometimes I can't understand myself.

*Crake*. No? What is there in your character that puzzles you?

*Regy*. I've knocked about the world all my life—been everywhere—seen everything—done everything. You'd call me a pretty smart, wide-awake fellow, wouldn't you, Crake?

*Crake*. [*Dubiously*.] Ye-es.

*Regy*. There's nothing of the fool about me, is there?

*Crake*. Not at all.

*Regy*. Then why do I keep on acting like a fool? Why do I go and land myself in one infernal scrape after another?

*Crake*. Ah, just so. Why do you?

*Regy*. [*Very confidentially*.] Sometimes, Crake, I fancy I'm more of a fool, than anybody suspects. I let Lady Poperoach twist me round her finger.

*Crake*. But you were clever enough to get out of that in the end.

*Regy*. Yes, because they caught Jack Percival. You don't think Lady Poperoach would let me walk out of the trap unless she was sure Jack would walk in—not likely. Poor Jack!

*Crake*. Hasn't the marriage between Mr. Percival and Miss Poperoach turned out quite—quite——

*Regy*. [*Chuckles.*] Yes—quite. I had a letter from Jack the other day. Three weeks ago Lady Poperoach took away his latch-key, and deliberately dropped it over the bridge into the Serpentine in Jack's presence.

[*Pulls out his own latch-key, gazes at it very affectionately, puts it back in waistcoat pocket, chuckles, reads letter.*

"Lady Poperoach unfortunately discovered Jack's rare collection of antique prints. She burnt the whole collection." [*Shakes hands cordially with himself.*

I can't be so very much of a fool after all, Crake, for I'm nearly forty and I've kept out of it till now. Poor old Jack! Stole his latch-key! Shake hands, Regy, dear old boy.

[*Shakes hands with himself.*

Well, Crake, I've enjoyed my chat with you. What the deuce to do with myself before dinner! [*Exit.*

*Crake*. [*Looking after him.*] If he lives till he's seventy I wonder whether he'll marry his cook? Oh, it's of no consequence—except to the cook.

*Enter* GUISEBURY.

Well, Duke, you may congratulate yourself—Endellion will turn out a splendid property after all. It's lucky the harbour was built just in time to develop the trade of the island.

*Guisebury*. Sybil always said it would. Crake, who was fool enough to advance the money?

*Crake*. What does it matter? It was a capital investment for him.

*Guisebury*. Who was it?

*Crake*. [*Uneasy.*] Well, Duke, I'd saved a considerable sum in your service, and after I'd left you, I felt ashamed of it, and when Sybil came to me and said she wanted the money I'd saved for her, to invest, I found that I could manage to raise enough to begin the breakwater, and as it was going on well, I've had no difficulty in getting the remainder.

*Guisebury*. [*Shakes his head.*] You're a thoroughly bad, unnatural father, Crake, to risk her money on such a worthless fellow as I. How can I thank you, Crake?

*Crake.* Virtue is its own reward, Duke. Virtue and five per cent. [*Exit.*

*Guisebury.* Yes, she was right. Everybody begins to respect me. I used to stand in such horror of being repected. It's rather a comfortable feeling after all.

DAVID *enters.*

*David.* He's there! Shall I give it to him myself? No, I've no dealings with him. [*Goes towards house, then repeats* SYBIL'S *words.*] There's a certain little passage, Mr. Ives, something about forgiveness. [*Stops, turns, goes up to* GUISEBURY.] I've something for you. They've brought me back the things that belonged to her. I dare not bring them to my house till I have made way with all the tokens of her occupation—dancing dresses and the like. When I was looking them through I found this letter—it's meant for you—you see she begun it and never finished it. [GUISEBURY *takes it, reads it.*] Is there anything in it that concerns me?

*Guisebury.* Read it.

[*Gives it to* DAVID; DAVID *reads it; shows emotion.*

*David.* You offered to make her your wife?

*Guisebury.* Yes.

*David.* She refused you?

*Guisebury.* Yes.

*David.* You loved her?

*Guisebury.* Yes.

[DAVID *offers his hand; a silent handshake between the two men;* DAVID *goes into house.*

He forgives me! If I could forgive myself. If I could once pass those little homes down there without remembering that my broken word robbed each of them of a husband, or a father!

MRS. CHRISTISON *creeps on in the dusk.*

*Mrs. Christison.* Your Grace, they're all come back from the dead—but my Mark is not with them.

*Guisebury.* Poor thing!

*Mrs. Christison.* They're all so old, so changed. You wouldn't know them.

*Guisebury.* Yes, yes, you must expect them to be changed. [*Soothingly.*]

*Mrs. Christison.* But why hasn't my Mark come back with them? There are all his old friends, Stephen and Captain Leddra——

*Guisebury.* [*Startled.*] What! Don't speak of them. There! Go away! You'll meet your husband some day! There! Don't say any more.

*Mrs. Christison.* But all the island is rejoicing. They were all like you. They wouldn't believe it at first. Nobody knew Captain Leddra—his wife didn't know him, but when she saw that it was himself indeed, she screamed for joy and hung about his neck.

SYBIL *enters.*

*Guisebury.* Woman! Be silent! Don't bring your mad tales here. Ah—my poor woman—your husband will come back some day. [*To* SYBIL.] Shall I never forget it! Shall I always be reminded of it! It's no use, Midge. I'm chained to look always backwards. But I cannot reach one hand or move one step to change the past.

[*Sinks upon rock in despair. Distant cheering from the beach below.*

*Sybil.* [*Creeps up to him.*] The woman's tale is not so impossible after all. Others have returned before—it is just possible that they may have escaped.

*Guisebury.* No! No! I've gone through it thousands of times—Besides the ship was broken up—the fragments were found.

*Sybil.* But if they had reached home after all!

*Guisebury.* Midge! [*Looks at her.*] My God! It's true!

*Sybil.* [*Pointing to the beach below.*] Look!

[*A bell rings loudly from below.*

*Guisebury.* Are they all saved?

*Sybil.* All the Endellion men—all are safe.

*Guisebury.* All! All! [*Bursts into tears.*]

*Sybil.* [*Touches him; he turns.*] So He bringeth them to their desired haven.

*Guisebury.* And me—to my desired haven.

*Sybil.* Listen! [*Faint cheers.*

CURTAIN.